THE
BEATLES
FAB FINDS OF THE FAB FOUR

Noah Fleisher

Published by

Krause Publications, a division of F+W Media, Inc.
700 East State Street • Iola, WI 54990-0001
715-445-2214 • 888-457-2873
www.krausebooks.com

To order books or other products call toll-free 1-800-258-0929
or visit us online at www.krausebooks.com

Cover images courtesy of Julien's Auctions and Heritage Auctions

ISBN-13:978-1-4402-4717-0
ISBN-10: 1-4402-4717-X

Cover Design by Dave Hauser
Designed by Dave Hauser
Edited by Paul Kennedy

Printed in China

10 9 8 7 6 5 4 3 2 1

CONTENTS

for the love of the music
NOAH FLEISHER

It was March of 2013 and I had a front row seat to a moment of stunning clarity. The object at hand was a copy of *Sgt. Pepper's Lonely Hearts Club Band* (Mono UK Parlophone PMC 7027, 1967) signed in big, bold, beautiful signatures by the band on the album's iconic center spread. That amazing piece sold for $290,500 in a Heritage Auctions Entertainment & Music Memorabilia Auction. I can assure you it was, and is, a thing of great magnificence.

The moment the signed album sold I knew the collecting world had changed.

All things associated with The Beatles—from rare records and autographs to band-used gear and personal items—have always been hot, and rightly so. This is, after all, the greatest rock 'n' roll band to ever exist. It's only right that the memorabilia surrounding these four amazing musicians should be the most sought after of any band. It wasn't until that 2013 auction, however, after I had been the Public Relations Director at Heritage for more than five years and after more than 14 years working in the business of antiques and collectibles, that I really began to understand that we're now in the Golden Age of Beatles collectibles.

Between my job and the friendships made with dealers and colleagues at other auction houses, I find myself uniquely positioned to try to make sense of what is now taking place with this new era of Beatlemania.

I've witnessed auction after auction filled with incredible Beatles material—much of it showcased within this book. I won't spoil here what's to follow. I will tell you, however, that we may never see a time for Beatles collectibles like we've seen in the last few years and what is yet to come. Fans who have held material since the band's inception are beginning to parse out their collections. Dealers that trade in the finest The Beatles had to offer are opening their vaults. The real game changer, however, may have been when Ringo Starr sold his collection at auction in late 2015, giving a market that needed no boost an incredible lift in terms of quality. Can it be too long before Paul McCartney, or the estates of John Lennon and/or George Harrison, decide to divest themselves of at least *a few* pieces of their considerable holdings? I hope not.

Of course, this book is not about things. It is about magic, how four lads from Liverpool, England, changed the musical world forever. And it is about our deep-seated desire to hold onto that magic.

First, The Music

I cannot remember when I heard The Beatles for the very first time—they were ubiquitous to AM radio throughout the 1970s when I was growing up—but I can remember when I was hooked on their music. I can also remember the song: It was spring 1979 and it was *Lucy In The Sky With Diamonds.*

In the bottom cabinet of the entertainment center in our suburban home in Richardson, Texas, to the right of the television, lived the family 8-track stereo. There were a handful of 8-tracks there, but I only remember one. It's clear as day. *The Beatles 1967-70 (The Blue Album).* The song was the fifth track. I learned that entire album by heart. I was hearing, for the first time, what would become the soundtrack of my life—the same way so many others had heard it before me and would after.

It was a pure connection, not one that was hoisted upon me—no one had said, "Noah, go sit down and listen to The Beatles. It will do your soul right." The music simply spoke to me.

So it was, a little more than 18 months later, in early December 1980, that I remember waking up to hear that John Lennon had died. Even in *Urban Cowboy*-crazed Texas, Lennon's death at the hands of Mark David Chapman outside *The Dakota* in Manhattan made everyone stop and pause. I heard on the radio that he was a member of the Beatles. I asked my mother which one he was.

"He wasn't the cute one," she said.

I had no idea the magnitude of what had just happened, and wouldn't for many years.

My youth rolled by, The Beatles continued as an enduring musical presence, but it wasn't until I was in high school—my senior year to be exact—that my friend Jason Boyd made me sit down one afternoon and listen to *Abbey Road.* Note for note, beat for beat, he dissected the album as we listened. He pondered John's state of mind while writing one song, or George's quiet brilliance on another. He marveled at Paul's rhymes and Ringo's under-appreciated virtuosity. Suddenly the music had context within a greater framework that decidedly needed greater investigation. The members of the band were now made real as men, they had names, stories, distinct personalities. It was a revelation. (I can also gladly report, almost 30 years later, Jason is still a good friend.)

As the years passed I have cycled through each of the band's albums numerous times. I have read biographies on all the members, and I have seen that the deeper I have gone that I cannot go deep enough. Whatever I think I know, there's always more. So after more than 35 years since first hearing The Beatles, *really hearing* the Beatles, I still feel as though I am hearing their music for the first time each time I put on *Sgt. Pepper's* or *The White Album* or almost any album these supreme geniuses so gra-

ciously recorded for all of us. It is, truly, manna from Heaven.

It is not only my opinion that The Beatles are the greatest band in history, it is the opinion of millions upon millions of people all over the world. It is not just me who considers the music of The Beatles to be the greatest music created in the 20th century, and so far into the 21st century, it is the consideration of successive generations. It's not just me who believes I have a special connection to the band, its members and its music—that they are speaking directly to me each time I hear them—it is the belief of anyone who has a good ear and good taste. I would even go so far right here and now to tell you that I find it hard to trust anyone that does not listen to The Beatles. I do, however, pray for their musical soul.

My wife Lauren would concur, I believe—she's got great taste in rock 'n' roll. I know my 10-year-old daughter would go one further; she has, in fact, told us that she could never marry a boy that didn't love the Beatles. She's going to be alright, I think.

I can never fully give voice to just how much I love The Beatles, how moved I am by their music, their lives and their seemingly endless impact on the world. I daresay there are more than a few of you out there that feel the same. Perhaps we can all just agree to this right here and now and stop trying. It's a given.

What It All Means

The story of The Beatles has been told in countless fashions. This story, though, what is happening right now, right before our very eyes, has not. If you know the world of antiques and collectibles, then you know it is vast and varied; it breaks down a million different ways, all uniquely reflective of the individual tastes of the person doing the buying. No more than a handful of individual entities or people have succeeded in carving out an entire niche for themselves, one that operates successfully and independently of any other markets. The Beatles are just such an entity. They join Marilyn Monroe, and maybe Elvis, as evergreen names. As the decades have worn on—as you will see in the chapters that follow—the value for the most prime, most rare Beatles memorabilia has skyrocketed, especially where instruments played by the band are concerned.

The main concern here, however, is not with value. It's with *context*. The Beatles price guide has been written, the guide to the greatest Beatles gear has been written, the story of the band's creation, rise and dissolution—as well as those of its individual members—has been written and re-written.

The story of John, Paul, George and Ringo has not been told, however, through their memorabilia and marketing. What this book attempts to do is provide, whether you are a seasoned vet or a neophyte in the ways of The Fabs, with an overview of what The Beatles are, how they became who they became and why they are still such an enduring and impactful presence in Pop Culture consciousness. It aspires to tell the story of the Beatles through an examination of the physical record, an anthropological study that contextualizes the band within a vast framework of relics spawned by unprecedented global fame and acclaim.

The effort is greatly enhanced by an extensive auction record that tracks the world of Beatles memorabilia. It is also aided by the legions of dedicated collectors who descend upon the various *Beatlefests* and Beatle conventions all over the world every year to buy from, trade and talk with the legions of dedicated dealers who have tracked down, identified, stratified and made available the mind-boggling amount of Beatles collectibles that are out there. The auction record, and the

values the memorabilia holds, reflects all that hard work and devotion.

The fact that so much Beatles memorabilia survives to this day, and is still so sought after, speaks not only to the immeasurable popularity of the band, but to its simply astounding reach into every single part of the globe. There is no corner of the planet that has not been touched by the boys from Liverpool. We feel as though we know the band; that the joys and heartbreaks they sing about are speaking directly to us. We all believe, in our heart of hearts, that were we able to sit down and spend just a little time hanging out with the boys, together or individually, that we'd end up good friends. At least *I* know it.

Like Buying a Memory

The Beatles are a band, and a market, in a class all unto themselves. This book is one of a long line to point this out. While this is, ostensibly, a book about collecting, I hope it transcends that characterization and entertains as it informs, celebrating the material by, from and about John, Paul, George and Ringo.

It's also important to note that this book, while highlighting the best of the best, strives also to highlight the affordable parts of the market. If you have a ton of cash, then you can go for better material. If you're just a fan who wants some neat stuff, you can take $1,000 and purchase on the lower side of rarity and build a satisfying grouping, hopefully with help from the examples presented here.

As with any collectible, and as any auctioneer or dealer will tell you, educating yourself is the key. Patience, study and a trusted ally will take you far.

"Do your research," said Darren Julien, the owner and namesake of Julien's Auction's in Los Angeles. "There's so much information online that can give you an idea of what an item is worth and if it's authentic. It's also very important to buy from a reputable auction house or dealer who knows how to vet the authenticity of an item."

Double your efforts at education the deeper you go into your research and the closer you get to buying. Measure twice and cut once, to borrow an adage. Know your limit and look for what you can afford. Listen to the experts:

"The provenance is the most important thing to look for on an item and make sure that it can be matched up to photographs or videos to ensure the items are authentic," said Julien. "When it comes to the Beatles instruments, the best resource is Andy Babuik's *Beatles Gear Book*. Andy has had access to the archives of the Beatles members and has done an impressive job of detailing the history of the items used by the band." (*Note: Babiuk is interviewed in Chapter 6 of this book.*)

With the Beatles market perpetually bullish over the course of decades, the cynic in us would quite reasonably fear an inevitable bear, but those in the know are confident that the Fab Four will continue to reign as the rare exception to the economic rule.

"The Beatles are not going anywhere," Julien said. "I think their legendary status and collectability will only continue to increase. Items that we see selling for $500,000 now, I believe, will be worth $2 million to $3 million in 50 years."

By respecting The Beatles' position in the market, by understanding their genius as artists, you may just be able to parlay that comprehension into a great Beatles acquisition down the road, one that respects your bank account and is a solid investment in your future. The Beatles are the pinnacle of the music memorabilia market. Learn from them and that education will pay off not just in what you collect from the Fab Four, but in everything else you turn your erudite collectors' eye toward.

This is a good time to be collecting Beatles—the material is out there, and available, from a variety of dealers and resources. Long the sole purview of conventioneers and hobby shop patrons, the collectibles market at-large has blossomed in the Internet age, fueling exponential growth in availability and the population of collectors themselves. Today only a keyboard and monitor is required for the comprehensive shopping experience. It's also important to note that there are a lot of collectors that have been in the business a long time. So long, in fact, that many of them are not buying any more or are starting to sell off their own collections.

If this strikes you as inherently sad, perhaps it is somewhat, but this is the nature of the business and the nature of collecting. One generation ages out and hopefully another is there to step into the breach. If there is no bridge, then a category can easily wither away. That does not seem to be a problem with Beatles collectibles. It is yet another clear indication of the band's cultural immortality.

In fact, it's a bonus, especially if you are a neophyte collector. There are tremendous resources out there to help you—this book among them—as well as an established dealer and collector network that, if it's smart (and I think it is) will do anything that it can to help you get established. It provides a living for some, a hobby for others and ensures the survival of the category.

If You Had to Choose

Is it really even possible to choose your favorite Beatles album? Why even ask such a question?

Let's say that you *have* to pick. Close your eyes, think of the band, name the first album that comes to mind. There you have it.

The White Album.

No, Revolver.

No, Sgt. Pepper's.

Okay, so if I really have to choose, then it's got to be *Abbey Road*. Really.

It's not because it's their best album musi-

recorded together. The acrimony that surfaced following Brian Epstein's death subsequently bled into the recording process for both *The White Album* and *Let It Be*, originally titled *Get Back*. These are both amazing albums, full of so much great music, but there is a certain disunion in the final product. There is no such problem with *Abbey Road*. While they were clearly heading to the end of the band's life together, all four members were hungry to get back into the studio and make an album in the way they made their greatest works to that date. The conflict of the past few years was deliberately put aside—as much as possible—and, as legendary producer George Martin insisted, discipline was strictly adhered to. The result was what is now considered the band's greatest masterpiece. It's hard to argue with the designation.

The process of recording the album was drawn out and somewhat agonizing for the band, done across several months and sessions in 1969, before they all dug in and recorded the meat of it in July and August of that year. What emerged, and is still broadly evident today, was spectacular, dense, holy and soaring. For one last shining moment the lads from Liverpool were a band once again and the music they produced was and is entirely without equal.

If it was not completely decided that *Abbey Road* was going to be the last thing the Beatles recorded, it seems as though they all had a feeling the end was near—and it was official by the time the album was released. Harrison himself was quoted in *Rolling Stone* on Sept. 2011 (posthumously) that "it felt as if we were reaching the end of the line."

Indeed they were, but what a way to go out. What a band. What an album. Yet, it wasn't really the end. In many ways it was only the beginning, as we see today.

I humbly submit the following book to you then. It's packed with great images, anecdotes and an attempt to tell the story of the greatest rock 'n' roll band the world has ever known via the material record. It was a daunting, rewarding task to wade through it all and attempt to codify it. Hopefully the record reads clear. At its heart is love for the band and its members, in its soul is a deep and abiding respect for the stunningly gorgeous, incredibly unique music they created. The world will never see its like again. We should all thank the stars of our stars daily that we've been fortunate enough to bear witness to their brilliance and to have had the infinitely great luck of being able to spend our lifetimes not only living with the original members of this band, but also listening to their music.

cally, though it may well be, even if the same could be said on any given day about any six of their other records. They were revolutionaries, yes?

Maybe I love *Abbey Road* so much because it is the first Beatles record that I listened to with mature ears. Maybe because the medley on the second side of the record blends into a single, gorgeous musical experience that has to be listened to, in order, all the way through—every time—or there is no harmony in existence. I'm not kidding. Nothing feels right.

I have listened to so much Beatles music over my lifetime, but the album I go back to over and over, the album that seems to define every period of my existence—the good times, the bad, the heartaches, the joy, the boredom and the excitement—is always *Abbey Road*. It has been there for me over and over again and it has never let me down. I have never tired of hearing it and I have never stopped being fascinated by the musical phrasing and the lyrical depth. It strikes me every time that, note for note, *Abbey Road* is the most perfect of all Beatles albums.

Abbey Road, while not being the last Beatles album released, was the last that the band

Image courtesy of Associated Press

SPECIAL THANKS

Special thanks go to many people for their help in compiling and supporting the effort that went into this book. First and foremost, thanks to Paul Kennedy, the Editorial Director at Krause Publications who first suggested the idea and whose guidance has been key. I would also like to thank Heritage Auctions – Steve Ivy, Jim Halperin, Greg Rohan and Paul Minshull, in particular – for its amazing archives and meticulous records, just as I would like to thank Darren Julien of Julien's Auctions, and his staff, for the images, the archives and the insight into the market. Andy Babiuk, the author of Collecting Beatles Gear very graciously gave of his time and energy, as did Jeff Augsburger, one of the greatest collectors of Beatles memorabilia in the business. Jeff gave generously of his time, expertise and photographs and is an enormously informative and entertaining source. Garry Shrum of Heritage Auctions, an old friend at this point, is one of the most knowledgeable people in the business when it comes to the band and I cannot thank him enough for his time and expertise. A special thanks also goes to Jonathan Scheier for his keen editorial eye.

Last of all, but certainly not least, the most personal of all thanks goes to my brilliant and beautiful wife Lauren Zittle and my amazing daughter Fiona Anne. Lauren is my first editor, my primary sounding board and a steady and abiding presence throughout this book and my life. Her help was crucial in getting this book into shape and I am indebted to her for her skill. My daughter Fiona is the light of my life and the joy of my heart. The fact that she thought it would be "cool" if I did this book was enough to make me say yes and the reason I made them both put up with the long hours it took write it and to put it all together. I love you and thank you both.

BEFORE FAME 1957-1962

Early Beatles Photograph: Taken by Paul's younger brother, Mike, this photo was taken in 1958 at a wedding reception at McCartney's aunt's home in Liverpool. George Harrison (left) was a mere 15 years old, and he looks it. Photo sold at auction for $1,000.
Image courtesy of Julien's Auctions

In his 2008 book, *Outliers: The Story of Success,* author Malcolm Gladwell posits the theory of the "10,000-Hour Rule," that achieving success and world-class expertise in any skill is largely a matter of practicing, the right way, for a total of around 10,000 hours. He cites The Beatles – among others like Bill Gates and Steve Jobs – as evidence of his theory.

It's difficult to argue with that. What is hard to define, though, as far as the Fabs are concerned, is what "the right way" means. We do know that

John Lennon School Photograph: *A very early image of Lennon, pre-fame, with classmates at Quarry Bank High School For Boys, 1957, when he was a regular kid with rock 'n' roll dreams. Sold at auction for $2,560.*
Image courtesy of Julien's Auctions

QUARRY BANK HIGH SCHOOL FOR BOYS,
CALDERSTONES, LIVERPOOL.
May 1957.

this period of practice came for The Beatles in the years before 1963, starting with the teenaged John Lennon and Paul McCartney's formation of The Quarrymen in 1957 (Harrison joined in 1958, famously being turned down by Lennon for being too young before he worked his way into the band with weeks of persistence) and continued as the band became The Silver Beetles and finally The Beatles, playing at the clubs first in Hamburg, Germany, and then across the UK.

What, exactly, was "the right way" they did it? The template for rock 'n' roll was Elvis Presley, it was Buddy Holly, Little Richard and Chuck Berry. It wasn't a group of boys from Northern England playing for post-war German kids in the burgeoning Hamburg club scene, but that's what it became. It also became the breeding ground for the 20th century's greatest Cultural Revolution and a story well worth telling.

It was spring of 1957 when John – age 16 – formed his famous skiffle group with a few friends from the Quarry Bank School. The band was short-lived. In 1959, with most of his Quarry Bank friends having left, Lennon, McCartney and Harrison were all of The Quarrymen left. Lennon soon enrolled at the Liverpool College of Art. The trio continued playing together as Johnny and the Moondogs, gigging whenever they could find a drummer. Those 10,000 hours started piling up, though the meat was soon to come.

In school, Lennon became friends with the charismatic and handsome artist Stuart Sutcliffe, a visual artist with a great sense of style and definite Rock 'n' roll attitude. Lennon persuaded him to buy a bass guitar in early 1960 and Sutcliffe suggested, in tribute to Buddy Holly, that the band change its name to the Beatals. That lasted a few

months before the name was changed to the Silver Beetles. The hours continued to accumulate. The band booked a tour as the backing band for a crooner named Johnny Gentle, changing to the Silver Beatles in the early summer of that year and, finally, to The Beatles by that August. It was around that same time that the band's early unofficial manager, Allan Williams, hired Pete Best to play the drums. The early core of the band, the famous first line-up, was in place.

The Beatles 1962 Mersey Beat Magazine: *An early appearance of the band in print in an important early regional rock 'n' roll magazine. Sold at auction for $7,680.*
Image courtesy of Julien's Auctions

Pieces of the Star-Club Stage, Dance Floor and Building Facade (Hamburg, 1960s): *Three incredible relics from the world famous Star-Club, which was razed in 1983: a piece of the grey and white marble dance floor; a piece of the wooden stage that hosted The Beatles, Jimi Hendrix and thousands of others ("Star-Club/Hamburg-St. Pauli" stamped upon it); and, a decorative piece of the façade. All in Very Good condition. Sold at auction for $812.*
Image courtesy of Heritage Auctions

In mid-August Williams secured for the now five-piece band a 3-1/2 month contract with Hamburg, Germany, club-owner Bruno Koschmider—Hamburg's red-light district had become a hotbed of rock 'n' roll and Koschmider's place, the Indra Club, was one of the scene's most happening spots. The boys famously crashed at the cramped, dirty Bambi-Kino, a converted theater. In a few weeks' time the Indra closed and the boys were booked into the larger Kaiserkeller club. They were soon wooed by Peter Eckhorn, the owner of the Top Ten Club and promptly fired by Koschmider when he found out they were double-timing him. Koschmider gave the boys a one-month termination notice and reported Harrison to German authorities for performing underage and lying on his visa.

Harrison was deported. Paul and Pete went to the Bambi Kino to get their belongings and, finding it totally dark, set fire to a condom in a concrete corridor for light while they packed – quickly. Paul and Pete said they did it for the light. Koschmider claimed it was revenge, and arson, and soon Pete and Paul were deported. John followed them back home in December and Stuart stayed in Germany with his girlfriend, Astrid Kirchherr, who would go on to become the band's official first photographer and perhaps their most famous early chronicler.

Does this all sound like "the right way" to practice for becoming the greatest rock 'n' roll band of all time? It does now. All the while, during this first period abroad, the boys played. They played for hours at a time, week after week. They had fun, partied like crazy and likely had one hell of a time. The key, though, is they were getting *good*.

Brushing off this minor early setback, the boys continued to play back home, notably at the Cavern Club, gaining in popularity and soon booking another residency in Hamburg. This would continue for the next two years. The band played constantly, ecstatically, un-self-consciously for hours and hours. It was a wild, unsupervised time of hedonism, amusement and – most importantly – *music*.

During the second Hamburg residency, Kirchherr cut Sutcliffe's hair in the tough, cool French style of the time, which was soon adopted by the other boys in the band. This was the evolution of the famous early leather look of the band – Lennon always referred to Sutcliffe as the band's stylist – so perfectly captured in Kirchherr's Hamburg portraits of the band.

-6-

§ 12 RECHT UND GERICHTSSTAND

Der Vertrag bleibt auch bei rechtlic! Klauseln wirksam.

Änderungen und Ergänzungen dieses Ve: Schriftform.

Für die Auslegung dieses Vertrages i: Recht maßgebend. Ausschließlicher Ge:

.............., den •....... Ha:

G.W. Lennon
James Paul McCartney
George Harrison
Peter Best

....

....

BERT KAEMPFERT PRODUKTION

VERTRAG
════════════

Zwischen

1) John W. Lennon   )
2) James Paul McCartney   )   als Gruppe genannt
3) George Harrison   )   The Beatles
4) Peter Best   )

wohnhaft

1) 251 Manlove Ave., Woolton 25, Liverpool
2) 20 Forthlin Rd., Liverpool 18
3) 25 Upton Green Speke, Liverpool 24
4) 8 Haymans Green, Liverpool 12

nachstehend "Gruppe" genannt,

und

der BERT KAEMPFERT PRODUKTION
    Hamburg, Inselstr. 4

nachstehend "Produktion" genannt,

wird folgender Vertrag geschlossen.

§ 1 Dauer und Gegenstand

Dieser Vertrag tritt am 1.7.1961 in Kraft und gilt bis zum 30.6.1962. Er verlängert sich jeweils um ein Jahr, falls er nicht von einer der Parteien drei Monate vor Ablauf einer Vertragsperiode gekündigt wird.

Gegenstand dieses Vertrages ist das Recht, Schallaufnahmen mit Darbietungen der Gruppe auszuwerten. Zu diesem Zweck verpflichtet sich die Gruppe, während der Vertragsdauer Titel zur Herstellung von Schallaufnahmen vorzutragen. Die aufzunehmenden Titel sollen im beiderseitigen Einvernehmen ausgewählt werden; kommt eine Einigung nicht zustande, so trifft die Produktion die Auswahl.

Die Gruppe steht dafür ein, daß sie das Recht an ihrem persön- lichen Vortrag der unter diesen Vertrag fallenden Schallaufnahmen niemandem übertragen hat und durch keine anderweitigen Bindungen gehindert ist, diesen Vertrag abzuschließen und zu erfüllen. Ins- besondere wird sie bei der gemeinsamen Auswahl der Titel darauf

-2-

(opposite) *This extraordinary contract is one of the most important Beatles documents in existence:* **The first recording contract signed by the group, in June 1961, for the session backing Tony Sheridan (as The Beat Brothers), which produced the "My Bonnie" single release, the recording that lead the boys, still struggling, to Brian Epstein. Of particular note is the fact that it is signed by original drummer Pete Best and is just one of three extant. Written in German, six pages total, this was executed between the group and the German music producer Bert Kaempfert. The Beatles were paid less than $20 each. They were called "The Beat Brothers" due to a stipulation in the contract that allowed Polydor to use a different group name, and Kaempfert felt "Beatles" would not be readily accepted in the German market. A modest success in Germany, "My Bonnie" did well back home in Liverpool, as Beatles fans began asking for it in record shops, including the store owned and managed by Brian Epstein. He paid a visit to the Cavern Club to see the band and within months had secured a music test with EMI producer George Martin, resulting in the recording of the group's first hit "Love Me Do." The contract sold at auction for $93,750.**

Image courtesy of Heritage Auctions

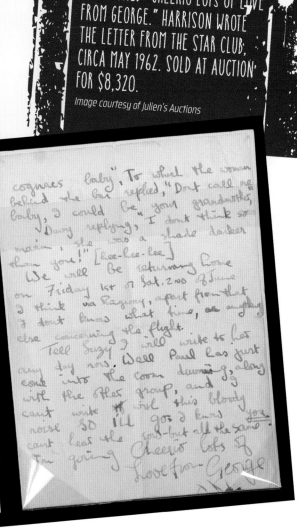

GEORGE HARRISON HANDWRITTEN LETTER: A HANDWRITTEN LETTER FROM HARRISON TO LINDA "LINDY" NESS, A FAN FROM THE CAVERN CLUB. THE LETTER READS IN PART, "WELL PAUL HAS JUST COME INTO THE ROOM DRUMMING ALONG WITH THE OTHER GROUP, AND I CANT [SIC] WRITE WITH THIS BLOODY NOISE..." AND SIGNED "CHEERIO LOTS OF LOVE FROM GEORGE." HARRISON WROTE THE LETTER FROM THE STAR CLUB, CIRCA MAY 1962. SOLD AT AUCTION FOR $8,320.

Image courtesy of Julien's Auctions

Astrid Kirchherr Large Format Photograph of John Lennon, "Black Portrait 1" (Hamburg, 1962): *A beautiful and very sad portrait of John. The photo was taken in 1962 at Stuart Sutcliffe's studio as John paid his respects to his deceased friend. John and Stuart met at Liverpool College of Art and soon shared a flat. His death greatly affected Lennon, as this image solemnly attests. This striking 20" x 24" image sold at auction for $1,000.*
Image courtesy of Heritage Auctions

The Beatles 1962 Line-up Signed Photograph: **A good photograph of The Beatles inscribed on verso by George Harrison, Paul McCartney and Pete Best, circa 1962, with additional handwritten notations in an unknown hand. Albert Marion, a local wedding photographer, took the photograph on Dec. 17 1961, during The Beatles' first professional photography session. Sold at auction for $4,800.**
Image courtesy of Julien's Auctions

In mid-1961, German producer Bert Kaempfert had taken notice of the band and contracted them to back English crooner Tommy Sheridan on a series of recordings for Polydor Records—most famously the first single they played on, "My Bonnie," an English folk song taught to German kids in school that Kaempfert thought would appeal to the German youth. The contract was for one year. The Beatles had busted their asses and ended up, miraculously they thought, with a record contract. They were listed on the record as "Tony Sheridan & The Beat Brothers," not The Beatles. Polydor didn't think the name would work in Germany and had a stipulation in the contract that they could change it as they saw fit. The boys didn't mind. They were recording artists now; that was what mattered.

The single didn't perform particularly well – peaking at number 32 on the German Musikmarkt chart. It did get them some notice, though, especially back in England where their notoriety had continued to grow – they were known for their electrifying live shows and brazen energy on stage.

Things got a little more complicated in late 1961, as Sutcliffe decided to leave the band and go back to art school in Germany to finish his studies. It was a fateful decision. The band suddenly needed a bassist. McCartney

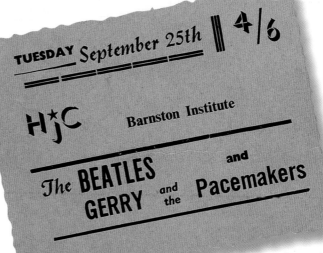

The Beatles and Gerry & the Pacemakers concert ticket for the September show at the Heswall Jazz Club. Sold for $1,434.
Image courtesy of Heritage Auctions

The Beatles, circa 1960, were still figuring things out – including their look and lineup. Here, from left, are John Lennon, George Harrison, Pete Best, Paul McCartney and Stuart Sutcliffe. This Best-signed photo sold for $675.
Image courtesy of Heritage Auctions

(right) **Meet The Beatles, Aintree Institute handbill, one of only four known to exist, sold at auction for $2,629.**
Image courtesy of Heritage Auctions

Jive Fans This Is It !

MEET THE BEATLES

every Saturday at

AINTREE INSTITUTE

(BUSES 20, 21, 22, 10, 61, 91, 92, 93, 95, 96 & 500 TO BLACK BULL, NEXT DOOR)

YES ! PAUL, JOHN, GEORGE AND PETE
will be playing for you exclusively at Aintree Institute,
every Saturday, starting 12th August 1961.

You must be there, too !

...rly and bring your friends !
...to 11 p.m.   Admission 4/-

...tute Your Saturday Dance Date

HESWALL JAZZ CLUB
BARNSTON INSTITUTE BARNSTON ROAD, HESWALL

NOTE THE DATE --
TUESDAY 25th SEPTEMBER, 1962

★ *Special Mid - Week Attraction*
7-30 p.m. --- 11-0 p.m.

Disc **J**ockey **D**erek **J**effery .... *introduces*

The North's TOP ROCK COMBO !!

★ *The Fabulous*
BEATLES
(Parlophone Recording Artists)
and MR. PERSONALITY Himself
GERRY AND THE ● Pacemakers

— plus the Week's TOP DISKS —

Admission by TICKET 4/6
AT THE DOOR   5/-

★ *Note the Date* ★
TUESDAY SEPTEMBER 25th

(below) **The Beatles spent the week of Monday, Aug. 26, through Saturday, Aug. 31, 1963, performing at the Odeon Theatre in Southport. It marked the third week in a row where The Beatles were the featured band performing two shows each night for separate audiences. The group's set consisted of "Roll Over Beethoven," "Thank You Girl," "Chains," "A Taste Of Honey," "She Loves You," "Baby It's You," "From Me To You" and "Twist And Shout." $388**
Image courtesy of Heritage Auctions

(left) **A from the Heswall Jazz Club, not far from Liverpool, refers to The Beatles as "Fabulous" in 1962. Little could the patrons of this famed club realize what the coming years would mean for their hometown boys. The handbill sold at auction for $1,912.**
Image courtesy of Heritage Auctions

ODEON THEATRE
SOUTHPORT

THE BEATLES and GERRY
& THE PACEMAKERS
2nd Performance at 8-40 p.m.
TUESDAY AUGUST 27

2

FRONT CIRCLE 6/6

A45

No Tickets exchanged nor money refunded
THIS PORTION TO BE RETAINED

RORY STORM
and the
Hurricanes

Presented by:-
DOWNBEAT
PROMOTIONS

54 BROADGREEN ROAD
Liverpool 13
STOneycroft 3324.

(above) **Before he joined The Beatles in August 1962, Ringo Starr played drums with Rory Storm and the Hurricanes, one of the most popular bands in the Liverpool and Hamburg club scene.**
Image courtesy of Heritage Auctions

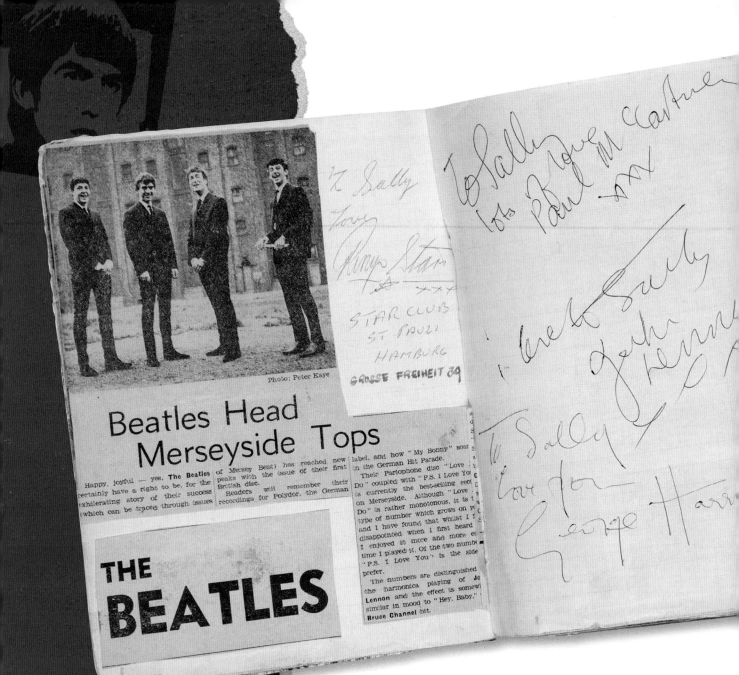

Beatles Head Merseyside Tops

Photo: Peter Kaye

Happy, joyful — yes, The Beatles certainly have a right to be, for the exhilarating story of their success (which can be traced through issues of Mersey Beat) has reached new peaks with the issue of their first British disc.

Readers will remember their recordings for Polydor, the German label, and how "My Bonny" soar in the German Hit Parade.

Their Parlophone disc "Love Do" coupled with "P.S. I Love You is currently the best-selling reco on Merseyside. Although "Love Do" is rather monotonous, it is type of number which grows on y and I have found that whilst I f disappointed when I first heard I enjoyed it more and more e time I played it. Of the two numb "P.S. I Love You" is the side prefer.

The numbers are distinguished the harmonica playing of J Lennon and the effect is somew similar in mood to "Hey, Baby," Bruce Channel hit.

THE BEATLES

A Fan's Autographed Scrapbook (UK, 1962-63): An incredible set of Beatles autographs from 1962 and a scrapbook of clippings lovingly put together by a young female fan named Sally. Provides great insight into a particular time and place: Liverpool and the north of England, circa mid-1962 to mid-1963, when "four of our own" were making their way into the big time. This archive brought $7,097.

Image courtesy of Heritage Auctions

graciously stepped in. Best was still on the drums. The hard work and the hours, by now thousands deep, had piled up.

By the end of their second residency in Hamburg, with 1961 drawing to a close, The Beatles were enjoying an ever-growing profile back home in Liverpool, echoing the growing influence of the Merseybeat movement. "My Bonnie" was popular with their Liverpool base, which flocked to local record stores asking for The Beatles record. One of the record storeowners was none other than Brian Epstein. The fact that kids were coming in and asking for the single peaked his already burgeoning interest – as the owner of the store he had heard of them already and had seen them profiled in a local music magazine. As the band was booked into The Cavern Club—this was in November 1961—he decided to check them out. It was a precipitous meeting.

The band was growing weary of the club lifestyle night after night, and Epstein liked what he heard enough to pursue the band for a few weeks before finally, in January of 1962, being appointed their official manager.

(below) Ringo Starr Antique Onyx Ring: *A circa 1920 10k yellow gold ring topped with a bezel set cushion shaped onyx. Ringo was photographed wearing the ring as early as 1960 and in hundreds of photos subsequent to that year. It sold at auction for $100,000.*
Image courtesy of Julien's Auctions

RINGO STARR PINKY RING: ONE OF THE EPONYMOUS RINGS THAT WAS NOT ONLY WORN BY STARR THROUGHOUT HIS CAREER AS A BEATLE BUT ALSO A RING THAT PLAYED A KEY ROLE IN RICHARD STARKEY BECOMING KNOWN THE WORLD OVER AS RINGO STARR. STARR WAS PHOTOGRAPHED WEARING THE RING AS EARLY AS 1961, WHEN HE WAS PLAYING WITH RORY STORM AND THE HURRICANES, BEFORE BECOMING A BEATLE. RINGO HAS SAID THAT HE BELIEVES HE WORE THIS RING DURING EVERY SHOW HE PLAYED AS A BEATLE. SOLD AT AUCTION FOR $106,250.
Image courtesy of Julien's Auctions

Vintage Peter Kaye Photograph:
This is a great publicity shot of the Beatles by photographer Peter Kaye, Liverpool, in 1962. Gone are the leather jackets, replaced by the suits that would come to define their early rise to fame. Printed on the back of the photo: "On location. First publicity shots ever." Sold at auction for $2,240.
Image courtesy of Julien's Auctions

Cavern Club Wood Sign: *An original sign from The Cavern Club in Liverpool. The company that demolished the building in 1973 that originally housed The Cavern Club saved the sign, which was then given to another builder who was a collector of curios. This premium piece of music history sold at auction for $15,360.*
Image courtesy of Julien's Auctions

RIBBON MICROPHONE
30/50 OHMS & Hi-Z RBT/
Made in England
RESLOSOUND LTD.

CAVERN CLUB STAGE USED MICROPHONE:
THIS RESLO-MODEL RBT RIBBON MICROPHONE, LATE 1950S/EARLY 1960S, FROM THE CAVERN CLUB, WHERE THE BEATLES PERFORMED 292 TIMES, MORE THAN AT ANY OTHER VENUE. IT WAS AT THE UNDERGROUND CLUB ON MATTHEW STREET THAT THE GROUP PERFECTED THEIR STAGE PRESENCE OVER THOUSANDS OF SONGS PERFORMED AND HUNDREDS OF HOURS SPENT ON STAGE. THIS PIECE OF MUSIC HISTORY, WHICH INCLUDED A SILVER METAL STAND, SOLD AT AUCTION FOR $10,625.
Image courtesy of Heritage Auctions

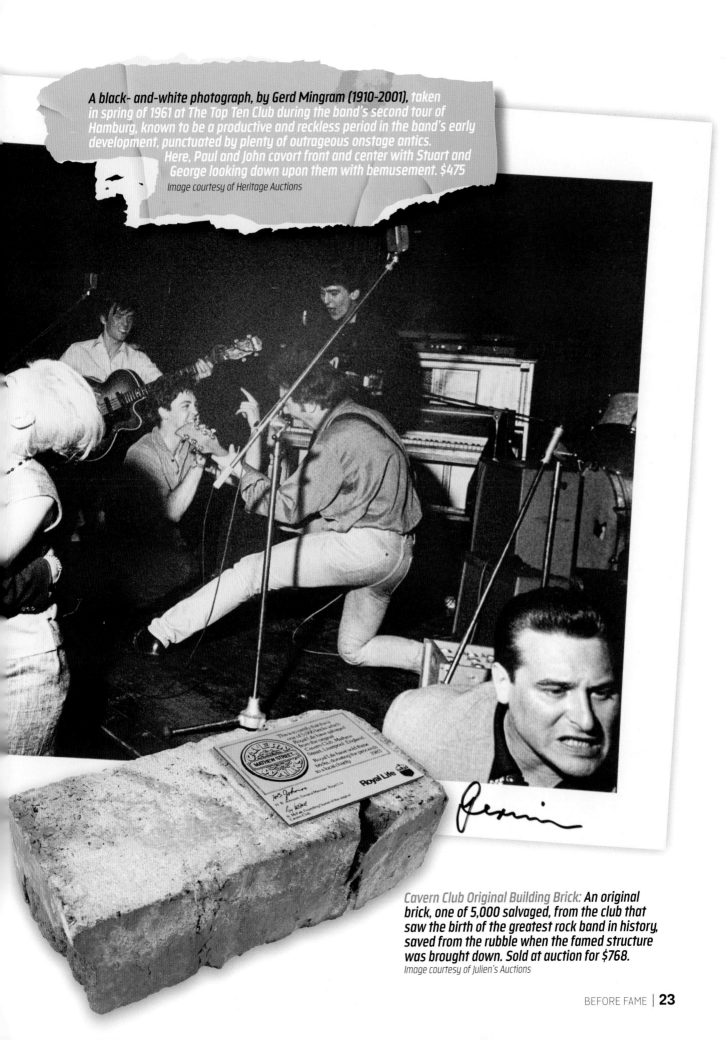

A black- and-white photograph, by Gerd Mingram (1910-2001), taken in spring of 1961 at The Top Ten Club during the band's second tour of Hamburg, known to be a productive and reckless period in the band's early development, punctuated by plenty of outrageous onstage antics.

Here, Paul and John cavort front and center with Stuart and George looking down upon them with bemusement. $475

Image courtesy of Heritage Auctions

Cavern Club Original Building Brick: An original brick, one of 5,000 salvaged, from the club that saw the birth of the greatest rock band in history, saved from the rubble when the famed structure was brought down. Sold at auction for $768.

Image courtesy of Julien's Auctions

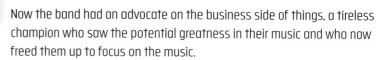

Now the band had an advocate on the business side of things, a tireless champion who saw the potential greatness in their music and who now freed them up to focus on the music.

In the months that followed, Epstein worked to free the band from their German contract, eventually negotiating with Kaempfert to get them out one month early in exchange for final recording sessions backing Sheridan in Hamburg.

Awaiting them in Germany, however, was tragic news: Kirchherr met them at the airport distraught, relaying the terrible information that Sutcliffe has died suddenly, just the day before, of what was later determined to be a brain hemorrhage. The boys, especially John, were stunned and broken. It was devastating news and deeply affected them all. Still, they soldiered on, finished their commitment and left Germany. One more piece of the puzzle was in place and the total hours put in toward mastery of their craft was approaching critical mass.

Back in England, with his eye on bigger fish than the Merseybeat scene, Epstein began looking for a mainstream label. After being rejected

Beatles at the Cavern Club Photo (1961): *The leather-clad lads, with Pete Best still in the band on drums, rock out in this vintage 8" x 10" photo, taken at the Liverpool club that first brought them to the attention of the world. Gloria Stavers took this well-known shot, noted on the back in pencil, "Paul and John get down to it." $750*
Image courtesy of Heritage Auctions

by Decca – being told that "guitar groups are on the way out" – Epstein managed to get The Beatles signed to EMI's Parlaphone label, working with producer George Martin. It would prove to be the beginning of the band's most important and productive creative relationship. They went into the studio for the first time on June 6, 1962, at EMI's Abbey Road Studios in London.

What became apparent to Martin, quickly, was that Pete Best was not a musician in the same league with John, Paul and George. Without knowing the boys were contemplating replacing Best already, Martin suggested they book a session drummer. The Beatles had a better idea: they would hire the drummer away from the band of friend and rival Rory Storm, whose drummer was a young man named Richard "Ringo" Starkey. They had all become friends in Germany, playing the same clubs, and the

Astrid Kirchherr Signed Large Format Photograph "The Beatles At The Hamburg Fun Fair" (Hamburg, 1960): *Perhaps the most iconic early photograph ever taken of the young Beatles, on their first visit to Hamburg, Germany, in the Fall of 1960. Kirchherr captures the boys as the very essence of cool and simmering genius. The print measures 23.5" x 18". Sold at auction for $4,750. Image courtesy of Heritage Auctions*

three remaining Beatles felt at home with Ringo both as a friend and a drummer. Ringo played on the original single for "Love Me Do," though he was replaced for other sessions— ones that yielded another recording of "Love Me Do," along with "Please Please Me" and "P.S. I Love You"—by drummer Andy White.

From these sessions the band released their first official single in the form of "Love Me Do," first with Ringo on drums and, in later pressings, with White's drums. It was October of 1962 and the single made it to number 17 on the Record Retailer chart. Their very first television appearance manifested a few weeks later when they performed on a regional show titled "People and Places." It was their first taste of success. They had put in the thousands of hours required to reach greatness and it was now within their grasp. That same month it all came together when Martin took them back into the studio – the core Fab 4 as they would become – to re-record "Please Please Me" at a faster pace, after which he would correctly observe to the boys, "You've just made your first Number 1."

By December 1962, with their final stint in Hamburg ending, fame was within their grasp. The Lennon-McCartney songwriting partnership had begun to blossom—effectively shutting out the songwriting and singing contributions of both Starr and Harrison for the next several years, which would eventually become a source of tension—and produce the gems that would make them legends.

(top) Astrid Kirchherr Signed Large Format Photograph of John Lennon and Stuart Sutcliffe, "Hamburg Fun Fair" (Hamburg, 1960): **A stunning shot of John Lennon, barely 20 years old, with fellow Beatle Stuart Sutcliffe, holding the bass John urged him to buy. This photograph by Astrid Kirchherr was printed in 2009 at almost two-feet wide. Sold at auction for $1,500.** *Image courtesy of Heritage Auctions*

(right) Astrid Kirchherr Signed Large Format Photograph of Paul McCartney and Stuart Sutcliffe, "Hamburg Fun Fair" (Hamburg, 1960): **A legendary portrait of Paul, with Stuart and his bass in the background. Kirchherr boldly signed the image in the lower left corner in silver marker. Printed 2009 by Grauwert, Hamburg, measuring 23.75" x 18.75". Sold at auction for $1,125.** *Image courtesy of Heritage Auctions*

Astrid Kirchherr Signed Large Format Photograph of Ringo Starr, "Chair" (Hamburg, 1962): Shot by Kirchherr in 1962, she captures Ringo's personality perfectly as he became the newest Beatle, after performing with Rory Storm and the Hurricanes. Measures 19.5" x 23.5". Sold at auction for $800. *Image courtesy of Heritage Auctions*

Ringo Starr Handwritten Postcard to His Grandmother from Hamburg, Signed "Richy" (Hamburg, November 9, 1960): *An amazing, incredibly early color photo postcard from Ringo to his grandmother, postmarked Nov. 9, 1960, bearing the handwritten message: "Dear Gramma. Arrived and having a great time in Hamburg. The weather hear (sic) is not to (sic) bad. We are playing in a big new club. The people hear (sic) are O.K. that (sic) all for now see you soon. Lots of Love. Richy xxxxx". At this time Ringo was performing at the Kaiserkeller with Rory Storm and the Hurricanes. This is one of the earliest Ringo manuscript items known. Sold at auction for $4,625.*

It was also at this time that Epstein, seeing the commercial potential in his brilliant young charges, pushed them to abandon the leather jackets and pompadours that constituted their early image. He encouraged them to dress a little more smartly and to clean up their onstage behavior. Gone were the days of blue jeans and boots, of smoking and swearing on stage, and here to stay were the days of neatly cut suits and the famous Beatle mop top haircut.

While the pre-Beatlemania days are a time rich with stories and apocrypha relating to the band, it is not a time that is too rich with collectibles relating to the boys. What exists largely are autographed postcards and letters to fans, signed photos, correspondence, some personal effects, pieces of equipment from the clubs where they played (as well as pieces of the clubs themselves) and, of course, Kirchherr's photography, which remain the most evocative and interesting documentation of those fascinating, wild early days of the greatest band in history.

If this period is one that draws you in as a collector, be prepared to pay for it. The dearth of material means that what exists is going to cost you, at the least, a few thousand dollars. The really good stuff—autographed pictures, personal effects and band-used equipment—is going to run in the five-figure range and much higher, depending on what you're after.

RINGO "RICHY" POSTCARD

Excerpted from The catalog for The Uwe Blaschke Collection, Sept. 2015, Heritage Auctions

The October through December 1960 season at the Kaiserkeller was an interesting time for the two bands performing there; Rory Storm and the Hurricanes (Ringo's first band), with more experience, were top-billed over the Beatles.

"They were professionals, we were still amateurs," John Lennon said. "They'd been going for years and they'd been to Butlins, and God knows what, and they really knew how to put on a show."

Each band was expected to play six hours a night so they would alternate sets, an hour at a time. This created quite a competition between the bands as they tried to top each other's performances. The Beatles and Ringo were aware of each other from meeting back in England.

"I met the Beatles while we were playing in Germany," Ringo would later say. "We'd seen them in Liverpool, but they were a nothing little band then, just putting it together... They were great in Hamburg. Really good – great rock. I knew I was better than the drummer they had at the time, and we started hanging out some..."

A bond was forming between four young Livepudlians plying their chosen trade in Hamburg that would eventually and literally rock the world.

"Pete [Best] would never hang out with us," Harrison related years later. "When we finished doing the gig, Pete would go off on his own and we three would hang out together, and then when Ringo was around it was like a full unit, both on and off the stage. When there were the four of us with Ringo, it felt rocking."

It would be August 1962 before the relationship became official and permanent, but the foundation was certainly laid on the fateful trip to Hamburg that "Richie" told his grandmother about in a postcard.

Note: All quotes taken from The Beatles Anthology (San Francisco: Chronicle Books, 2000).

Astrid Kirchherr Signed Large Format Photograph of John Lennon, Stuart Sutcliffe and George Harrison, "Truck" (1960): *With George and John in their newly acquired Hamburg leathers and Stuart in his James Dean shades, this is another classic Kirchherr image of the early band. Measures 19.5" x 23.5". Sold at auction for $1,500.* Image courtesy of Heritage Auctions

EARLY FAME AND BEATLEMANIA

1963-1966

For The Beatles, with their hardest days behind them and their best music ahead of them, the early part of their fame—from their meteoric rise up the British charts to their appearance on Ed Sullivan to their hectic touring, recording and filming schedule—saw the full unleashing of their commercial potential. The juggernaut of the Beatle brand was unstoppable.

BOLD SIGNATURES HIGHLIGHT THIS BEAUTIFUL 1965 BEATLES TOUR PROGRAM DEPICTING THE BAND AS THEY WERE SEEN IN THEIR SATURDAY MORNING CARTOON. SOLD AT AUCTION FOR $19,200.

Image courtesy of Julien's Auctions

16/50

**Paul McCartney and John Lennon
photograph taken by Mike McCartney,
Paul's brother:** *In the photograph, Lennon and McCartney are said to be writing the song "I Saw Her Standing There," which was written in the McCartneys' front parlor. Apocryphal or factual? Who cares! It's a great image. Numbered 16/50 in the lower left margin and signed by the photographer in the lower right. Sold at auction for $6,875. Image courtesy of Julien's Auctions*

They were much more than just a brand, however. They were making ever more spectacular music, growing and maturing by the minute. Their longstanding influences—Elvis, Chuck Berry, Little Richard, Jerry Lee Lewis—were still and always would be important, but the tide of popular music was changing as The Beatles worked their way musically toward the end of their days touring. They were a huge factor in determining the direction of that tide, but the British invasion they spearheaded brought with it a flood of great artists, not to mention the profound impact the music of Bob Dylan had on the boys, especially John. They were quickly to become the greatest band of the day and they were on the cusp of making the music that would ensure their spot as the greatest ever.

On Aug. 14, 1965, the Beatles returned to the scene of their historic American TV debut on the Ed Sullivan Show and performed "I Feel Fine," "I'm Down," "Ticket to Ride," "Act Naturally," "Yesterday" (sung by Paul, accompanied by a string quartet from Sullivan's orchestra), and "Help!". *They were a group of fully mature musicians at this point, about to make the turn toward Rubber Soul that would totally break open the world of rock 'n' roll. This ticket from the taping is in Excellent condition and sold at auction for $11,350.*

Image courtesy of Heritage Auctions

The Ed Sullivan Show Debut Rehearsal Schedule. This 8" x 11" pink dittoed sheet dress rehearsal schedule for the show is a wonderful piece of history. It lists, in order, every segment of the show including all acts and commercials. It is signed "John Lennon" and "Paul McCartney" near the listing of their first set, and "Ringo Starr" near the listing of their second set. The autographed schedule was obtained by Noreen Fay, a member of the acrobatic troop Wells & Four Fays, who had the unenviable task of closing the show after the Beatles finished performing their huge hit "I Want To Hold Your Hand." Sold at auction for $11,250.

Image courtesy of Heritage Auctions

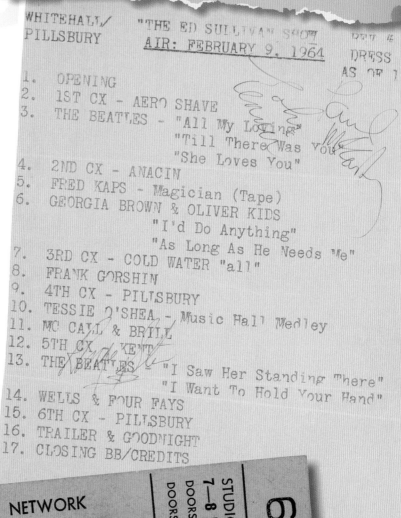

WHITEHALL/
PILLSBURY

"THE ED SULLIVAN SHOW"
AIR: FEBRUARY 9, 1964   DRESS
                               AS OF 12:0(

1.   OPENING
2.   1ST CX - AERO SHAVE
3.   THE BEATLES - "All My Loving"
                   "Till There Was You"
                   "She Loves You"
4.   2ND CX - ANACIN
5.   FRED KAPS - Magician (Tape)
6.   GEORGIA BROWN & OLIVER KIDS
                   "I'd Do Anything"
                   "As Long As He Needs Me"
7.   3RD CX - COLD WATER "all"
8.   FRANK GORSHIN
9.   4TH CX - PILLSBURY
10. TESSIE O'SHEA - Music Hall Medley
11. MC CALL & BRILL
12. 5TH CX - KENT
13. THE BEATLES - "I Saw Her Standing There"
                   "I Want To Hold Your Hand"
14. WELLS & FOUR FAYS
15. 6TH CX - PILLSBURY
16. TRAILER & GOODNIGHT
17. CLOSING BB/CREDITS

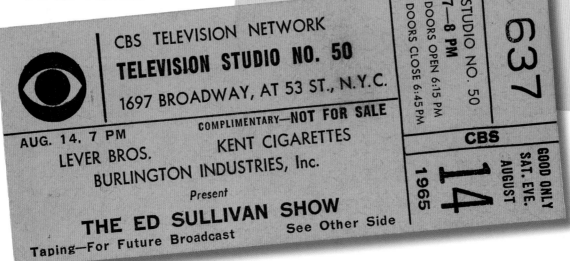

CBS TELEVISION NETWORK
TELEVISION STUDIO NO. 50
1697 BROADWAY, AT 53 ST., N.Y.C.

COMPLIMENTARY—**NOT FOR SALE**

AUG. 14, 7 PM

LEVER BROS.   KENT CIGARETTES
BURLINGTON INDUSTRIES, Inc.

Present

THE ED SULLIVAN SHOW

See Other Side

Taping—For Future Broadcast

STUDIO NO. 50
7—8 PM
DOORS OPEN 6:15 PM
DOORS CLOSE 6:45 PM

637

CBS

GOOD ONLY
SAT. EVE.
AUGUST

14

1965

February 9, 1964
THE NIGHT THEY APPEARED ON ED SULLIVAN

Excerpted from The Uwe Blaschke Collection catalog, Sept. 2015, Heritage Auctions

It was The Beatles' first live performance in America and 73 million Americans tuned in to The Ed Sullivan Show to witness the young lads from Liverpool. (Note: the population in the United States was approximately 190 million in 1964.) America was glued to its TV sets as we heard the solemn-faced Ed Sullivan mention that The Beatles had received a congratulatory telegram from Elvis and the Colonel.

In his introduction, he said: "Now yesterday and today our theater's been jammed with newspapermen and hundreds of photographers from all over the nation, and these veterans agreed with me that the city never has the excitement stirred by these youngsters from Liverpool, who call themselves The Beatles. Now tonight, you're going to twice be entertained by them. Right now, and again in the second half of our show. Ladies and gentlemen, The Beatles. Let's bring them on."

The girls in the audience started screaming the second he finished. The cameras then focused on The Beatles as McCartney counted-in to an energetic performance of "All My Loving." That song was followed by Paul crooning a ballad from The Music Man titled "Til There Was You". (That probably won a lot of the young girls' moms over.) They closed out this historic first American performance with the infectious "yeah yeah yeahs" of their hit "She Loves You." Every time they sang "wooo" or shook their heads, the screams got even louder.

They ended their first set with formal bows. About 30 minutes later, Ed Sullivan announced, "Ladies and Gentlemen, once again..." This time John, Paul, George, and Ringo performed both sides of their mega-hit Capitol single, "I Want to Hold Your Hand" and "I Saw Her Standing There." They then put down their instruments and walked over to shake hands with Sullivan. Performance over. History made. Payback complete for the "colonies" split from England nearly 200 years before. America was once again "owned" by the British. And this was just round one of the invasion; The Beatles opened the door for numerous British acts to make it in America.

As an aside, there was another act on that night's show- five members of the Broadway cast of Oliver! appeared and performed two songs from the hit musical. The actor who played the part of the Artful Dodger was a young British actor and singer named Davy Jones. Of course, he would soon make millions of girls scream for him as a member of the Monkees. He later said of that night: "I watched The Beatles from the side of the stage, I saw the girls going crazy, and I said to myself, this is it, I want a piece of that."

THE BEATLES

An early Dezo Hoffman photo of the Beatles was blown up to life size, 65" x 77", to create this impressive poster. The poster, in Very Good condition, sold at auction, for $275.
Image courtesy of Heritage Auctions

The year 1963 would be crucial in the band's history. With a new look, a new sound and a new album released in the UK in March of that year—the Please Please Me LP that yielded the megahit "She Loves You"—they were simply taking over the British music scene. They were playing bigger and bigger venues, making frequent appearances on British television (including several appearances on the BBC that resulted in the Live at the BBC recordings) and recording their follow-up album, With The Beatles.

When With The Beatles came out in August of 1963, led by the single "I Want to Hold Your Hand," the band must have finally gotten an inkling of what was awaiting them. They were fully confident in their abilities as musicians, discovering the genius of their churning musical attack—a la Chuck Berry and Little

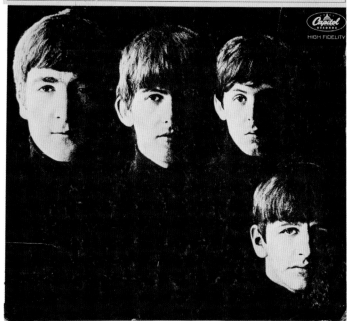

Richard—that would come to define the early years. Lightning was striking. All that was left was to catch those bolts in a bottle.

The best place to catch those bolts, as far as the boys and their manager could see, was America, a prize that had eluded them up to this point. They now had money, they had burgeoning respect, but what they really needed was America. What they didn't know was that America, too, needed them. At the end of 1963, with European stardom firmly in hand, Epstein and The Beatles made plans to cross the pond.

The early relationship between America and The Beatles—as defined in the press and by Capitol Records, the imprint of EMI that controlled the rights to The Beatles in America—was tepid, at best. Beatlemania had fully caught on in England, but it was seen as a childish fancy by the US press, when it was noted at all. To top it off, Capitol Records had declined to release any Beatles music in the U.S. all through 1963. Finally, in early 1964, they released the single "I Want to Hold Your Hand." The impact was massive, overwhelm-

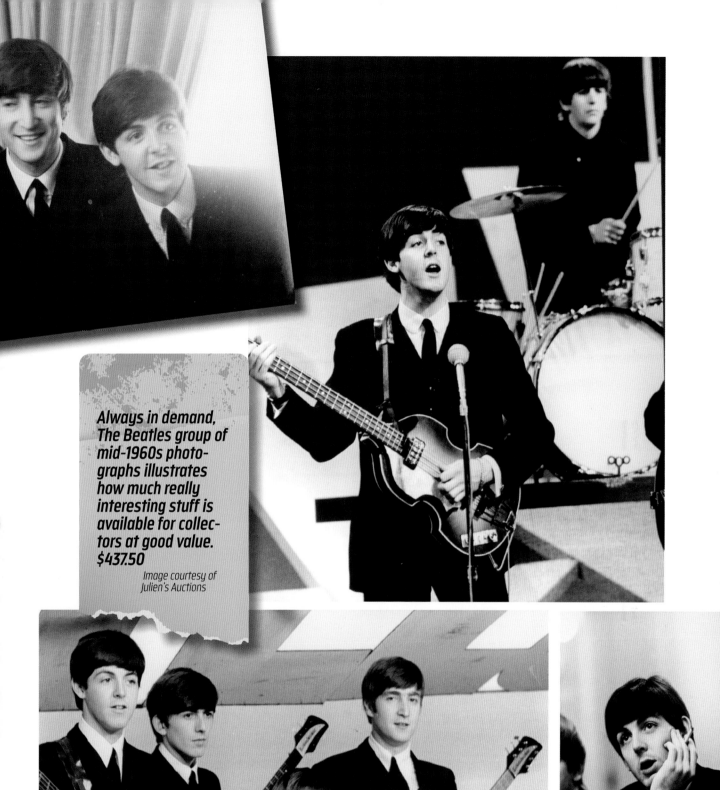

Always in demand, The Beatles group of mid-1960s photographs illustrates how much really interesting stuff is available for collectors at good value. $437.50

Image courtesy of Julien's Auctions

ing and historic. It raced to number one and sold 1.5 million copies in three weeks. There had been Pop phenomena before, but nothing like this.

So it was, on Feb. 9, 1964, that the band was booked onto the very popular and influential Ed Sullivan Show. The anticipation was gigantic, second only to Elvis's first appearance on the show in 1956. On Feb. 7, 1964, The Beatles boarded a Pan-Am jet to cross the Atlantic.

We know the boys were nervous on the flight, and we know they wondered aloud whether anyone would know who they were. We all know what it was like when they landed—pandemonium, hordes of screaming fans and whirring TV cameras. It was the defining moment of the British Invasion as the true Kings set foot upon American soil. The wave of popularity they rode into JFK Airport in New York was only to build over the next few days.

(top) An assortment of black-and-white photographs of the Beatles from the 1960s offers neophyte collectors an easy and fun gateway into Beatles collecting. Sold at auction for $192. Image courtesy of Julien's Auctions

(above) The Beatles "Our World" photograph: $384
Image courtesy of Julien's Auctions

(above) *A nice grouping of affordable Beatles photographs. $187.50*
Image courtesy of Julien's Auctions

(below) *The Beatles group of career and personal photos: Various looks at the band together, apart and in personal moments. Find this for $192 at auction? I say snap it up!* Image courtesy of Julien's Auctions

Beatles In Dallas Photos and Negatives:
The Beatles arrived in Dallas, Texas on Sept. 18, 1964. On hand to meet them was Dallas Times Herald photographer John Mazziotta, who snapped this group of more than 100 shots. Mazziotta's 10 year-old daughter, Jan, wanted to attend the concert, but safety issues kept her at home, so as compensation, she was gifted the collection of original negatives taken of the band. This incredible and rare look at the band at an historic moment sold at auction for $18,750.
Image courtesy of Heritage Auctions

For two days the band was ensconced at The Plaza Hotel. If they thought their first American trip was going to include sightseeing and tourism, they were quickly disabused of the thought. The hotel was overrun with fans and reporters, all trying anything they could to get a glimpse of the boys. There could be no question in their minds that America knew who they were. The CBS switchboard was inundated with requests for tickets from all over the map, including Walter Cronkite and President Nixon, who both were looking for tickets for their daughters.

At 7:59pm ET on Feb. 9, 1964, America was a country that was still stunned and reeling from the assassination of President Kennedy a mere 11 weeks prior. At 8pm ET, as 73 million Americans gathered around their television sets—that's 60% of all TVs in the country at that time—America moved past its grief and embraced the Modern era. The energy of America's youth, dampened by the sorrow and fear of the previous November, exploded in joyous rapture. The future had arrived and it was playing guitars on the small screen.

IN THE DAYS JUST BEFORE BEATLEMANIA HIT FULL FORCE, JOHN LENNON WROTE THIS LETTER TO A FAN, CIRCA 1963. TODAY IT'S WORTH AT LEAST $4,800.
Image courtesy of Julien's Auctions

'Swinging Lunch Time Rock Sessions'
AT THE
LIVERPOOL JAZZ SOCIETY,
13, TEMPLE STREET (off Dale Street and Victoria Street).
EVERY LUNCH TIME, 12-00 to 2-30
RESIDENT BANDS:
Gerry and the Pacemakers,
Rory Storm and the Wild Ones,
The Big Three.

Next Wednesday Afternoon, March 15th
12-00 to 5-00 Special
STARRING—
The Beatles,
Gerry and the Pacemakers
Rory Storm and the Wild Ones.

Admission—Members 1/-, *Visitors* 1/6

" Rocking at the L. J. S. "

The Victor Printing Co. 730 West Derby Road, Liverpool, 6

(above)
An early Beatles concert handbill featuring Ringo's old band Rory Storm and the Wild Ones. Sold at auction for $640.

Image courtesy of
Julien's Auctions

Inside a mid-60s press event attended by the Beatles. Sold for $320.
Image courtesy of
Julien's Auctions

(left) The Beatles Something New album cover artwork proof: $192
Image courtesy of Julien's Auctions

BEATLES SHEA STADIUM CONCERT POSTER (1965): A LARGER VERSION OF THE NEW YORK CITY-AREA HANDBILL, ANNOUNCING SHOWS FOR THE BEATLES, HERMAN'S HERMITS, THE DAVE CLARK 5, THE KINKS AND MOODY BLUES, AND THE NEW YORK FOLK FESTIVAL STARRING CHUCK BERRY AND JOHNNY CASH. FINE CONDITION. RARITY HAS ITS COST, AS WITH THIS PIECE AT $11,250.

Image courtesy of Heritage Auctions

Not a whole lot of props from "A Hard Day's Night" seem to show up at auction, making those that do stand-out. This "prop ram" brought a premium price at $3,200.
Image courtesy of Julien's Auctions

Imagine having a ticket to the last Beatles show, not using it and then knowing that you missed history. That's all I can think about seeing this magical slip of paper. Their final live performance—aside from their impromptu rooftop performance atop Apple Records in January 1969—was played at San Francisco's Candlestick Park on Aug. 29, 1966. The ticket features headshots of each of the boys and admits one to the upper stand reserve with a face value of $4.50. At auction the ticket sold for $625.

Image courtesy of Heritage Auctions

Just 10 days after the release of their seventh LP, Revolver, and in the midst of their "Bigger than Jesus" controversy, The Beatles played to a crowd of some 25,000 fans at Suffolk Downs, a famous horse track located in East Boston, on Aug. 18, 1966. $812.50

Image courtesy of Heritage Auctions

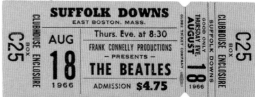

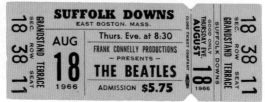

Pouring rain drenched 23,000 hardcore fans at the Beatles concert at Busch Memorial Stadium Aug. 21, 1966, the band's only appearance in St. Louis. This unused 5" x 2" black and red on pink printed ticket is in fantastic condition and sold for $1,375.

Image courtesy of Heritage Auctions

All bets were suddenly off. Once savaged by critics, ridiculed by the old guard, and deemed a momentary obsession of young girls, The Beatles had arrived. And the early 1960s had found its mirror. It's important to consider the scope of the impact The Beatles had. After Ed Sullivan, Capitol began to re-lease Beatles music en masse, whatever they could do to capitalize on the band's meteoric rise, however short-lived they thought it would be. The music continued to be good, with hints of the genius that the Lennon-Mc-Cartney partnership would produce. The fact was, the boys were so busy touring that they just didn't have the time to make a full studio album. It was the beginning of their frustra-tion with touring, one that would ultimately result in them giving it up.

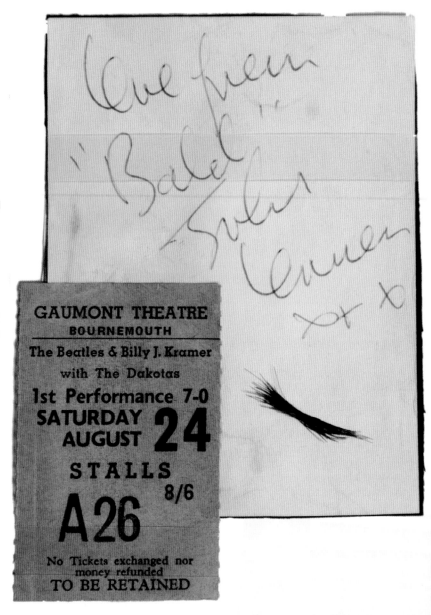

There has long been a fascination with and a market for locks of hair. Your writer has always found the pursuit somewhat creepy. For the record I am completely against the owner of this hair eventually creating a musician army of John Lennon clones. John has played along nicely in the inscription, signing it "Love, from 'Bald' John Lennon." It sold at auction for $25,600. Image courtesy of Julien's Auctions

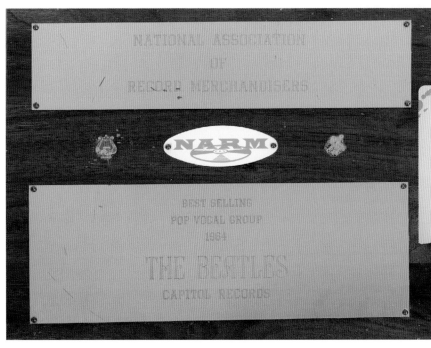

A National Association of Record Merchadisers (NARM) award presented to The Beatles Capitol Records for Best Selling Pop Vocal Group in 1964. Given by the great Neil Aspinall to an Apple employee in the 1980s. Sold at auction for $5,120. Image courtesy of Julien's Auctions

Beatles bass drum head from Madame Tussauds wax museum in London: *This drum head was famously an exact replica of the drum head used by Ringo when The Beatles played on "The Ed Sullivan Show" for the first time in 1964. The Beatles gave Madame Tussauds the drum head for display in her museum in 1964. The drum head was hand painted by Edwin Stokes, who also painted five of the seven original Beatles drum heads. The drum head sold at auction for $40,625.* Image courtesy of Julien's Auctions

Beatles full set of self-signed forgeries: *These forgeries occurred when one member of the band was responding to fan mail apart from his other three band members. The set consisting of four notes and cut sheets where the first Beatle signer was the signer of the remaining three signatures. All circa 1964. Fantastic piece of early Beatlemania, priced at premium for $14,080.* Image courtesy of Julien's Auctions

Iconic photograph of The Beatles by Robert Freeman. Sold at auction for $1,250. *Image courtesy of Julien's Auctions*

(right) A gold record for "I Want To Hold Your Hand," given to a Ringo Starr and signed on the back by George Harrison sold at auction for an impressive $68,750. *Image courtesy of Julien's Auctions*

A baseball signed by The Beatles on August 15, 1966. *The ball was the second of three signed that evening at DC Stadium for the Senators' equipment manager, Fred Baster. The autograph ball is a hit with collectors, selling at auction for $100,000. Image courtesy of Julien's Auctions*

Original photographs of The Beatles from across all periods of the band's career, with more focusing on the early part of their fame. $1,152.
Image courtesy of Julien's Auctions

For the time being, however, Beatlemania was in full effect. The names and faces of the band were everywhere and on everything. They couldn't go out in public without being mobbed. This was the price of fame, however, and their marketing prowess in effect may well be what kept the band in the public consciousness during these hectic days before their musical talents fully matured and/or were fully recognized.

"Everybody wanted something to do with them at the time," said Darren Julien, the namesake of Julien's Auctions in Los Angeles. "It's what helped keep them alive. They were a brand, too, a business. There were all these things being made and, as people began to realize the importance of the band, they began to hold onto the material more and more. The good pieces became collector's items."

You also see, in this period, that The Beatles did their best to satisfy fan demand. The record label kept re-issuing the same

(Above) The Beatles "A Hard Day's Night" soundtrack album cover proof sold at auction for $375.
Image courtesy of Julien's Auctions

(left) A highly coveted one-sheet movie poster from The Beatles' movie "Help" sold at auction for $1,920. Image courtesy of Julien's Auctions

Beatles Band Signed Shirt: *A vintage light gray short-sleeved shirt with a Beatles logo silk-screened onto the right breast signed by John, Paul, George and Ringo in blue ink on the right side. The exact date of the signing of this shirt is unknown, but we know it was very hard to get them to sign anything ensemble after 1963. This rare find sold at auction for $11,350.*

Image courtesy of Heritage Auctions

A John Lennon autograph from the mid-1960s. $1,920
Image courtesy of Julien's Auctions

A BLACK-ON-BLACK-STRIPE SUIT WITH SIX-BUTTON-FRONT CLOSURE, AND FOUR BUTTONS AT EACH CUFF, LINED IN RED AND BLACK PLAID SILK WITH MATCHING TROUSERS WORN BY RINGO IN THE 1964 FILM "A HARD DAY'S NIGHT" DIRECTED BY RICHARD LESTER. MAYBE NOT AN ICONIC OUTFIT FROM THE FILM, BUT IT WAS IN THE MOVIE AND A BEATLE WORE IT. 'NUFF SAID! SOLD AT AUCTION FOR $50,000. *Image courtesy of Julien's Auctions*

songs, with a few new ones mixed in, on different albums, and The Beatles signed as many things as they could.

Whether it was in public, on a film shoot of some kind, backstage at a concert or simply answering a fan letter, the amount of amateur images and autographs increased exponentially with their fame. In fact, the demand quickly became so great that the band first turned to their original Road Manager and Personal Assistant, Neil Aspinall, who would become the head of Apple Corps—the entity that controls The Beatles licensing to this day—to start signing for the whole band.

In terms of collectibles, especially autographs (detailed in this book in Chapter 8), it means a lot more items are available. It also means there are a lot more fakes, so be very careful about your source for buying, especially if that source is unverifiable or offers no guarantee.

"At that time they were signing more than they had previously," said Julien. "You also see from that period a lot of the signatures that Neil Aspinall did for them. These aren't fakes, exactly. They're just not near as valu-

"Beatles '65" Gold Record Award: Presented to the band to commemorate the sale of more than $1 million worth of the Capitol LP "Beatles '65." *Released in December of 1964, it became the fastest-selling album of the year, selling more than a million copies in its first week and displacing Elvis Presley's latest soundtrack from the #1 spot. The award sold at auction for $7,170.*
Image courtesy of Heritage Auctions

John Lennon's bathrobe was originally sold by Lennon's house-keeper, Dorothy "Dot" Jarlett, who said Lennon gave her the robe for her son. Jarlett worked for Lennon at Kenwood, his country mansion in Surrey, England, where he wrote some of the best-known Beatles songs. Any item that got this close to a Beatle is worth a minor fortune – in this case $10,625.

Image courtesy of Julien's Auctions

Ringo's personal copy of the film script for "Beatles Two," which became "Help!" (UA, 1965). *With handwritten notations Ringo's personal recollections on the film are very entertaining, from the Julien's Auctions catalog: "I think because I loved films I was less embarrassed than the others to be in one," said Starr. "John really got into the movie, too... The storyline to Help! was written around me and the theme of the ring, and of course, Kaili. I had the central part. I think it helped that I was enthusiastic about the first film... A hell of a lot of pot was being smoked while we were making the film." The script sold at auction for $10,625.* Image courtesy of Julien's Auctions

able. Early on I don't think anybody thought they were going to be as big as they were so nobody thought much of having an employee sign some autographs."

Eventually the flow would slow to a trickle and the only autographs that serious collectors and dealers will take nowadays are those that come with a verifiable story and/or a picture.

There are tiers of value in every collectible category and The Beatles are no different. Whether it's merchandising, autographs, awards or instruments, know what you're getting. The Beatles were a huge business at the time and that meant that a lot of decisions would be out of their control and result in items and images with their names and signatures on it.

"I think, at the time, they were so busy that other people were making certain decisions for them, especially business," said Julien. "Their management tried to do right by the band, but no matter how careful they were, certain things would escape and the material that surfaced from it is authentic to the time period, but not to the band or its licensing."

The solution to this is simple, especially if you are actively looking to buy: go to reputable, verifiable sources for your Beatles material. There are good dealers and auctioneers out there, and price guides and reference materials aplenty. If an image or a piece of merchandising seems too good to be true, it probably is. A little study and a little guidance go a long way and can save a good bit of money.

So 1964 ended and 1965 found the band still as popular and busy as ever. They were making films, appearing on TV, recording whenever they could and, most of all, touring relentlessly, all to massive crowds and seething throngs of fans—mostly young girls. Amidst all this hubbub, however, the first fully mature Beatles songs began to emerge, as evidenced by several songs on Help!, released in August of 1965.

The real revolution would begin, however, with the December 1965 release of Rubber Soul. It marked the first time that The Beatles went into the studio and recorded an album consecutively.

BEATLES "A HARD DAY'S NIGHT" RIAA WHITE MATTE GOLD RECORD AWARD (CAPITOL 5222, 1964): RELEASED IN JULY OF 1964, "A HARD DAY'S NIGHT" WAS A MONUMENTAL MOMENT FOR THE BAND. WRITTEN BY JOHN LENNON, ITS TITLE TAKEN FROM A QUIP BY RINGO STARR, THE SONG SHARED ITS TITLE WITH THE BAND'S FIRST FEATURE FILM. THE PLAQUE STATES: "PRESENTED TO THE BEATLES TO COMMEMORATE THE SALE OF MORE THAN ONE MILLION COPIES OF THE CAPITOL RECORDS POP SINGLE RECORD 'A HARD DAY'S NIGHT'." SOLD AT AUCTION FOR $3,750.

Image courtesy of Heritage Auctions

BEATLES "REVOLVER" RIAA GOLD ALBUM AWARD: PRESENTED TO THE BEATLES BY THE RIAA TO COMMEMORATE THE SALE OF MORE THAN $1 MILLION DOLLARS WORTH OF THEIR GROUNDBREAKING 1966 ALBUM. THE BAND'S SEVENTH STUDIO RECORDING, REVOLVER MARKED THEIR ENTRANCE INTO PSYCHEDELIA, AS WELL AS GEORGE HARRISON'S EMERGENCE AS A SONGWRITER WITH HIS CONTRIBUTIONS TO THREE TRACKS. IT'S OFTEN CITED AS ONE OF THE GREATEST ALBUMS IN POP MUSIC HISTORY. IT HAS BEEN CERTIFIED PLATINUM FIVE TIMES OVER, AND THEN SOME, I IMAGINE. THE AWARD SOLD AT AUCTION FOR $7,170.
IMAGE COURTESY OF HERITAGE AUCTIONS

(right) Beatles Rubber Soul RIAA Gold Album Award: *Presented to the Beatles by the RIAA (Recording Industry Association of America) to commemorate the sale of $1 million worth of the Fab Four's December 1965 LP. Recorded in just four weeks in order to be on the market for Christmas, the album exhibited a sound influenced by contemporary Folk Rock. It became a major artistic achievement, a commercial and critical success and marked a turning point for the band's sound. The award sold at auction for $7,170.* Image courtesy of Heritage Auctions

THE BEATLES: COLLECTION OF STORYBOARD AND IDEA SKETCHES FOR "THE BEATLES" CARTOON SERIES:
46 TOTAL SHEETS, EACH SKETCH DONE IN PENCIL WITH SEVERAL NOTATIONS DONE IN RED. IN VERY GOOD CONDITION. THE BEATLES ANIMATED TELEVISION SERIES RAN FOR THREE SEASONS, BETWEEN 1965 AND 1969, WITH A TOTAL OF 39 EPISODES—AND WAS STARTED BEFORE 1965, HENCE ITS INCLUSION IN THIS CHAPTER. WORD AMONG THOSE IN THE KNOW IS THAT THE BAND HATED THE SHOW AT FIRST, BUT GREW FOND OF IT IN LATER YEARS. SOLD AT AUCTION FOR $1,250.

Image courtesy of Heritage Auctions

over the course of several weeks. They were off the road and working furiously. What emerged is nothing less than their first full work of genius. The music was so good, and so mature, musicians and fans alike took notice of what was happening. It may have been hard to put a finger on, but The Beatles had managed to blend all their early influence, all the present influence and all their own quirks, to produce an album of depth and quality that fully transcended the image of the jolly moptops.

By 1966, touring had begun to exhaust the band and fame had begun to make them a lightning rod. It was a claustrophobic existence for the boys, being on the road all the time, playing the same music over and over, having no privacy and being creatively stifled.

Author Hunter Davies, in his book *"The Beatles: The Authorized Biography,"* writes of the times: "They were trapped in their dressing room during a

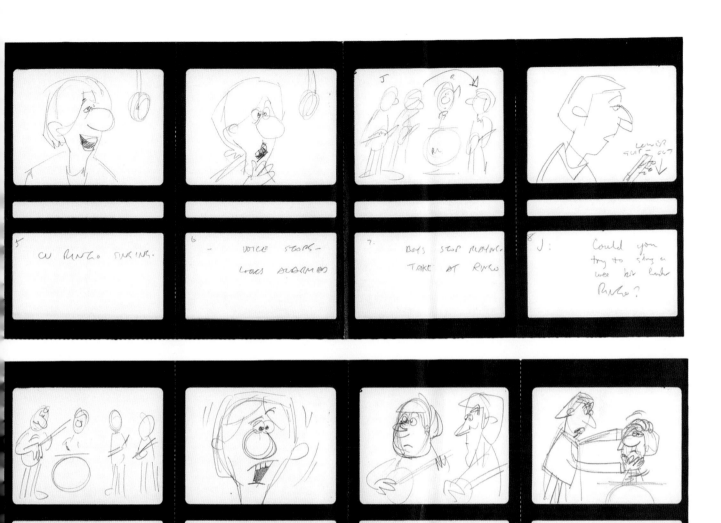

Non-stop touring was taking its toll on The Beatles by 1966. As the cover for the program to The Beatles concert at Dodger Stadium in Los Angeles on Aug. 28, 1966, illustrates, the boys were growing up and no longer teen idols. The Beatles were serious musicians and the burden of travel and fame was beginning to weigh on them. Program and tickets sold at auction for $512. *Image Courtesy of Julien's Auctions*

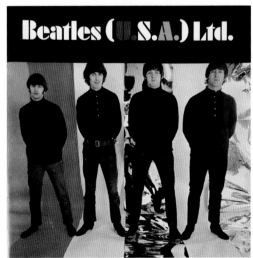

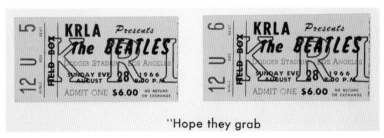

"Hope they grab

The Beatles released a specially recorded Christmas message to the members of The Official Beatles Fan Club each year from 1963 to 1969. The sleeve for this 7" flexi disc from that first year is signed in ballpoint: "To All the 'Kelly'/ family - Fred - Gladys/ Barbara - Arthur - Paul and/ RED/ best of Luck from/ George Harrison (a smile and a song)/ your friend -/ buddy -/ Pal." Arthur Kelly was a lifelong friend of George's and a member of his first band. Fred and Gladys were Arthur's parents, Paul and Barbara were his siblings, and Red was his brother-in-law. Sold at auction for $2,375.

Image courtesy of Heritage Auctions

(opposite) The original owner of these photographs was on a family vacation in the Bahamas in early March 1965 while the Beatles were on location filming HELP! They met the band and were allowed broad access. The result is this candid collection of original color photographs and 35MM negatives. Most photos show filming on the beach, with John, Paul, George and Ringo in numerous shots. Shots were also taken around the white sports car Paul used during filming and other locations in the Bahamas. $2,500

Image courtesy of Heritage Auctions

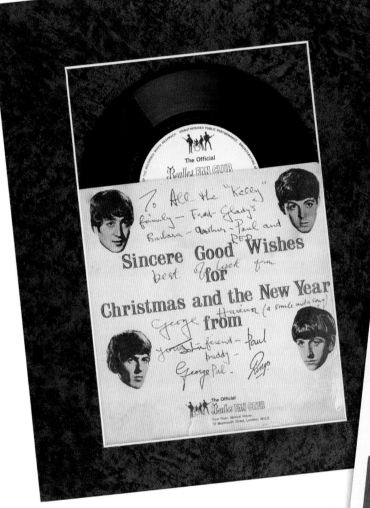

The Helen Shapiro Tour Handbill, from March 2, 1963, was the last tour on which The Beatles were not the top act on the bill. The Shapiro tour ended on March 3, which was two days after John and Paul wrote "From Me To You" on the tour bus. The band's third single was recorded on March 5, 1963. The handbill sold at auction for $1,625. Image courtesy of Heritage Auctions

On Nov. 4, 1963, the Beatles played a Royal Command performance in London for the Queen Mother and Princess Margaret. The group was number seven on a 19-act bill, but they were definitely the main event. During the rehearsals in the days leading up to the show, members of the Beatles became friends with many of the other performers, including American singer and pianist Buddy Greco—so much so that when Greco presented George Harrison and John Lennon with a copy of his most recent recording, Harrison returned the gesture with an autograph and Lennon by giving away his cap. This black wool seaman's cap has the initials "J.L." written on the lining in black ink, and was carefully stored and preserved by Greco for decades. An incredible artifact relating to a key moment in Beatles (and music) history, it sold for $8,066.

Image courtesy of Heritage Auctions

FRENCH AFFICHE MOVIE POSTER FOR THE LANDMARK FILM HELP! (UNITED ARTISTS, 1965) STARRING THE BEATLES AND DIRECTED BY RICHARD LESTER. IN UNRESTORED STATE, OVERALL FINE /VERY FINE CONDITION, THIS POSTER SOLD AT AUCTION FOR $550.

Image courtesy of Heritage Auctions

(below) Help! (United Artists, 1965) Half Sheet (22" X 28"): *Starring The Beatles, John Lennon, Paul McCartney, George Harrison, Ringo Starr, Leo McKern, Eleanor Bron, Victor Spinetti, and Roy Kinnear. Directed by Richard Lester. This half sheet is partially restored with good color. For a half sheet in this condition expect to pay around $350. Image courtesy of Heritage Auctions*

performance. There was the mad dash, guarded by hordes of police and bodyguards, to the hotel. There they stayed, with the outside world locked out, till the time came for the next move. They never went out in the street, to a restaurant or for a walk."

It was a hellish way to try and make art. At the same time, The Beatles were facing controversy over the famous, short-lived release of Yesterday and Today, now known as the Butcher Cover, featuring the band dressed in white smocks and covered with dismembered baby dolls and pieces of meat—it was done to be humorous and break the boredom of

The Beatles 1964 Netherlands Concert Poster. Sold at auction for $128.
Image courtesy of Julien's Auctions

Astrid Kirchherr Signed Large-Format Photograph of George Harrison, "Soup" (London, 1964): *A sweet, humorous photograph taken on the set of A Hard Day's Night of the notoriously picky eater George Harrison. The photograph is signed and printed 2009 by Grauwert, Hamburg. A great find by for an astute collector for $800.*
Image courtesy of Heritage Auctions

RADIO EUROPA Nederland Eurovox Studio NIJMEGEN

PROGRAMMARELAIS FESTIVAL BLOKKER 1964

6 JUNI THE BEATLES

This is the original artwork mock-up used for The Beatles '65 album. The images and the layout capture the personality of band very well. Sold at auction for $896.

Image Courtesy of Julien's Auctions

the tedious, numerous photo shoots the boys were called to do. It also may or may not have been a not-so-quiet protest against Vietnam or Capitol Records, depending on what you read.

It was conceptual, weird and way out of line with mainstream American thinking, where it was released. Reaction was immediate; complaints poured in and the copies were pulled. The original albums were covered with a tamer image and re-released. Those original albums now are known as "First State" issues and worth quite a bit if the serial number is low and the album is sealed or otherwise in mint condition.

Around the same time, in March of that year, Lennon made his famous comment about Christianity dying and The Beatles being "more popular than Jesus" to a British magazine. The comments languished at first, but soon began to stir up serious controversy in America.

Amidst all of this, The Beatles recorded and released the sublime and impeccable Revolver album in August of 1966, truly a hallmark of modern music and one that shows that The Beatles were the early masters of the emerging studio technology. The Lennon-McCartney partnership was in full flower, the production was out of this world and the music was consistently brilliant.

The Beatles Come to Town (Pathé, 1963): One Sheet movie poster for this early Beatles short concert film, shot by Pathé News, in Technicolor, of the band at the ABC Cinema in Manchester, Lancashire on Nov. 20, 1963. The film was distributed in the U.S. in 1964 with two printing variations in the posters. Although both styles are very rare, this is the more difficult to find. Very Fine condition. Sold at auction for $3,346 Image courtesy of Heritage Auctions

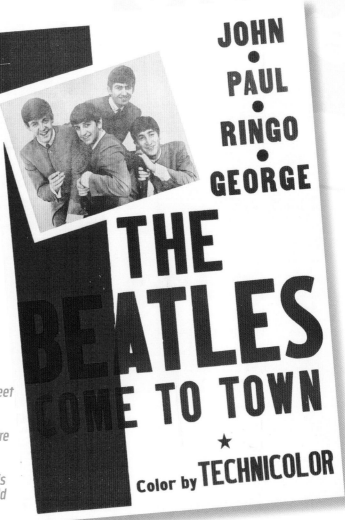

The reception stateside was muted, as the band was mired in the controversy over Lennon's comments, but the impact had been made. Clearly their place was making music at their own pace, without the burden of performing. A few days after Revolver was released, Aug. 29, 1966, The Beatles played their last live concert at Candlestick Park in San Francisco. Their days of touring, which they had come to despise, were officially over.

The Beatles were no longer just teen idols, no longer young men on a fanciful journey through the pop charts. They were fully grown men, mature musicians whose work was a major influence on a burgeoning group of musicians looking for rock glory. They were growing with their fans and they were breaking the mold with every new release.

The first part of their lives as the world's greatest rock band was over. Good things lay ahead, musically—some of the greatest music ever written or recorded—while the road of their personal lives was about to get much rockier. The end was already written in the stars, or rather the music, but what an end it would be.

Vintage Collection in Framed Display (US, 1964): *Wonderful grouping of five large-size and 12 smaller pinbacks; eight original Topps trading cards with both black-and-white and color waxpack wrappers; a full, unused A Hard Day's Night premiere ticket, dated Aug. 12th (1964) at the Embassy Theatre; a guitar-shaped pin; a round brooch with a silver bezel; and the A Hard Day's Night 7" 33 rpm record and picture sleeve. Great material at a good auction price of $193.75*
Image courtesy of Heritage Auctions

PEAK MUSICAL PERIOD and THE END

LATE 1966-1970

History has taught us that the end of The Beatles was writ large on the heels of their last gig in August of 1966 at Candlestick Park. There were so many contributing factors, when all was said and done, that there is as much myth as there is fact about what ultimately went down. What matters in the end, at least in terms of this book, is the music and the collectibles.

THIS STUNNING ITALIAN YELLOW SUBMARINE MOVIE POSTER (55" X 78") SOLD AT AUCTION FOR $2,868.

Image courtesy of Heritage Auctions

"John Lennon Listening To The White Album" by photographer Ethan Russell. **Not sure if I would want to have been there with him listening, but I love getting a look and trying to guess what he was thinking. $125.** *Image courtesy of Julien's Auctions.*

Musically, while their albums signaled the emergence of four distinct musicians and people, the results they achieved as a band has no pound-for-pound equal in the history of rock 'n' roll, and I would stand on Mick Jagger's coffee table and yell it.

Here's what the boys released in the three-year period between 1967 and 1970: *Sgt. Pepper's Lonely Hearts Club Band*, *Magical Mystery Tour*, *The Beatles (The White Album)*, *Yellow Submarine*, *Abbey Road* and *Let It Be*. It's a stunning and humbling run, despite the acrimony and mistrust that was building during the latter three records.

There is a certain magic to the memorabilia that emerged from the period, as well. The Beatles marketing juggernaut continued to produce, and the Saturday morning cartoon featuring the band kept them in front of the

(above) An RIAA-certified "gold" record award presented to The **Beatles to commemorate the sale of more than $1 million worth of the Capitol Records long-playing record album Rubber Soul. Sold at auction for $7,040.** *Image courtesy of Julien's Auctions*

Vintage and press photographs capture the group from January 1967 during the filming of the promotional clip for "Strawberry Fields Forever," continuing through their final group photo session with Ethan Russell at John's home, Tittenhurst Park, on Aug. 22, 1969. A steal at auction for $400.
Image courtesy of Heritage Auctions

eyes and in the minds of the younger generation. In terms of hard and fast pieces of memorabilia, however? It's a tough go. There are things that can be found, but signatures and instruments are much more rare from this period.

"The truth is that they really weren't together much anymore except in the studio," said Darren Julien, CEO and President of Julien's Auctions in Los Angeles. "As the '60s wore on they were spread out doing their own thing. They all wanted to have their own separate careers at that point and were chasing that."

The result is a dearth of material from the time, minus straight marketing and ephemera, and that lack, today, equals value. The rare signatures from the period that were all signed together, at the same time, bring significant money—into the tens of thousands and up into the hundreds of thousands of dollars—depending on the signatures themselves and what they're signed on. After these things, you begin to see more premium placed on photo archives, individual band member-used items and Beatles-as-a-group-used items.

"This is a period that you see a lot of individual things from the band members," said Julien. "That's where you see a pair of sunglasses or eyeglasses from John, or a suit one of them wore."

Ringo Starr wore this suit to the premiere for what is, arguably, the band's most famous film, "Yellow Submarine". It sold at auction for $34,375 at auction.
Image courtesy of Julien's Auctions

A pair of John Lennon's gold tone Algha glasses, often referred to as Lennon's "Granny" glasses. Given to a fashion designer at the Ad Lib club in London in the 1960s. Lennon gave her the specs to help her read the menu. Lennon began wearing this style of glasses after being cast in How I Won The War (UA, 1967). Few accoutrements are more associated with John than his glasses. Sold at auction for $25,000.
Image courtesy of Julien's Auctions

A brief glimpse inside Apple Corp *via some corporate transparencies for the marketing for the release of Sgt. Pepper's. A good auction buy for the right collector at $384.*

Image courtesy of Julien's Auctions

B6-AC0018

B6 ACO O21

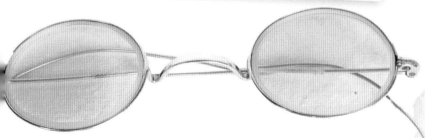

A PAIR OF JOHN LENNON'S PRESCRIPTION "GRANNY" GLASSES, GOLD-TONE WIRE-RIM GLASSES WITH CABLE TEMPLES, CIRCA 1967. LENNON WORE THESE IN THE SUMMER OF '67 BUT FOUND THE LENSES TOO SMALL. SOLD AT AUCTION FOR $25,600.

Image courtesy of Julien's Auctions

WHEN RINGO AND GEORGE QUIT THE BAND

Excerpted, with permission, from Listverse.com
"10 Untold Stories from the Wild Days of The Beatles"
Nolan Moore, Sept. 29, 2014

Thanks to a mix of egos and economics, Paul McCartney left The Beatles in April 1970, ending the most famous musical act in history. But Paul wasn't the first member to leave the band. That honor goes to Ringo Starr, who quit back in 1968 while The Beatles were recording their famous The White Album.

In addition to its influence on Charles Manson, The White Album marked a particularly dark period for The Beatles. George was trying to assert himself musically, Paul was becoming rather bossy, and John kept bringing Yoko Ono into the studio, which threw off the band's groove. As a result, there was a lot of fighting, resulting in band members recording by themselves. In the words of Paul, the White Album was actually the "tension album."

That tension boiled over on August 22, 1968, when Ringo called it quits. Everyone was fighting, Paul had mocked his drumming, and he was feeling like an outsider. Frustrated, Ringo approached John and said, "I'm leaving the group because I'm not playing well, and I feel unloved and out of it, and you three are really close." Lennon was flabbergasted. "I thought it was you three!" he shouted. When Ringo approached Paul, he got the same exact response.

Nevertheless, Starr borrowed Peter Sellers's yacht, sailed for Sardinia, and spent two weeks on the high sea writing "Octopus's Garden." In the meantime, Paul filled in for Ringo, drumming on "Back in the USSR" and "Dear Prudence." But eventually, the band sent Ringo a telegram proclaiming him the best drummer in the world and begging him to come back. And when Starr returned, he found flowers spread across his drum set, spelling out the words, "Welcome Back, Ringo."

The good mood didn't last. In 1969, George was getting angry at Paul for suppressing his songs and was furious at Lennon for taking Yoko's advice over his. It also didn't help that a documentary crew was filming every little flare-up. Finally, things exploded when Lennon told the press that Apple was going bankrupt. An enraged George confronted John, and the two ended up getting into an actual fistfight. Sick of all the shenanigans, Harrison decided it was time to go.

"See you 'round the clubs," he said as he stormed off. Lennon, always one to add fuel to the fire, made a joke about replacing George with Eric Clapton.

The four were able to smooth things over for a little while, and George returned to finish Let It Be and Abbey Road. Sadly, though, time was running out for The Beatles, and in just a matter of months, the dream would finally be over.

You also cannot discount the fact that The Beatles had become increasingly cognizant of the inherent worth of their *things*. It's always been well known that Paul McCartney is a great collector and has kept most of his memorabilia, instruments and assorted collectibles since the beginning. The same is true of the other members of the band. By the time they had settled into their role as the greatest rock 'n' roll band in history, they also realized that there was a premium on not only their signatures, but also on anything they touched. They now were millionaires and could control what emerged and what didn't.

Julien is well positioned to have seen the collecting prowess of the Beatles first-hand, having sold Ringo Starr's collection in late 2015.

Yellow Submarine album cover artwork proofs sold at auction for $896.
Image courtesy of Julien's Auctions

One-of-a-kind production cel set-up *of four original hand-painted cels featuring all four Beatles and the Yellow Submarine placed over a printed background for presentation purposes. A set-up featuring all four Beatles together is rare – add the Yellow Submarine to that and you have something special. A Holy Grail piece, with paint, in Fine condition. $7,767.50*
Image courtesy of Heritage Auctions

Two large format contact sheets containing 65 images in all, featuring locations throughout The Beatles' hometown of Liverpool, including the docks, the train station and The Cavern Club. The spots were used in the film, Yellow Submarine. Sold at auction for $500.
Image courtesy of Heritage Auctions

(below) So very cool and so very rare! An original hand-painted color model cel focusing on the Beatles in their "everyday" outfits from the groundbreaking psychedelic animated movie, Yellow Submarine (United Artists/King Features, 1968), replete with color instructions written in ink and china marker on the acetate. Note the special instructions for Ringo's many rings! Excellent condition. Sold at auction for $14,340.
Image courtesy of Heritage Auctions

"The Beatles themselves certainly kept their things from this period," he said. "The amount of storage they all had, and have, for their items is vast. It was different early on, as they didn't have the means to store anything properly. As they progressed, they took better care."

What this means for collectors is that you better be ready to spend big for the choicest material.

The scarcity of memorabilia that emerges in the final period, in direct contrast to the Beatlemania and touring years, also reflects the larger feeling of The Beatles toward the world and their fame. They were simply worn out after the first part of the 1960s, and it shows in press photos of the maturing young men. When they quit performing to focus only on recording, the music shifted into overdrive while the interpersonal and business dynamics of the band changed drastically.

It also, where the memorabilia is concerned, marks what seemed to be a disconnection from the fan. The band had poured half a decade into their fans, into their concerts, into being available to everyone. Now, as free agents, they didn't need to do anything they didn't want and a big part of what they didn't want to do was deal with the mobs at their every public turn. The result is less photos, less autographs and less related material. What there is from the time, however, is highly coveted.

At first there must have been a profound sense of relief. The grind was over. They had the money, they had the fame and they had the power to do whatever they wanted. They did travel and they did do a lot of drugs

BACK IN THE USSR

Excerpted, with permission, from Listverse.com
"10 Untold Stories from the Wild Days of The Beatles"
Nolan Moore, Sept. 29, 2014

In 1966, after John made his infamous "more popular than Jesus" quip, angry Americans rampaged, bashing and burning piles of Beatles albums. And conspiracy theories abound, lambasting the boys from Liverpool for connections with the Illuminati.

However, nobody feared The Beatles more than the Soviet government. Recognizing their rebellious attitudes and Western ways as a threat, the USSR banned the sale of Beatles albums and punished anyone caught listening to this "capitalist pollution." This only created a black market for contraband albums.

Like many illegal items, Beatles records were smuggled into Russia by sailors, actors, and the occasional Party official. The albums were then sold for a hefty price. Vinyl discs could cost Soviet citizens up to two weeks pay.

Some enterprising outlaws devised an ingenious solution: etch the music onto X-ray film with the help of a modified record player. These jerry-rigged disks were covered in images of fractured arms and cracked pelvises, causing fans to refer to the albums as "music on the bones" or "records on ribs."

Other musicians received the X-ray treatment, but there was something special about The Beatles.

According to Mikhail Safonov of the Institute of Russian History, "Beatlemania washed away the foundations of Soviet society. The Beatles brought us the idea of democracy." Inspired by the Fab Four's fashion sense, teens used army boots and hand-me-down coats to copy the Beatles' signature collarless look. Men grew their hair long, kids started their own rock bands, and anyone who challenged The Beatles was viewed with disdain—even government officials.

The state fought back as hard as it could. Students caught listening to The Beatles could be expelled from college. One Russian school put the band on trial and broadcasted the little drama for all the USSR to hear. And anyone sporting a mop-top could be nabbed by the police and given a quick haircut. But despite all these efforts, The Beatles remained.

The USSR collapsed, and Paul McCartney played his first performance in Moscow in 2003.

A sculpted bust from Tittenhurst Park, former home of John Lennon and Ringo Starr. **This bust was featured in a number of images from what would be The Beatles last photo shoot together as a group before officially breaking up the following year. Images from this last shoot were later used on the cover for the album "Hey Jude" (Apple, 1970). The sculpture offered here can be seen prominently featured on the left side of the album's front cover. An incredible witness to Rock history. $35,200.**

Image courtesy of
Julien's Auctions

The Beatles "Let It Be" movie publicity stills. Sold at auction for $192.
Image courtesy of Julien's Auctions

SGT. PEPPER'S LONELY HEARTS CLUB BAND SPENT 175 WEEKS ON THE AMERICAN BILLBOARD CHARTS AND PRODUCED A NUMBER OF CHART-TOPPING SINGLES AS WELL. THIS GOLD RECORD, COMMEMORATING MORE THAN $1 MILLION IN RECORD SALES, FOR THE ALBUM SOLD AT AUCTION FOR $8,125.
Image courtesy of Heritage Auctions

Yellow Submarine animation cel of John Lennon. Auction price: $1,600.
Image courtesy of Julien's Auctions

Yellow Submarine animation cel of Paul McCartney. $1,920
Image courtesy of Julien's Auctions

AN RIAA—CERTIFIED "GOLD" RECORD AWARD PRESENTED TO THE BEATLES TO COMMEMORATE THE SALE OF MORE THAN ONE MILLION COPIES OF THE SINGLE "GET BACK." SOLD AT AUCTION FOR $10,880.
Image courtesy of Julien's Auctions

PRESENTED TO
THE BEATLES
TO COMMEMORATE THE SALE OF MORE THAN
ONE MILLION COPIES OF THE
APPLE RECORDS
POP SINGLE RECORD
"GET BACK"

CERTIFIED
RIAA
SALES AWARD

and they did relax for the first time since being teenagers. They also wrote and recorded *Sgt. Pepper's Lonely Hearts Club Band*, the most mind-blowing record album the world had heard at the time, and still one of the greatest.

During the recording process for *Sgt. Pepper's* the band was getting along well, they enjoyed the process of recording and discovery and, with the help of George Martin, used their emerging prowess with technology, tape looping and world instruments to create a unique soundscape that restructured rock 'n' roll and Pop Music from the bottom up. They had re-defined themselves again, they had created a definitive masterpiece for the ages and they—and the rest of the world—knew it.

It is also obvious from the songs on the album that the styles of Lennon, McCartney and Harrison—with Ringo emerging, too—as distinct song voices within the Beatle dynamic were becoming quite pronounced. This, combined with their evolution as human beings, started the countdown clock to the end.

After *Sgt. Pepper's*, the band embarked upon *Magical Mystery Tour*. Not only was it to be a

The back panel of Lennon's famous psychedelic painted caravan featuring the "Sgt. Peppers Lonely Hearts Club Band" drum logo. Lennon purchased the caravan in 1967 as a gift for son Julian's fourth birthday. Lennon had the caravan custom painted with a Sgt. Pepper theme by The Fool who also painted his famous psychedelic Rolls Royce in a similar motif. Lennon and family reportedly used the caravan for vacations before it made its final journey back to the garden of Tittenhurst Park in Ascot where it remained until Lennon's assassination. Ringo Starr acquired the caravan and had it fully restored in 1983 by John Pockett. This portion of the caravan features a back window with drape, and the chains that originally held the back gate, but most iconic is the bold Sgt. Pepper logo featured on the back panel. Sold with a framed image of the caravan as it was kept at the Starr's English country home in Surrey. An amazing piece of Beatles history: $125,000.

Image courtesy of Julien's Auctions

John Lennon and Yoko Ono Original Signed Bed-In Drawing: *A wonderfully evocative signed drawing from John and Yoko's famous bed-in in Montreal. The message of this one is very clear: "Hair Peace." The famous crusaders and newlyweds have signed it clearly. Hard to imagine a better, more spot-on piece of Lennon/Ono activism. It doubles as Modern Art with Yoko's involvement and brought a Modern Art price of $185,000 at auction.*

Image Courtesy of Julien's Auctions

Beatles Yellow Submarine "Lucy in the Sky with Diamonds" Production Drawing (United Artists/King Features, 1968): **An original, museum-worthy concept drawing for the Sea of Phrenology featured in the "Lucy in the Sky with Diamonds" sequence in Yellow Submarine. Graphite and colored pencil, the drawing is an epic 15" x 10.5". Amazing detail and one of the rarest forms of artwork from this film gives a rare glimpse into the making of the avant-garde, Beatles-inspired movie. $1,972.**

Image courtesy of Heritage Auctions

sublime album full of great, emotionally mature tunes of incredible depth, McCartney had an idea to make a film out of it. It was to be unscripted, off the cuff and full of "magical" adventures —a reflection of the LSD-influenced free form art of the day. Or maybe the boys were just so rich and famous that no one could tell them "no."

The end result was more legendary music and a really bad "film," aired on the BBC in December of 1967. Critics panned it, people didn't get it at all and the band was embarrassed by it. Ultimately, however, this was far from the worst thing that befell The Beatles in 1967. Tragedy struck Aug. 27, 1967, when manager Brian Epstein died from a drug overdose. Epstein's death rocked the band to its core. Epstein had handled every part of their business dealings since the beginning. He had profited handsomely off of the work, but he made sure the band did well, too, especially in the areas of merchandising and concerts.

When the band stopped touring, however, Epstein's roll changed. They needed Epstein to keep things rolling when they were touring. Someone needed to handle the contracts, the travel, the venues and the money, and it was all Epstein. Once The Beatles were fully a studio band, the need for Epstein to do all those things diminished considerably. He was making 25% of what the band made and, after expenses, splitting the rest between the musicians. It was a relationship the Beatles were comfortable with because of his dedication to them, their dedication to him, their history together and his influence on their lives. It was also a relationship that was clearly going to have to change.

Did this contribute to Epstein's death? It's impossible to know what did it, or if it was even on purpose, though Epstein was known to have flirted with suicide before. What is clearly known is that he was addicted to prescription drugs—Preludin, an upper that all the band members talked about taking in the early days to stay up all night and play their epic early shows, in particular—and led

Ringo's custom Ludwig silver sparkle drum kit used in the 1967 "Hello, Goodbye" video made for and played on The Ed Sullivan Show to help Sullivan celebrate the re-naming of CBS-Studio 50 to The Ed Sullivan Theater. The drums were built in October 1967 for the video and sent to London for the Paul McCartney directed video shoot that took place on Nov. 10, 1967 at the Saville Theatre in London. Sold at auction for $115,200. Image courtesy of Julien's Auctions

*The Beatles "Let It Be" Movie Poster, in Very Fine condition. **The film's soundtrack was nominated for an Academy Award. Sold at auction for $2,880.** Image courtesy of Julien's Auctions*

Set of eight Lobby Cards for "Let It Be" (United Artists, 1970), *the documentary film of the band as it made the album Let It Be and slowly fell apart. This movie was originally quite obscure, due to rights issues, so original paper related to the 1970 release is quite sacred. Very Fine condition, these sold at auction for $597.50.*

Image courtesy of Heritage Auctions

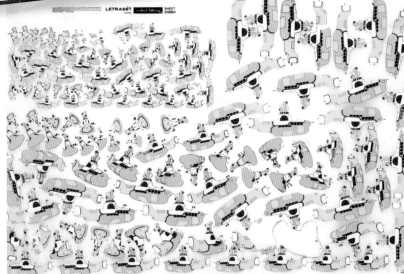

With less than a year to finish Yellow Submarine, a technique using Letraset stickers was used to depict the submarine traveling in certain sequences. These rare sheets of production stickers are highly sought by collectors. This one is missing only one Yellow Sub. It realized $1,912.

Image courtesy of Heritage Auctions

MAGICAL MYSTERY TOUR PARTY

Excerpted from The catalog for The Uwe Blaschke Collection, Sept. 2015, Heritage Auctions

All the Beatles and their partners attended the costume ball.

John was an Elvis-style rocker while Cynthia Lennon dressed as a Victorian lady. Paul and Jane Asher wore matching King and Queen outfits. Ringo was a Regency gentleman and Maureen Starkey an Indian maiden. George came as an Errol Flynn-style swashbuckler while Pattie Harrison was in an Eastern Princess costume later described by Cynthia as "incredibly sexy in an eastern dancer's seven-veils-and-not-much-else outfit."

At the party, the 19 year-old singer Lulu, who was riding high on the success of her movie and single To Sir With Love, came dressed as Shirley Temple in a blond wig and carrying a large lollipop. Seeing a drunken John Lennon ignoring his wife and concentrating his attention on the sexily-dressed Pattie Harrison, Lulu went over to John and scolded him in a loud voice, waving her lollipop in the air at him.

The normally-macho Lennon sat quietly and contritely with his head bowed, taking the criticism. Cynthia later wrote about the incident: "It was such a lovely sight, Lulu cornering John and giving him what for. John was much taken aback by Shirley Temple's serious lecture on how to treat his wife."

BEATLES COMPLETE MAGICAL MYSTERY TOUR FANCY DRESS PARTY INVITATION (LONDON, DECEMBER 1967): A VERY COOL FOUR-PANEL FOLDOUT INVITATION ON CARDSTOCK SHOWCASING THE PSYCHEDELIC DESIGN OF THE TIME. TEXT READS, IN FULL: "MAGICAL MYSTERY TOUR FANCY DRESS/ THURSDAY 21 DECEMBER AT 7:45PM/ ROYAL LANCASTER HOTEL BAYSWATER ROAD/ ENTRANCE TO WESTBOURNE SUITE/ TELEPHONE 262-6787/ NO ADMITTANCE WITHOUT THIS CARD." SINCE THE BEATLES TYPICALLY CELEBRATED CHRISTMAS WITH A PARTY, JOHN SUGGESTED THEY HAVE A COSTUME BALL FOR THE LAUNCH OF THEIR MAGICAL MYSTERY TOUR MOVIE, SCHEDULED TO BE SHOWN ON BBC TELEVISION DEC. 26, 1967, AND INVITE FRIENDS, FAMILY, AND THE FILM CREW THIS IS A RARE AND VERY DESIRABLE INVITATION FOR THAT PARTY. NEAR MINT CONDITION. $1,125.

Image courtesy of Heritage Auctions

A Platinum Record presented to The Beatles for the confirmed sale of more than 1 million copies of Abbey Road. Sold at auction for $2,560.

Image Courtesy of Julien's Auctions

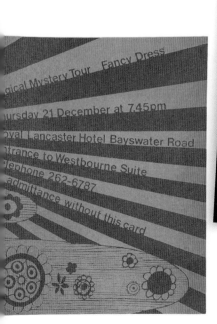

A "Good" condition UK half-sheet movie poster related to the theatrical release of "Let It Be." At auction, this brought $768.

Image Courtesy of Julien's Auctions

a complex life. In the end, no matter the reason, it was an overdose of barbiturates and alcohol that took him, a lethal combination he probably used to try and counteract the effect of the Preludin. At 32 years old he was gone. He had been an anchor for the boys for years, especially when it came to settling disputes. Now they were adrift.

The band knew it, too. When the news came down, they were all attending their first Transcendental Meditation workshop in Wales led by the Maharishi. They promptly cut the retreat short and made their way back to London.

"I knew that we were in trouble then," John Lennon told *Rolling Stone Magazine* in 1970. "I thought, we've (expletive) had it now."

A limited-edition digital photograph featuring an alternate version of the iconic Beatles album cover for *Sgt. Pepper's Lonely Hearts Club Band* **(Parlophone, 1967). Ringo holds a tuba, Paul kneels left of the bass drum. Alternate "audience" members include Einstein, Gandhi and Bette Davis. Featured on the History Channel series Pawn Stars, which added some notoriety, but not a ton of value. Still, at $1,250 it's a great piece and a good buy.** *Image courtesy of Julien's Auctions.*

Famed American caricaturist Al Hirschfeld captured the most famous celebrities in the world, including The Beatles with this ink-on-paper, 13 x 15, piece that sold at auction for $15,000.

Image courtesy of Heritage Auctions

Al Hirschfeld's limited-edition lithograph of George Harrison on Japanese rice paper sold at auction for $9,375.

Image courtesy of Julien's Auctions

Al Hirschfeld's limited-edition lithograph of Ringo Starr on Japanese rice paper sold at auction for $3,750.

Image courtesy of Julien's Auctions

BEATLES CARTOON SERIES

The Beatles cartoon series was an instant hit on ABC-TV, running from 1965 through 1967, then in reruns in 1968 and 1969. To expedite production in the wake of Beatlemania, episodes were produced at different studios in Australia, the UK and Canada.

Largely due to the decentralized production of The Beatles, original material is very difficult to find and only rarely comes to auction.

The Beatles reportedly did not care for the animated series and were less than enthusiastic about the idea of an animated feature film, ultimately declining to be involved in the production of Yellow Submarine (1968). However, they changed their minds upon seeing completed footage from the movie, and years after The Beatles broke up, John Lennon admitted that he "got a blast" out of watching reruns of the cartoon series.

This show ran for 39 episodes.

The Beatles Cartoon Series Animation Cel: A medium shot of the cartoon John Lennon from The Beatles cartoon. From episode #10 ("Long Tall Sally/I'll Cry Instead," November, 1965). Excellent condition. $1,912 at auction. Image courtesy of Heritage Auctions

Al Hirschfeld's limited-edition lithograph of John Lennon on Japanese rice paper sold at auction for $8,750.
Image courtesy of Julien's Auctions

Al Hirschfeld's limited-edition lithograph of Paul McCartney on Japanese rice paper sold at auction for $12,500.
Image courtesy of Julien's Auctions

Part of an auction grouping, here is an original animation cel and background art from The Beatles popular Saturday morning cartoon show in the mid 1960s. The cel from Season 1, Episode 10, "Long Tall Sally", shows all four Beatles walking in profile behind a sinister-looking butler. On the verso of the background art piece the animator Frank Andrina has signed, dated, and inscribed the work to his friend and colleague Kent Melton, a legendary animator himself, adding to the value of this group. In Very Good original condition. These brought $4,750.
Image courtesy of Heritage Auctions

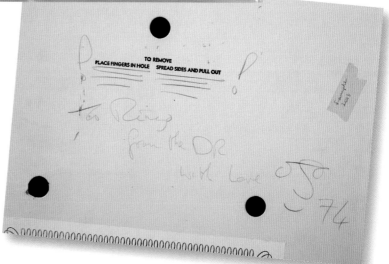

*John Lennon gave this multi-cel setup depicting Ringo with a Blue Meanie to Ringo. **On the back he signed it: "To Ringo/from the Dr/with Love" with Lennon's iconic caricature doodle and "74." Sold at auction for $10,240.***
Image courtesy of ulien's Auctions

The band went ahead with the release and premier of *Magical Mystery Tour*. The album was a hit, the movie was not, the band bid farewell to a terrible end to 1967 and, in February of 1968, split for Rishikesh, India, to pursue their interest in Eastern philosophy and leave the material world behind. It was one of the most productive and interesting periods of the band's history (and maybe the most important moment for meditation and Eastern Philosophy the Western World has ever experienced) and —though it ended in disillusionment and disappointment—it would yield the band's next brilliant, if disparate work, *The White Album*.

By the time The Beatles released *The White Album*, it had been a year since new music had been heard from them. It came out under the name *The Beatles*, which is still its "official" name, but no fan this writer has encountered has ever referred to it by that name. At 20 songs long spread over two LPs, it was a revelation and it was dissonant—the work of four distinct voices. The fact of the matter is,

however great the album turned out, there was incredible tension in the air between the band members while it was being recorded, a process that lasted from May through October.

It is well documented that it was during the recording of *The White Album* that creative differences started to break out between the band members. Without Epstein around, the arguments were intense. Things quickly deteriorated when Lennon broke the cardinal rule of the recording studio— no wives or girlfriends—and let his new girlfriend, Yoko Ono, attend the sessions. It was less than helpful, as has been well documented. Things got worse when George Martin took a sudden leave of absence, sound engineer Geoff Emerick quit and Ringo decided that he'd simply had enough

Abbey Road spent 129 weeks on the American charts. This gold record presented to The Beatles commemorates more than $1 million worth of sales. Sold at auction for $5,937.

Image courtesy of Heritage Auctions

THE APPLE SCRUFFS

Excerpted, with permission,
"10 Untold Stories from the Wild Days of The Beatles"
Nolan Moore, Listverse.com, Sept. 29, 2014

Wherever The Beatles went, they were hounded by rabid fans. While filming A Hard Day's Night, several scenes were interrupted. When performing at Shea Stadium, girls tried to storm the stage. And when the group visited the British Embassy in Washington, D.C., an 18-year-old Beverly Markowitz sneaked up behind Ringo and snipped off some of his hair.

However, none of their fans were as devoted as the Apple Scruffs. Named for their big, thick coats, the Scruffs waited on the front steps of Apple Headquarters every single day, longing for a glimpse of one of their idols. There were about 20 Scruffs, most of them young British women who'd given up their jobs to follow The Beatles full-time. Some of the members included Margo Stevens, the leader of the group, and Sue-John, named for her huge crush on Lennon. But a few Scruffs stood out from the crowd, like 63-year-old Emma Eldredge, Carol Beford from Texas, and a gay New Yorker named Tommy.

Sometimes, the Scruffs took their obsession too far. Once, they spotted an open window on Paul's house, grabbed a ladder, and climbed inside. After wandering around, they made off with a pair of pants, one of his tapes, and some of Linda McCartney's photos. Infuriated, Paul tracked them down and demanded his things back. He knew they'd done it because real thieves "would have taken more expensive things."

But mostly, the Apple Scruffs were a harmless bunch. They printed their own fan magazine and created cards for club members. They even helped The Beatles from time to time. For example, their breaking-and-entering stunt inspired Paul to write "She Came in Through the Bathroom Window." Most importantly, their dedication and devotion helped The Beatles cope in their final days when things were getting rough. At the very least, they certainly encouraged George who later dedicated a sweet song to his favorite fans.

and quit the band. The fact that he soon came back—after pleading from George—to finish the album did little to settle the simmering tensions.

Critics didn't overwhelmingly love *The White Album* when it came out, nor did the band, but history has assured its place in the annals of great rock music. Simply put, it was a masterpiece.

After the experience in 1968 of making *The White Album*, Paul conceived of a project for the band with them going back to a simpler form of writing and recording in the studio, with less technology and an eye toward filming the sessions and returning to live performing when the recording was over. The album and the documentary would be called *Get Back*. The world knows the album and the film as *Let It Be*.

While *Let It Be* is usually listed as the Beatles final album, because it was the last new Beatles music released while they were all still alive—1970—it was really the band's penultimate record, having been recorded in 1968 and early 1969, well before *Abbey Road*, which was recorded throughout the spring and summer of 1969 and was released in late-September 1969.

Let It Be, both the film and the LP, are equal parts brilliance and mess. Needless to say, Paul's desire to create an atmosphere like the old times not only failed, it was all captured on camera. The music and the footage show four men struggling mightily to get along with each other and to fight whatever personal demons are dogging them. It got so bad that it was now Harrison who left the band, agreeing only to come back and finish if the other members would agree to go back to Abbey Road Studios and finishing recording the material. They all agreed and he returned. The sessions were finished with the help of musician Billy Preston and led to the memorable rooftop recordings of the band on top of the Apple Records HQ in London, their famous last live performance.

The album, when it was released in May of

A Beatles Abbey Road Standup Display, 1969: *Truly rare and very desirable Abbey Road standup display with all four members, totally intact. These are usually damaged in some form or another when they show up, so price will descend accordingly – at least at auction. $550.*
Image courtesy of Heritage Auctions

The Beatles ("The White Album") sold more than 9.5 million copies in the United States. **This Gold Record Award (Apple 101, 1968) commemorates the sale of more than $1 million in sales for the double album that debuted at No. 1 in the UK on Dec. 7, 1968. The album spent 155 weeks on the Billboard Top 200 list. $6,875**

Image courtesy of Heritage Auctions

Vintage 1960s Kodak M26 Instamatic movie camera, owned and used by John Lennon *during the mid-60s to capture many memories at his Kenwood home in Weybridge, England. Initially acquired from the collection of Lennon's first wife, Cynthia. Sold at auction for $3,525.*

Image courtesy of Heritage Auctions

A huge 9" x 9" production cel from Yellow Submarine (United Artists/ King Features, 1968) with the Chief Blue Meanie dominating the scene and all four Fabs, plus Jeremy Boob, walking off in the distance. A true "wow" piece from the film. $3,585.

Image courtesy of Heritage Auctions

1970, had been handed over to legendary producer Phil Spector—whose own tortured tale is best told elsewhere—who added backing vocals and strings. While all the members agreed to it at the time, Paul McCartney would fight the release in court for several years before finally settling in 1975. *Let It Be... Naked* was released in 2003 and featured a much more stripped-down sound the way McCartney always insisted they meant it to be.

So what is left to cover from the band, musically? Only their greatest work of art, the finest rock 'n' roll album ever recorded: *Abbey Road*.

As the band spiraled toward dissolution—all the members had already begun recording separately and pursuing other ventures—and in the wake of the disastrous *Get Back* sessions, Paul went to George Martin and suggested they make one last album in the fashion they used to do it. Martin agreed, but only on the condition that all the members of the band agreed to let him produce the record the way he

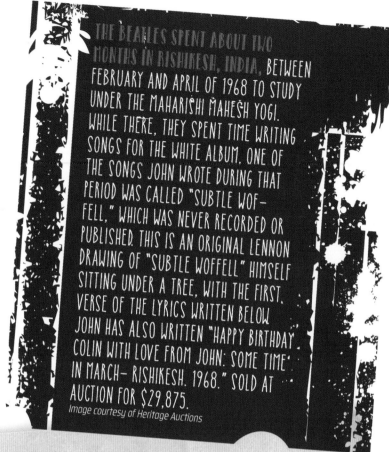

THE BEATLES SPENT ABOUT TWO MONTHS IN RISHIKESH, INDIA, BETWEEN FEBRUARY AND APRIL OF 1968 TO STUDY UNDER THE MAHARISHI MAHESH YOGI. WHILE THERE, THEY SPENT TIME WRITING SONGS FOR THE WHITE ALBUM. ONE OF THE SONGS JOHN WROTE DURING THAT PERIOD WAS CALLED "SUBTLE WOFFELL," WHICH WAS NEVER RECORDED OR PUBLISHED. THIS IS AN ORIGINAL LENNON DRAWING OF "SUBTLE WOFFELL" HIMSELF SITTING UNDER A TREE, WITH THE FIRST VERSE OF THE LYRICS WRITTEN BELOW. JOHN HAS ALSO WRITTEN "HAPPY BIRTHDAY COLIN WITH LOVE FROM JOHN: SOME TIME IN MARCH— RISHIKESH. 1968." SOLD AT AUCTION FOR $29,875.
Image courtesy of Heritage Auctions

beneath the deep Ambrosia tree
the Subtle Woffell lies,
and he will sing to comfort thee
under the purple skies.

happy birthday Colin
with love from John:
Some time in March-Rishikesh,
1968.

wanted to and that the boys adhered strictly to this.

Abbey Road was recorded over the course of 1969, in a few different bursts. For the most part the recording was harmonious, relatively, but the old tensions were still there. Paul and John continued to get into arguments, and Yoko's presence continued to piss everyone off but John. By the time the recording sessions were over and the album was tracked (on Aug. 1, 1969, the last time all four Beatles would be in a studio together), the Beatles were all but done for. John was the first to officially quit, on Sept. 20, 1969, one week before the album was released. That was kept quiet from the public, however, with news of the band's official split not fully surfacing until McCartney announced he was leaving the band in April of 1970. The Beatles were over.

Abbey Road's greatness speaks for itself—it is the best-selling Beatles album of all. It combined the very best of the technological innovativeness of the Beatles and Martin while harkening back to simpler days and straight up rock songs. The famous medley on side two, reportedly largely hated by Lennon – listed by *Rolling Stone Magazine* in 2014 as #23 on the list of greatest Beatles songs—is perhaps the most famous recorded 16 minutes in rock 'n' roll. Whatever critics thought at the time and whatever the band may have thought of it, fans loved it and love it to this day. History bears this out.

In just one decade, 10 years, the Beatles re-shaped popular music with every major recording they produced. Their legacy, sealed by *Abbey Road*, is unchallenged to this day.

This is a hand-made sign from the Montreal Bed-In For Peace that took place in the Queen Elizabeth Hotel in Montreal, May 1969. *This was the second anti-war Bed-In by John Lennon and Yoko Ono. The first took place in Amsterdam. This piece, reading "MURRAY THE K COMES ON MONDAY," was signed and dated at the event by John and Yoko, and made especially notable for the mention of famous American radio personality "Murray The K" Kaufman. This sign was affixed to the wall of the Montreal hotel suite, to the left of the bed (John's side), and appears prominently in photographic and video records of the event, including the film of the recording of "Give Peace A Chance", where the sign can be seen directly between John and Tommy Smothers as they play their guitars. John wrote "John Lennon 1969" and drew a caricature of himself and Yoko in bold black marker. Yoko added her signature just below in blue marker. Sold at auction for $75,000.*
Image courtesy of Heritage Auctions

POST-BREAKUP
1970 TO PRESENT

A Beatles limited edition lithograph sold at auction for $384.
Image courtesy of Julien's Auctions

So the bad news, as 1970 wore on, was that The Beatles were done. The primary force behind the 1960s Cultural Revolution was gone. Suddenly the coolest people at the party had split and the rest of us were left staring at our drinks.

The Beatles, intentionally or not, were the lens through which the tumultuous decade had been focused. The 1970s dawned with a sinister aspect, haunted by war and new breeds of rock 'n' roll that trended from the hard driving to the funky and the glam, all of it a result of the Fab Four's brilliance. Into the vacancy stepped bands like Pink Floyd, Led Zeppelin and the Velvet Underground, with solo acts like David Bowie and Elton John keeping pace. Rock had taken on a thousand different aspects as it raced toward Punk Rock. Without The Beatles there to dictate the direction, the box was left wide open and musicians rushed into the void.

It was all in an attempt to start a revolution that would rival the impact of the Beatles. There was a lot of great music, across all genres, but none of them came close.

Fortunately for the world, the band did not stop making music—they just did it apart and under their own names. In fact, they had all been working on solo projects before the band's ultimate dissolution, so it was no great leap for them to score with fans as solo artists. That none of their various solo projects ever rivaled the size and scope of their Beatles fame is to be expected, but their respective runs (and stories) are impressive across the board. If they emerged from the band's breakup confused and worried, all of them soon found out that the premium of talent that

The Beatles (1970s) Personality Poster, 23" x 35", unrestored, released after the boys said their final goodbyes. A good auction deal at $38.

Image courtesy of Heritage Auctions

Beatles Anthology 1 RIAA Multi-Platinum Record Award (Apple/EMI 7243, 1995), presented to Jeff Abrams commemorating more than 6 million copies sold of the compilation album, cassette and CD that proved the Beatles only get more popular with age—this was in 1995 after all. $625.

Image courtesy of Heritage Auctions

Two album posters released for the 30th Anniversary of The White Album in 1998 and a poster for The Beatles: Anthology 2 released in 1996. Very Fine condition. $95.

Image courtesy of Heritage Auctions

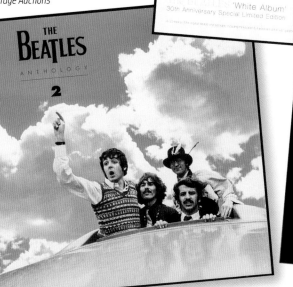

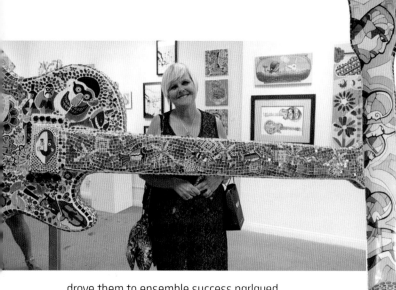

Yellow Submarine guitar sculpture: A 10-foot Beatles "Yellow Submarine" Gibson Les Paul guitar sculpture created by artist Juliana Martinez and signed on the side. The tile mosaic sculpture has the Beatles members on the front, together with a yellow submarine, marine life and clown musician imagery similar to the Yellow Submarine album art. Exhibited in 2014. The sculpture sold at auction for $20,000.
Image courtesy of Julien's Auctions

drove them to ensemble success parlayed quite nicely into solo fame.

Also, as the '70s wore on, the boys reunited in various ways by appearing on and writing for each other's albums. The fact is, they had grown up together and had myriad good times together in the 1960s. They had bonded, as musicians and friends, and that never went away, especially between John and Ringo. It's well known that they all kept in touch throughout the decade, even John and Paul. It was clear by the end of John's life that he had nothing but good feelings left for their accomplishments. We can only guess as to if the boys would have recorded together again had Lennon lived.

"After the troubles they had during The White Album," said Darren Julien, "a lot of that went away in their later years and they were just friends."

It also made quite a difference in the collectibles market. As a band in the last part

Sleek limited-edition Japanese red vinyl 1980s releases in the original mono format of Please Please Me, With The Beatles, A Hard Day's Night, The Beatles For Sale, Help!, Rubber Soul, Revolver, Sgt. Pepper's Lonely Hearts Club Band, The White Album and Yellow Submarine. Note that The Beatles and Yellow Submarine never came out in mono in the US. All in Mint or Near Mint, sold with four photos and a poster for $750.
Image courtesy of Heritage Auctions

A grouping of four, autographed 45 picture sleeves, one from the solo career of each Beatle, beautifully signed on their respective covers by John Lennon, Paul McCartney, George Harrison and Ringo Starr. This is a clever idea for a post-breakup grouping. $5,640

Image courtesy of Heritage Auctions

of their time together, they boys were isolated from each other and their fans. The weight of fame, business and music weighed too heavily. Once those burdens were gone, however, the members of the band were suddenly available again to their fans – at least in certain ways. They did not hesitate to sign autographs, records, photos and much more, all in the name of their solo pursuits. The result is a broad selection of material that relates to each individual member.

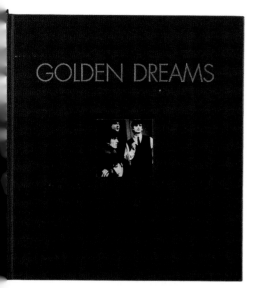

(left) *The Beatles Golden Dreams Limited Edition #1582/2500 (Genesis Publications, Ltd., 1994), by photographers Max Scheler and Astrid Kirchherr.* **A photographic journey accompanying The Beatles during the filming of A Hard Day's Night in Liverpool, 1964. Limited slipcase edition book presents Kirchherr's and Max Scheler's unpublished pictures of The Beatles, the Liverpool music scene's early-1960s explosion and the phenomenon of the Merseybeat. Signed by Kirchherr and Scheler. Sold at auction for $425.**

Image courtesy of Heritage Auctions

GOD SAVE US

JOHN LENNON

STEREO

Apple Corps Ltd. 3. Savile Row London W1.

Custom Recording

JEALOUS GUY RSI
GIMME SOME TRUTH.RSI
GIMME SOME TRUTH RS2
HOW RSI
I DON'T WANT TO BE A SOLDIER
RSI

JOHN LENNON

STEREO

Apple Corps Ltd. 3 Savile Row London W1.

Custom Recording

**A John Lennon
Imagine acetate
record sold for $576**
Image courtesy of Julien's Auctions

JOHN

Lennon, as his final decade wore on, revealed himself to be the most flawed—some would say, the most human—of all the band, and people either loved him or hated him for it, at least at first. His foibles and failings have been very well documented. It's safe to say, I think, that today Lennon is widely and rightly beloved.

Lennon was very public in his life, at least during the first five years after The Beatles. He recorded a ton of interesting music and was very politically active. He, arguably, had the most success early after the breakup, releasing Plastic Ono Band in 1970 and following that up with Imagine in 1971, his most successful solo outing and his most beloved solo single.

His political maneuvering, however, drew the ire of the U.S. government, particularly Richard Nixon, who feared his counter-culture influence. The government started a five-year campaign to get Lennon deported, ostensibly because of a 1968 marijuana conviction in England, but more likely for his protests against the Vietnam War. At any rate, it ended in 1976 when Lennon was granted citizenship.

The early peak of Lennon's solo career was the beloved album Imagine. *Included with that landmark album was a 22" x 32.5" poster, showing John at his iconic white piano. This one has been signed with a large, long autograph right across the piano. Near Mint condition and sold at auction for $13,750.*
Image courtesy of Heritage Auctions

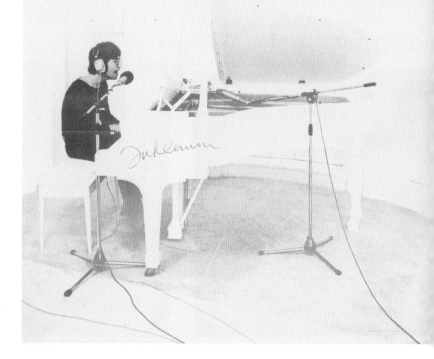

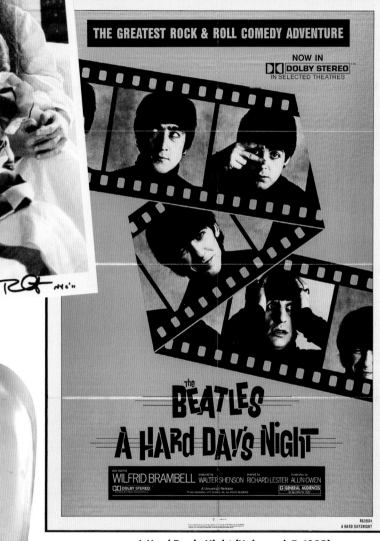

Bob Gruen signed photograph of the Lennon Family, also signed by Yoko. *Gruen is a famed Rock photographer who also served as Lennon's personal photographer during his post-Beatles life in Manhattan. Gruen is, perhaps, most famous for his shot of Lennon wearing the "New York City" T-shirt. $320*
Image courtesy of Julien's Auctions

Welcome to the World! Yoko Ono

JOHN, SEAN + YOKO ONO LENNON · NYC · 1975

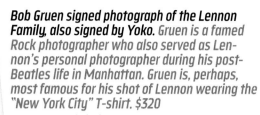

THE GREATEST ROCK & ROLL COMEDY ADVENTURE

NOW IN
DOLBY STEREO™
IN SELECTED THEATRES

the
**BEATLES
A HARD DAY'S NIGHT**

also starring
WILFRID BRAMBELL   produced by **WALTER SHENSON**   directed by **RICHARD LESTER**   screenplay by **ALUN OWEN**
[DOLBY STEREO]   A Universal Release   [G GENERAL AUDIENCES]

A John Lennon and Yoko Ono owned tabletop jukebox made by J.P. Seeburg Corporation, Type 3W-1. Chrome plated, coin operated, with 50 selections including The Beatles. Originally sold by Lennon's estate in a charity auction. In 2014 it sold at auction for $5,760.
Image courtesy of Julien's Auctions

A Hard Day's Night (Universal, R-1982) one sheet (27" x 41") *from the 1982 re-release of the film. Starring The Beatles (John Lennon, Paul McCartney, George Harrison, Ringo Starr), Wilfred Brambell, Victor Spinetti and Norman Rossington. Directed by Richard Lester. Unrestored poster sold at auction for $42.*

Image courtesy of Heritage Auctions

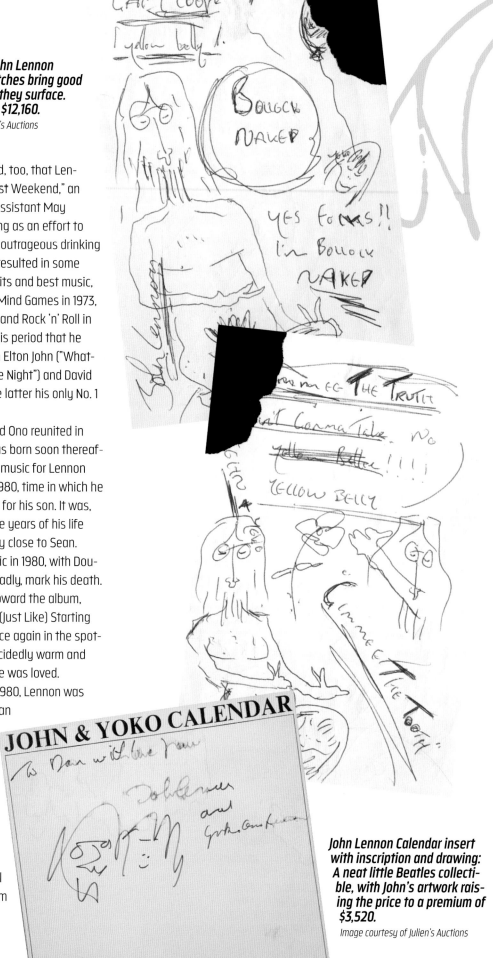

Highly coveted John Lennon drawn erotic sketches bring good prices whenever they surface. This one realized $12,160.

Image courtesy of Julien's Auctions

It was during this period, too, that Lennon had his infamous "Lost Weekend," an 18-month affair with his assistant May Pang—with Yoko's blessing as an effort to save their marriage—and outrageous drinking and partying. The period resulted in some of Lennon's wildest exploits and best music, especially in his work on Mind Games in 1973, Walls and Bridges in 1974 and Rock 'n' Roll in 1975. It was also during this period that he notably collaborated with Elton John ("Whatever Gets You Through the Night") and David Bowie ("Fame"), giving the latter his only No. 1 single in the U.S.

Importantly, Lennon and Ono reunited in 1974 and Sean Lennon was born soon thereafter. It led to a hiatus from music for Lennon that lasted from 1975 to 1980, time in which he devoted himself to caring for his son. It was, arguably, the happiest five years of his life and he was obviously very close to Sean.

Lennon's return to music in 1980, with Double Fantasy, would also, sadly, mark his death. While critics were tepid toward the album, fans flocked to the tune "(Just Like) Starting Over" and Lennon was once again in the spotlight and the vibe was decidedly warm and fuzzy. He was back and he was loved.

On the night of Dec. 8, 1980, Lennon was shot outside his Manhattan home, the Dakota building, by Mark David Chapman, a deranged fan who Lennon had signed an autograph for a few hours earlier. At the age of 40, on the eve of a comeback, he was gone. It's a death that still evokes great sadness from all generations of fans.

John Lennon Calendar insert with inscription and drawing: A neat little Beatles collectible, with John's artwork raising the price to a premium of $3,520.

Image courtesy of Julien's Auctions

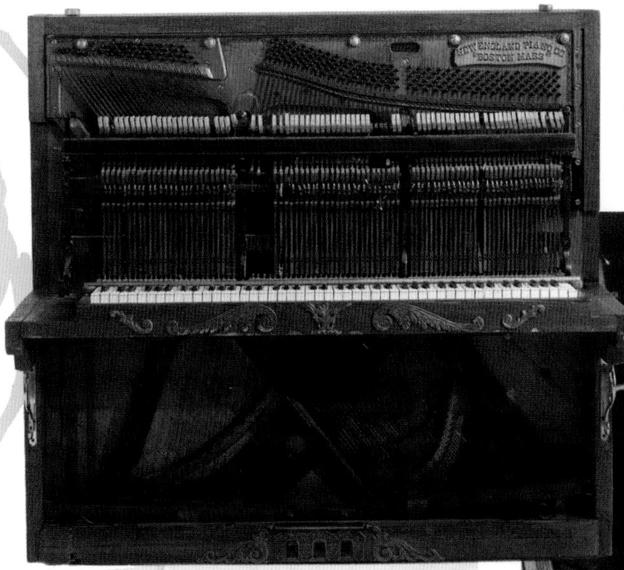

John Lennon played this upright piano from New York's legendary Record Plant recording studio. It sold at auction for $25,600.

Image courtesy of Julien's Auctions

LENNON MUSIC
1370 AVENUE OF THE AMERICAS
NEW YORK, NEW YORK 10019
212-586-6444
TELEX: 148316

July

1.west.72.nd street.apt.72.
new york.new york.10023.

Dear Leila,

Dont shout,and excuse typing...it's better than my writing! Well its me/him/it...wondering how you are..got your address from mater. I know you seem to think i was callous(?) about harry,i wasnt.I only ever got vague messages about anything...especially late 73 thru the whole of 74...being as 'ow i was having a slight case of the dylan thomas's(or brendan behans' for that matter).I finally attained mimi's goal in life, 'to suffer in luxury'...remember her always saying that?.No?well i do.

I know you've had it ruff....enuff to never get in touch.well whatever you think about me,i am,as i wrote mater,STILL ME.i.e.the same as when we knew each other...only now i'm 34...and you're 38.it's that simple.all the rest is bullshit.

Yoko and i/me(?) are having a baby...in oct...we hope..perhaps we could all get together somewhere or other(not in an 'office'') and compare notes...how many do you have?

I'm sad about harry.death is a drag for everyone but the dead.

please write..you can complain if you like!

love ,

the one who got away...

John

p.s.phone: 0101 212.595.4329.

(above) A John Lennon typed and signed letter written on Lennon Music stationery. "July" is handwritten at the top of the page, and the letter is signed "John" with a small self-portrait. The letter reads in part, "I know you seem to think I was callous (?) about harry, i wasn't. I only ever got vague messages about anything... I know you've had it ruff...enuff [sic] to never get in touch. well whatever you think about me, i am, as i wrote mater, STILL ME." What was the issue and how was John callous? We'll never know anything, except that this letter realized $5,625 at auction.

Image courtesy of Julien's Auctions

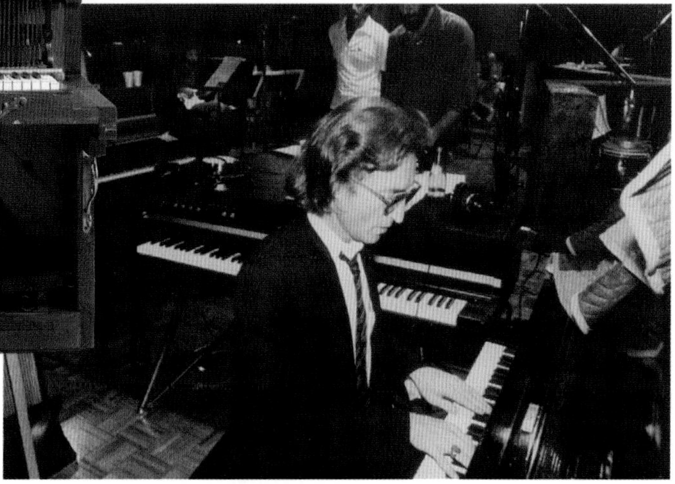

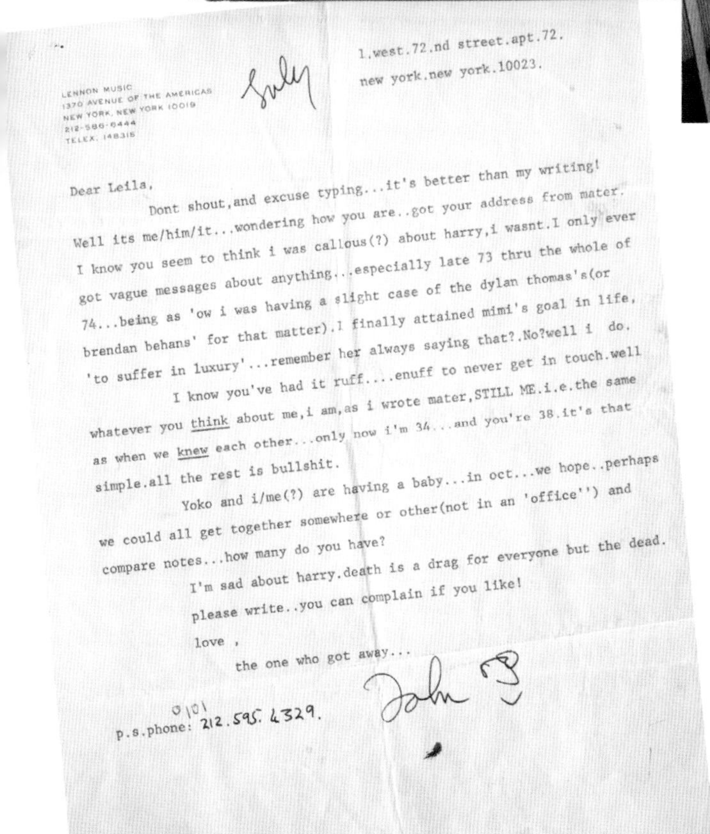

A Lennon handwritten letter to "Mark" on Apple memorandum stationery **in black ink and reads in part, "Dear Mark I knew you didn't want to ask us to the party – we could read your face/mind, we felt as bad as you!" and signed "Love John & Yoko" with Lennon's caricature portraits of himself and wife Yoko Ono with a guitar. Sold at auction for $15,000 .** *Image courtesy of Julien's Auctions*

Apple

MEMORANDUM

To: Mark

From: West door

Date: any time

Subject: to be continued

Dear Mark

I knew you didn't want to ask us to the party? – we could read your face/mind, we felt as bad as you! about it?! please don't worry about it – i might find an old amplifier for you – your a sensitive guy so we understand,

See you on the roof

love

John + Yoko

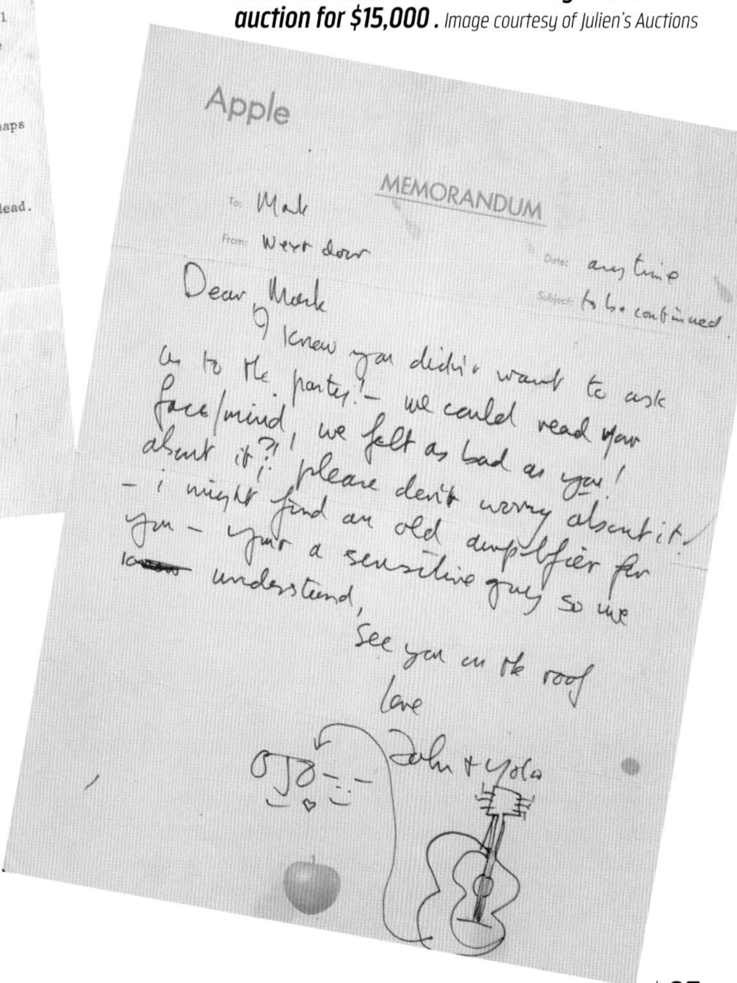

(below) Imagine: John Lennon (Warner Brothers, 1988) movie poster for an important Beatles film that clued a lot of Gen-Xers in to the amazing story and talent of John. Starring John Lennon, Yoko Ono, Paul McCartney, Ringo Starr, George Harrison, David Bowie and Phil Spector. Directed by Andrew Solt. $90

Image courtesy of Heritage Auctions

(above) John Lennon "Bag One" Art Exhibition Catalog (New York: Lee Nordness Galleries, 1970. This limited edition portfolio featuring reproductions of the 14 lithographs offered by the gallery in the Bag One Suite sold for $312. The exhibit drawings were originally created by Lennon as a wedding present for wife Yoko Ono and depict scenes from their wedding, bed-in and quite intimate erotic episodes from their honeymoon.

Image courtesy of Heritage Auctions

(righgt) The Beatles: Yoko Ono Lennon Signed Check: 8" x 3.5", London, Sept. 4, 1980. Drawn on the National Westminster Bank Limited, Ono orders payment of £400 to Inland Revenue from Ono Music Ltd. Stamp cancelled twice. In Very Good condition, expect to pay in the range of $275 for a similar piece. *Image courtesy of Heritage Auctions*

A John Lennon Happy Xmas (War Is Over) acetate record sold for $448

Image courtesy of Julien's Auctions

A print of famous photo of John Lennon by Bob Davidoff taken a few years after the band split sold at auction for $75.

Image courtesy of Heritage Auctions

AN ORIGINAL 20" X 30" WAR IS OVER POSTER, 1971, CREATED TO PROMOTE BOTH JOHN AND YOKO'S ANTI-VIETNAM WAR PEACE CAMPAIGN AND THEIR "HAPPY XMAS (WAR IS OVER)" SINGLE. THESE POSTERS WERE DISPLAYED ALL OVER NEW YORK CITY FOR A BRIEF PERIOD AND HELPED PUT JOHN ON THE FBI'S "UNDESIRABLE ALIENS" LIST. EXCELLENT CONDITION, THIS ONE BROUGHT $594 AT AUCTION.

Image courtesy of Heritage Auctions

WAR IS OVER!

IF YOU WANT IT

Love and Peace from John & Yoko

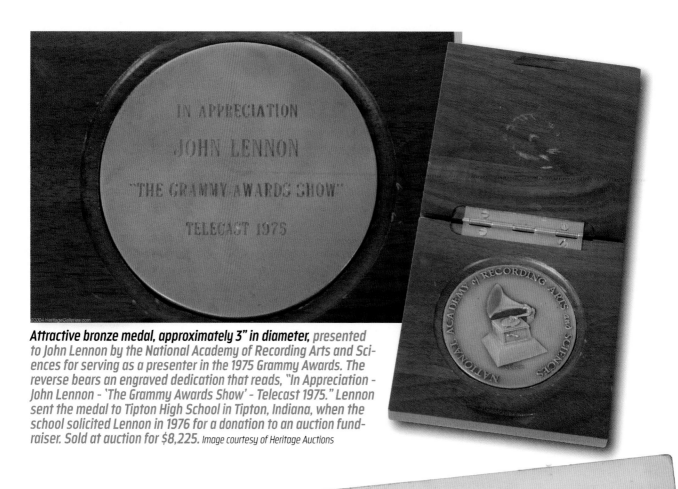

Attractive bronze medal, approximately 3" in diameter, presented to John Lennon by the National Academy of Recording Arts and Sciences for serving as a presenter in the 1975 Grammy Awards. The reverse bears an engraved dedication that reads, "In Appreciation - John Lennon - 'The Grammy Awards Show' - Telecast 1975." Lennon sent the medal to Tipton High School in Tipton, Indiana, when the school solicited Lennon in 1976 for a donation to an auction fundraiser. Sold at auction for $8,225. *Image courtesy of Heritage Auctions*

When it comes to the collectibles from Lennon's solo career, albums, autographed albums and signed photos play a prominent role. Personal items are harder to come by as Yoko and Sean Lennon followed John's example, keeping almost everything. Lennon solo memorabilia tends to fetch a premium at auction, given the rarity. As always, do your research and buy from a reliable source. Scammers and forgers have also figured out that Lennon memorabilia can bring a pretty penny.

John Lennon signed the back of this copy of "The White Album" while appearing as a celebrity guest host for the Helping Hands Marathon at WFIL Television studios in Philadelphia May 1975. Also included is a picture of Lennon signing the album. At auction a collector paid $5,975.

Image courtesy of Heritage Auctions

John Lennon Gold Record Award *for the sale of more than 500,000 copies of the album and cassette of Mind Games, John's seminal solo album. $1,152. Image courtesy of Julien's Auctions*

A Gold Record given to "John Ono Lennon" for the sale of more than $1 million worth of Walls & Bridges. $7,680.
Image courtesy of Julien's Auctions

John Lennon Some Time In New York City acetate records. $576.
Image courtesy of Julien's Auctions

John Lennon Imagine album artwork proofs offer a very cool inside look at the development of the artwork from Lennon's groundbreaking and still influential album. A collector paid $896.

Image courtesy of Julien's Auctions

A JOHN LENNON HANDWRITTEN, TWO-PAGE LETTER SENT TO HIS COUSIN LEILA IN 1977. THE LETTER READS IN PART, "... SENDING XMAS LETTER AFTER I BECAME A MILLIONAIRE — WELL I ALSO GET 1000 OR SO LETTERS A DAY... SEAN IS 17 MONTH, WALKING AND SOOO BEAUTIFUL... (BY THE WAY I'M 36 — WOULD YOU BELIEVE IT?)." SIGNED "HIMSELF. LOVE JOHN" WITH A SMALL SELF-PORTRAIT AND THE POSTSCRIPT "I SELDOM WRITE LETTERS MYSELF." WHEN HE DID, HOWEVER, THEY WERE OF GREAT INTEREST AND NOW ALWAYS BRING A PREMIUM. THIS LOVELY LITTLE MISSIVE REALIZED $11,875 AT AUCTION.

Image courtesy of Julien's Auctions

Dear Bob Hanson
the address for
photo is
LENNON
105 BANK ST
N.Y. N.Y
10014.
Thank you have a good trip
OE!
J Lennon

105 bank st
ny;ny;10014.

Dear Bob,

yes!we do remember all of you!!thank you very much for sending the photo'.
we framed it and it now hangs in the kitchen.all the best to all of you,hope spain
was fun.CONGRATULATIONS to your daughter;we send our best wishes for a happy future.

thanks again,

john lennon/yoko ono

Lennon/ono
105 Bank St.
N.Y.C. 10014

Bob Hanson
District Sales Manager
Hunt-Wesson Foods Inc.
Grocery Sales
6630 Harwin, Suite#110
Houston, Texas 77036

*John Lennon photograph
by Bob Gruen. $1,024*
Image courtesy of Julien's Auctions

A group of John's correspondences including a handwritten note on a brown sheet of paper signed by Lennon to Bob Hanson with Lennon's address in New York. The photo, with John and Yoko on the right, captures a wonderfully innocent and fun moment in an airport. Sent to them by Bob, John and Yoko framed the photo and hung it in their kitchen. $8,750.
Image courtesy of Julien's Auctions

A color portrait of Paul and Linda on a vintage 1990 MPL postcard, signed in blue ballpoint by both. It brought $562.

Image courtesy of Heritage Auctions

PAUL McCartney always has been and always will be the most accessible of the Beatles. He is the most widely known and certainly the most beloved. Perhaps it's his knack for catchy, relatable songs. Perhaps it has been his continued, concerted effort since 1970 to demystify himself as a rock star and come off more as a family man who happens to be one of the greatest songwriters that has ever lived—no big deal.

In terms of solo Beatle efforts, none of the other members of the band can touch McCartney when it comes to post-band success. McCartney had begun working on solo projects early in his career, as far back as 1966 doing film scores, and in fact released his first solo album—the distinctly atypical McCartney in 1970—just as he announced The Beatles were officially done.

A 1965 HOFNER VIOLIN BASS SIGNED BY PAUL MCCARTNEY ON THE PICK GUARD IN HAMBURG AT A 1991 PRESS CONFERENCE FOR THE RELEASE OF HIS CONCERT DOCUMENTARY FILM GET BACK. NOTE THAT PAUL ONLY SIGNED THIS, NOT PLAYED IT. IF HE DID PLAY IT, IT WOULD SURELY BRING MORE THAN THE $8,750 IT REALIZED AT AUCTION.

Image courtesy of Heritage Auctions

A promotional neon lamp created by Capitol Records in 1976 and given to record stores to promote the album Wings Over America. Manufactured by Neo-Art Inc. of Los Angeles. $3,840.
Image courtesy of Julien's Auctions

Paul McCartney signed Epiphone McCartney model guitar sold at auction for $4,160.
Image courtesy of Julien's Auctions

(above) Paul and Linda McCartney signed photographic postcard (4.25" x 5.75"). The pair have inscribed, "To Joanne/love/Linda McCartney/Paul McCartney." Joanne was the niece of Bruce Foxton, a member of the English band, The Jam. Sold at auction for $625.
Image courtesy of Heritage Auctions

Give My Regards to Broad Street (20th Century Fox, 1984) movie poster. *This writer remembers well going to see this movie at the mall in Richardson, Texas, as a teenager. Starring Paul McCartney, Bryan Brown, Ringo Starr, Barbara Bach, Linda McCartney, Tracey Ullman, Ralph Richardson, and Jeremy Child. Directed by Peter Webb. $28.*

Image courtesy of Heritage Auctions

He spent the rest of the 1970s recording and touring with Wings, producing some of his biggest hit records and best overall work – Ram in 1971, Red Rose Speedway and Band on the Run in 1973, Venus and Mars in 1975 and the groundbreaking Wings at the Speed of Sound in 1976—before the band petered out in 1980.

McCartney has subsequently spent the last 37 years quietly putting together a prolific and stellar catalog. He has worked at a pace of roughly one full album's worth of new material a year and has swung back and forth between rock, jazz, symphony, electronica and standards then right back to rock again.

While John gained as much notoriety for his outrageous opinions, antics and political protesting post-Beatles as he did for his music, Paul simply went about the business of being a musician. In fact, the most criticism he's taken for a public comment was soon after Lennon's assassination. When asked what he thought of it, he said: "It's a drag." Taken out of context, it came off callous. McCartney was, of course, wrecked by the news, as were we all. In retrospect, his comment pretty well sums it up.

A BLACK-AND-WHITE PORTRAIT OF THE LINDA MCCARTNEY PHOTO USED FOR THE COVER OF THE FLAMING PIE ALBUM, SIGNED IN BLACK FELT TIP: "CHEERS!/ PAUL MCCARTNEY." $750.

Image courtesy of Heritage Auctions

To our parents

After the Beatles breakup, Paul McCartney signed this copy of Sgt. Pepper's Lonely Heart's Club. A rare find. At auction it brought $3,840.

Image courtesy of Julien's Auctions

(above) A large signature on a 7" x 11" sheet of onion-skin paper with a printed "To our parents" at center, signed above: "To EVA/ love Paul McCartney." Presented with a B&W glossy press photo of McCartney. $500.

Image courtesy of Heritage Auctions

Paul McCartney signed left-handed Hofner HI-Series "B-Bass" guitar in the familiar sunburst violin design. **Neatly autographed in black felt tip on the pearloid pickguard. Obtained on Oct. 1, 2005, while Paul was appearing in a series of concerts at Madison Square Garden. Sold at auction for $6,875.**

Image courtesy of Heritage Auctions

PAUL McCARTNEY
COMPOSER/ARTIST

(left) *Paul McCartney signed 272-page songbook published in 1981 by Pavilion Book: $1,024.*
Image courtesy of Julien's Auctions

(below) *Paul McCartney signed Hey Jude album. $1,920.*
Image courtesy of Julien's Auctions

Through more than 50 hit tunes in his life, dozens of gold records and a tour itinerary that has repeatedly taken him around the world to play in front of millions of people, it's not out of bounds to say that he has become the most beloved musician in rock history. McCartney is ageless and brilliant; he's admirable as a family man, as a husband and as a businessman on top of his greatness as a musician.

So what about Paul-related collectibles and memorabilia? There is plenty out there when it comes to autographs, photographs, posters, signed records and gold records — beware fakes! — but precious little personal material related to Paul. Every guitar he has played, every piece of clothing he has worn and most of his correspondence has stayed with him and his family. If you look beyond this, however, there is plenty to choose from; you just have to be willing to choose your price range. If you can afford it today, at whatever level, then it's a good idea to get in. Once Paul is gone—which hopefully will not be for a long time—then it all becomes more valuable.

Paul is and always has been a keen collector, especially of his own material. In fact, he may own what is the holy grail of all music collectibles: his 1961 Hofner violin bass guitar. It is the most famous of all Beatles instruments and the most recognizable. What would it bring if Sir Paul ever wanted to auction it? I can't even hazard a guess.

A left-handed modern Hofner "Mersey" electric HI-Series B-Bass guitar, signed on the pickguard by Sir Paul McCartney on Oct. 5, 2005. Unused and in its original case, with original cable and tools. Excellent condition. Such is the power of being a Beatle that just signing a bass that looks like the bass you play is worth $10,000 at auction.
Image courtesy of Heritage Auctions

PAUL McCARTNEY'S BEAUTIFUL 5-INCH SIGNATURE GRACES THE COVER OF THE US TOUR PROGRAM FOR HIS 2011 ON THE RUN TOUR. $750. *Image courtesy of Heritage Auctions*

Paul McCartney and Wings album cover alternative artwork proof for *Band on the Run*, McCartney's breakout post-Beatles record. $125.

Image courtesy of Julien's Auctions

GEORGE

Harrison was "The Quiet Beatle" and, undeniably, a completely fascinating person. He was the youngest in the band and it took him the longest to master his instrument and his voice, but when he did the result was some of the very best music The Beatles would make as a band, especially in the second part of their careers together; and his first solo recording after the band split up — 1970's three-disc masterpiece All Things Must Pass, certainly this writer's favorite of any post-Beatle album recorded by any of the members — stands as likely the greatest recording released by a Beatle after the end of the band.

Harrison also was the most reluctant to be famous. In the early days of the band, in terms of establishing a rapport with the band's growing fan base, it seemed to be Harrison who was always returning correspondence. He came off as normal and relatable, but as the band's career progressed—and their fame mounted—he began to fear the rabid crowds of irrational teens that would melt at the sight of them. A few close calls were all he needed to develop a lifelong fear of stalkers, a fear not made any easier by the murder of Lennon in 1980. One can't help but imagine that his worst fears were realized on Dec. 30, 1999, when a deranged stalker broke into his house in the English countryside. He was hospitalized with more

This George Harrison Gretsch guitar, a 1962 Chet Atkins Tennessean, **was given to Ringo Starr by Harrison's family after Ringo participated in the Concert for George in London on the one-year anniversary of George's death in 2001. A small gift card to Ringo read: "Dear/ Richy/Happy Christmas/ & Love you loads/2002 from Oli & Dhani/x". Just an incredible and moving piec of Beatles memorabilia. Sold at auction for $179,20**

Image courtesy of Julien's Auctions

A George Harrison autograph on a lyric sheet of one of his greatest songs, "Something." What's not to love? Likely signed after the band split, then paired with a copy of Abbey Road. $2,560 at auction. *Image courtesy of Julien's Auctions*

SOMETHING
(George Harrison)

Something in the way she moves
Attracts me like no other lover.
Something in the way she woos me.
I don't want to leave her now.
You know I believe and how.

Somewhere in her smile she knows
That I don't need no other lover.
Something in her style that shows me.
I don't want to leave her now.
You know I believe and how.

You're asking me will my love grow.
I don't know, I don't know.
You stick around now, it may show.
I don't know, I don't know.

Something in the way she knows
And all I have to do is think of her.
Something in the things she shows me.
I don't want to leave her now.
You know I believe and how.

George Harrison

George Harrison and Ringo Starr 2000 Mercedes-Benz CLK 55 AMG two door notchback coupe: This particular Mercedes-Benz was purchased new by George Harrison and then later, touchingly, purchased by Ringo Starr directly from Harrison's estate after his passing in 2001. The title reads both George Harrison and Ringo Starr. Mileage: 10,729. The car, driven by two of the greatest musicians to ever write and play, sold at auction for $70,400.
Image courtesy of Julien's Auctions

than 40 stab wounds, though still managed to quip, in a statement released soon after the attack, that his assailant "...wasn't a burglar, and he certainly wasn't auditioning for the Traveling Wilburys."

George was the most pure musician in the band and his solo work—begun in 1968 with two recordings, Wonderwall Music and Electronic Sound—was hit and miss from a critical and fan standpoint. All Things Must Pass was an obvious triumph, which Harrison himself described as being a continuation of his time with the Beatles, including the classic "My Sweet Lord." It was as if, bottled up for so many years behind Lennon and McCartney, all of Harrison's creativity burst forth in an amazing rush. The result is an album that is still simply sublime even today, a gorgeous mediation on life, love and death.

1973's Living in the Material World would provide his last hit for a few decades with the tune "Give Me Love (Give Me Peace on Earth)," after which time he would record and tour with a variety of bands and musicians and then quietly retreat into family life to raise

GEORGE HARRISON SIGNED "LAST SUPPER" PARODY PHOTOGRAPH (1973): A 10" X 7" B&W AND COLOR GLOSSY PHOTO OF GEORGE HARRISON'S "THE LAST SUPPER" PARODY. HARRISON, STANDING, IS DRESSED AS A PRIEST WEARING A SIX-SHOOTER, IN THE MIDST OF OTHERS SEATED (INCLUDING RINGO STARR) AT A LONG BANQUET TABLE ON THE FRONT GROUNDS OF A TUDOR-STYLE MANSION IN CALIFORNIA, SIGNED IN BLACK INK ON THE WHITE TABLE CLOTH AREA: "TO SARAH/ LOVE FROM GEORGE/ HARRISON." THIS PHOTO WAS USED AS THE INSIDE LEFT GATEFOLD COVER FOR GEORGE'S 1973 ALBUM LIVING IN THE MATERIAL WORLD. THE OTHERS AT THE TABLE PLAYED ON THE ALBUM. GEORGE EXPLAINED, TAKEN AS A WHOLE, THE VARIOUS DETAILS IN THE PHOTO REPRESENT THE "GROSS ASPECTS" OF THE MATERIAL WORLD. WHAT WOULD GEORGE THINK TO SEE THIS PHOTO BROUGHT $1,675 AT AUCTION?

Image courtesy of Heritage Auctions

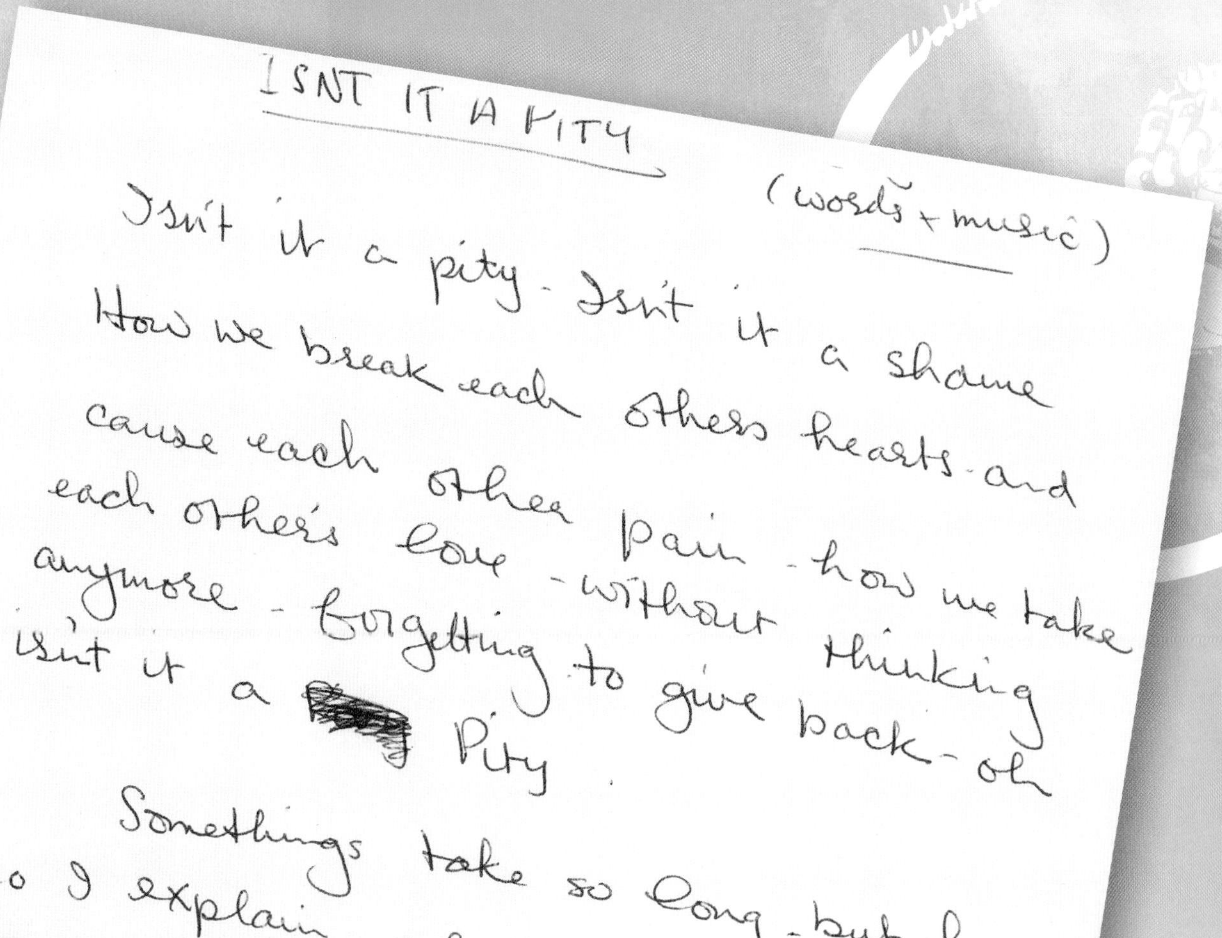

ISNT IT A PITY

(words + music)

Isn't it a pity - Isn't it a shame
How we break each others hearts and
cause each other pain - how we take
each other's love - without thinking
anymore - forgetting to give back - oh
isn't it a Pity.

Somethings take so long - but how
do I explain - when not too many
people can see were all the same
and because of all their tears -
their eyes cant hope to see -
the beauty that surrounds them
isn't it a pity.

repeat (1) ~~instrumental~~

The complete lyrics to one of Harrison's greatest, most heartfelt songs, "Isn't It A Pity." While the song was released on George's landmark All Things Must Pass album—and as a double "A" side with "My Sweet Lord"—in 1970, George originally wrote it in the mid-1960s. Beatles lore has it that it was turned down for inclusion in Revolver, Sgt. Pepper's Lonely Hearts Club Band, and Let It Be. This is an amazing thing to think about, as the song is so closely identified with George now, and is so powerfully evocative of his up-front spirituality and empathy. It's interesting to think about how it would have sounded had the band recorded it for one of those records. These lyrics match almost perfectly, line by line, the set shown on page 171 of George's autobiography I Me Mine. Sold at auction for $87,500.

Image courtesy of Heritage Auctions

George Harrison photograph taken by Richard Avedon sold at auction for $448. *Image courtesy of Julien's Auctions*

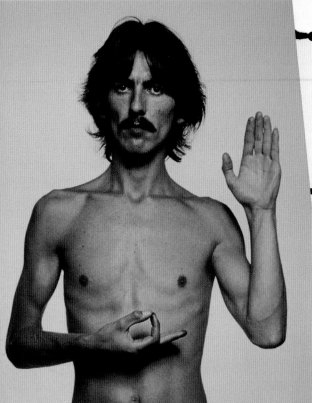

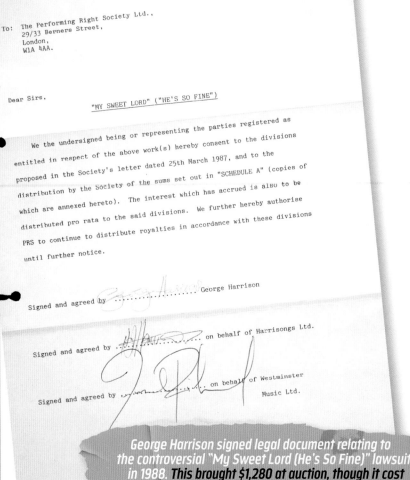

Date: 1988

To: The Performing Right Society Ltd.,
     29/33 Berners Street,
     London,
     W1A 4AA.

Dear Sirs,   "MY SWEET LORD" ("HE'S SO FINE")

We the undersigned being or representing the parties registered as entitled in respect of the above work(s) hereby consent to the divisions proposed in the Society's letter dated 25th March 1987, and to the distribution by the Society of the sums set out in "SCHEDULE A" (copies of which are annexed hereto). The interest which has accrued is also to be distributed pro rata to the said divisions. We further hereby authorise PRS to continue to distribute royalties in accordance with these divisions until further notice.

Signed and agreed by .... George Harrison

Signed and agreed by .... on behalf of Harrisongs Ltd.

Signed and agreed by .... on behalf of Westminster
                                                          Music Ltd.

George Harrison signed legal document relating to the controversial "My Sweet Lord (He's So Fine)" lawsuit in 1988. This brought $1,280 at auction, though it cost George considerably more to settle the lawsu *Image courtesy of Julien's Auctions*

his son Dhani. He re-surfaced again in the late 1980s with the hit record Cloud Nine and his No. 1 single "I Got My Mind Set on You," a remake of James Ray's 1961 recording of the same name. This led Harrison in 1998 directly to The Traveling Wilburys, the Super Group of Tom Petty, Bob Dylan, Roy Orbison, Jeff Lynne, and Harrison, which turned on a new generation of fans to the music of all its members.

In terms of collectibles, there is not a lot related to the notoriously private Harrison. There are autographed photos and posters, signed checks and a slim variety of other material. As far as personal items go, however, there is precious little. Harrison, too, kept much of his best stuff. On the occasion that things from his personal collection have surfaced, they have always been from someone who knew him well and who he and his family trusted—like Ringo (as you'll see in the section dedicated to Ringo's solo years) —and will always bring top dollar.

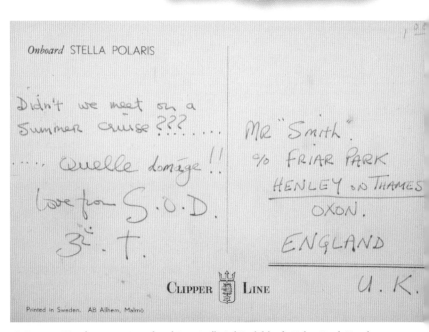

Onboard STELLA POLARIS

Didn't we meet on a summer cruise ???.....
..... Quelle domáge !!
Love from S.O.D.
ॐ. T.

Mr "Smith".
% FRIAR PARK
HENLEY ON THAMES
OXON.
ENGLAND
U. K.

CLIPPER ✠ LINE

Printed in Sweden. AB Allhem, Malmö

A George Harrison postcard written to "Mr 'Smith' c/o Friar Park Henley on Thames Oxon. England U.K." The postcard reads in full "Didn't we meet on a/ summer cruise???..../......Quelle domáge!!/ Love from S.O.D. /(om symbol). t." The postcard is from a ship called the Stella Polaris. Cryptic and clever. Undated though likely post-split. It brought $1,024. *Image courtesy of Julien's Auctions*

A VERY GOOD CONDITION SIGNED COPY OF GEORGE'S 1987 SOLO ALBUM "CLOUD NINE", AMONG HIS BEST. GOOD SONGS LIKE "WHEN WE WAS FAB" AND "GOT MY MIND SET ON YOU" SAW GEORGE BACK ON TOP OF HIS GAME AND TURNING ON A WHOLE NEW GENERATION OF FANS TO HIS NUMEROUS EXCELLENT SOLO EFFORTS. THIS COPY BROUGHT $2,250. *Image courtesy of Heritage Auctions*

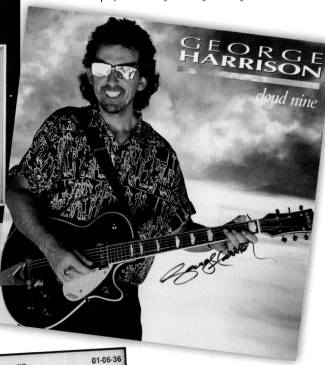

George Harrison signed bank check order form (London, July 25, 1974) **ordering two books of 50 checks for the Harrisongs Ltd. Account. Harrisongs Ltd. was a music publishing company set up by George in 1964 (originally named Mornyork). Sold at auction for $1,250.**
Image courtesy of Heritage Auctions

George Harrison signed Apple Publishing Limited check (London, July 3, 1973), *made payable to "George Alexander" for £112-8. George Alexander was the first songwriter signed by The Beatles to Apple Music Publishing in 1967. Sold at auction for $1,875.*
Image courtesy of Heritage Auctions

Richard Starkey, aka Ringo Starr, signed check (1971), orders payment of £44.25 to Dick James Music from Apple Publishing Ltd. Dick James (1920-1986) was a British music publisher who worked with The Beatles early in their career. In 1969, James sold his company, Northern Lights, which included all of rights to The Beatles' songs, causing friction between him and the band. $625. *Image courtesy of Heritage Auctions*

RINGO

I will go out on a limb here and say that Ringo is obviously the most charming of the Beatles, always has been. In fact, it's largely his charm that kept him in the public eye after the prolific and highly successful first few years of his solo career, which saw Ringo chart seven different songs in both the U.S. and the U.K. After that point, and largely through the last 40 years, Ringo has had almost no presence on the record charts, though he has remained a beloved figure in the popular consciousness.

There is no doubt that Starr's credit as The Beatles drummer assures him a place in Rock history, yet there seemed to be some debate over the decades as to whether Ringo was actually that good of a drummer. When compared with drummers like Keith Moon or John Bonham, Ringo is nowhere near as flashy. To expect

Ringo Starr's 1989 All-Starr band Ludwig Drum Kit. Sold at auction for $64,000. *Image courtesy of Julien's Auctions*

CBS Records neon "Ringo" sign: *Nice promotional item for Ringo's 1973 debut solo self-titled album. $1,024*
Image courtesy of Julien's Auctions

Buck Owens guitar gifted to Ringo Starr: *Okay, if your humble author could choose one single piece out of this book for his own personal collection, this may well be the piece, which materially marries the Bakersfield sound with the Beatles long after the band recorded Owen's "Act Naturally." The guitar, model number 319. 12190 100, with Owen's iconic red, white and blue striped finish, is inscribed "To My Friend,/Ringo/All we had to do was/ Act Naturally/ Your Friend, Buck Owens/ March 27, 1989." On that date Owens and Ringo recorded a version of "Act Naturally" at Abbey Road Studios. In 1963 Owens version of the song was his first No. 1 hit on the country charts, and in 1965 Starr recorded the song for the Beatles album Help! $51,200.*
Image courtesy of Julien's Auctions

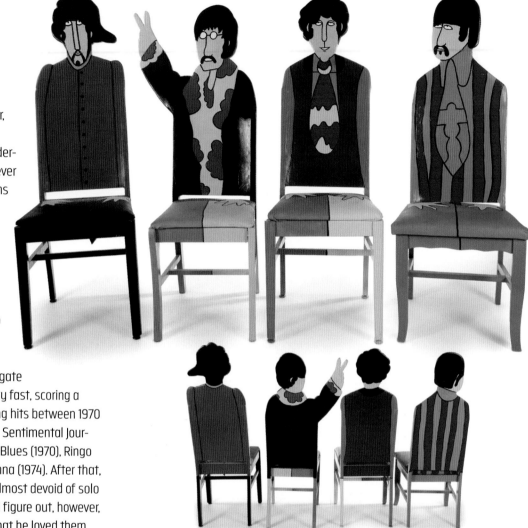

A set of four handmade figural chairs made by Todd Fendos depicting John, Paul, Ringo and George from Yellow Submarine. Eagles guitarist Joe Walsh gave the chairs to Ringo, his brother-in-law, sometime in the 1980s or 1990s. Priced at a premium: $22,500. Image courtesy of Julien's Auctions

flash from Ringo, however, as a Beatle or as a solo artist, is simply to misunderstand his intent. Ringo never played over-the-top drums because he simply didn't have to. His philosophy was to play what was necessary, no more, and it worked beautifully. There is a deceptive simplicity in his musicianship and it takes patience to understand its beauty.

Ringo came out of the gate post-Beatles breakup very fast, scoring a series of decently charting hits between 1970 and 1974 from his albums Sentimental Journey (1970), Beaucoups of Blues (1970), Ringo (1973) and Goodnight Vienna (1974). After that, however, the charts are almost devoid of solo Ringo hits. What Starr did figure out, however, is that people love him, that he loved them and that his presence was more than enough to earn him ongoing public adoration. He threw himself into a few acting gigs, appearing on the albums of his friends and, in the late-1980s, assembled Ringo Starr's All-Starr Band. The All-Starr Band concept, consisting of Ringo on tour with a rotating cast—a veritable Who's Who—of famous musicians, was a great coup. The band

Ringo Starr signed check. $768
Image courtesy of Julien's Auctions

Ringo Starr Painting by Peter Max (1999): A terrific original Max portrait of Ringo in silk-screen and oil, signed "Max 99" in the upper left. Excellent condition. From the collection of David Fishof, founder of the Rock 'N' Roll Fantasy Camp, and producer and co-creator of the All-Starr Band concept with Ringo. $6,875
Image courtesy of Heritage Auctions

RINGO STARR'S PATEK PHILIPPE WRISTWATCH: AN 18K YELLOW GOLD "MOONPHASE" AUTOMATIC WRISTWATCH BY PATEK PHILIPPE IS ALREADY A VERY VALUABLE TIMEPIECE, BUT RINGO STARR WORE THIS ONE. WHAT'S THE PREMIUM ON THAT? ABOUT $100,000, GIVE OR TAKE $25,000. SUCH A WATCH WITHOUT THE HISTORY GOES FOR $25,000–$50,000 NORMALLY. RINGO'S WATCH BROUGHT AN INCREDIBLE FINAL PRICE REALIZED OF $179,200.

Image courtesy of Julien's Auctions

Ringo signed program from the 1992 All-Starr Band tour sold with a used ticket stub from a performance at the Iowa State Fair on Saturday, Aug. 22, 1992. $162.

Image courtesy of Heritage Auctions

has traveled, in one form or another, whenever Ringo has wanted for the last 30 years.

The market for Ringo collectibles, and by association all Beatles collectibles, got a massive shot in the arm in December of 2015 at Julien's Auctions in Los Angeles, when Darren Julien and his company offered "Property from the Ringo Starr and Barbara Bach Collection," marking the first time a Beatle had personally consigned his collection to auction. The results were spectacular— many of the items offered are featured in this book—to the tune of $12+ million. It needs to be noted, too, that Ringo and Barbara donated all the proceeds to charity.

"Yoko did a sale at Sotheby's in the '80s," said Julien, "but it wasn't really that much stuff. Ringo is the first one to sell so much."

The collection included an incredible array of material that spanned Ringo's career as a Beatle, as a solo artist, as a friend to the other Beatles and many other musicians and included a few different incredible Beatles-

A SGT. PEPPER THEMED MANNEQUIN GIFTED TO RINGO. A LITTLE STRANGE FOR YOUR WRITER'S TASTES, BUT IT'S WORTH $3,520 TO A COLLECTOR AT AUCTION, LARGELY BECAUSE IT WAS OWNED BY THE ONE AND ONLY RINGO.

Image courtesy of Julien's Auctions

A whimsical Ringo limited-edition print titled "Chef Alamode". Numbered 93/100 in pencil lower left with a corresponding holographic sticker, and signed "Ringo 05." $500.

Image courtesy of Heritage Auctions

Ringo Starr owned Hofner Violin bass, circa 1968-1971, Model 500/1 with gold decal logo on headstock, engraved Hofner blade pickups, large cream pearl control panel, and cream teacup knobs. $23,040 at auction.

Image courtesy of Julien's Auctions

Black-and-white photo of a long-haired and bearded Ringo standing behind white curtains, boldly signed in black felt tip: "Ringo" with an added star symbol. $500

Image courtesy of Heritage Auctions

RINGO STARR'S NUDIE COAT. $2,560 AT AUCTION.

Image courtesy of Julien's Auctions

used instruments, including his original Pearl drum set and a variety of other pieces of different importance.

"Ringo was great to work with," added Julien. "He was very open to the process and talked a lot about the stories behind the pieces in the auction."

This is a bonus for the Beatle collector, as good Beatles material always brings more good Beatles material out of the woodwork. It also establishes a baseline value for material, great and small, that originates from an actual member of the band—a fact sure to put a premium on every lot in the sale. The savvy collector can work backwards on value from the totals established by the auction and get a good sense of what their collection is worth, if they are experienced, or what it should cost them to start collecting. The prices that were realized in the auction were by turns fair and by turns astonishing, reflecting the relative rarity of each item.

The Concert for Bangladesh (20th Century Fox, 1972) movie poster. Film starred Eric Clapton, Bob Dylan, George Harrison, Billy Preston, Leon Russell, Ravi Shankar, Ringo Starr, Klaus Voormann and Badfinger. Directed by Saul Swimmer. $131.

Image courtesy of Heritage Auctions

The Greatest Concert Of The Decade
NOW YOU CAN SEE IT AND HEAR IT...
AS IF YOU WERE THERE!

apple presents
THE CONCERT FOR BANGLADESH

ERIC CLAPTON · BOB DYLAN · GEORGE HARRISON · BILLY PRESTON · LEON RUSSELL · RAVI SHANKAR
RINGO STARR · KLAUS VOORMANN · BADFINGER · PETE HAM · TOM EVANS · JOEY MOLLAND
MIKE GIBBONS · ALLAN BEUTLER · JESSE ED DAVIS · CHUCK FINDLEY · MARLIN GREENE · JEANIE GREENE
JO GREEN · DOLORES HALL · JIM HORN · KAMALA CHAKRAVARTY · JACKIE KELSO · JIM KELTNER
USTED ALIAKBAR KHAN · CLAUDIA LENNEAR · LOU McCREARY · OLLIE MITCHELL · DON NIX
DON PRESTON · CARL RADLE · ALLA RAKAH Directed by Saul Swimmer

Produced by George Harrison and Allen Klein   Music Recording Produced by George Harrison and Phil Spector   Technicolor®

G ALL AGES ADMITTED General Audiences   apple/20th century-fox release   Original Sound Track Available On Apple Records

(right) This amazing suit from the iconic designer Nuta Kotl-yarenko, professionally known as Nudie Cohn, was made for Bob Dylan, who later gave it to his friend Ringo Starr. The ornate, rhinestone-covered suits were popularly known as "Nudie Suits" and became favorites of such Country stars as Porter Wagoner, George Jones and Glen Campbell. Cohn designed the memorable costume worn by Robert Redford in the 1979 movie, Electric Horseman. At auction, this Ringo-owned suit sold for $22,500.

Image courtesy of Julien's Auctions

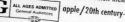

Ringo Starr owned Rickenbacker 12-string guitar. Worth $32,000 to a determined bidder.

Image courtesy of Julien's Auctions

THE BEATLES

GIBSON JOHN LENNON J-160E PEACE MODEL GUITAR. $1,600

Image courtesy of Julien's Auctions

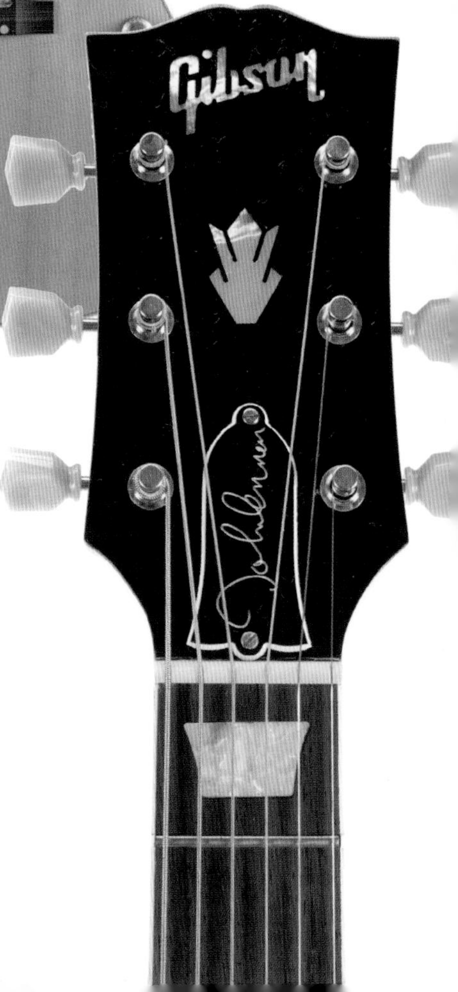

INSPIRED AND REPLICA GUITARS

A limited-edition Paul McCartney 1964 Texan Epiphone acoustic guitar. The reissued guitar was a collaboration between Epiphone and McCartney to replicate his 1964 Texan, the guitar he wrote "Yesterday" on and used to perform on The Ed Sullivan Show. A beauty of an acoustic for $4,480. *Image courtesy of Julien's Auctions*

Epiphone
performance is our passion

645 Massman Drive

Nashville, Tennessee

37210 USA

Epiphone, a part of the Gibson family of brands.

LIMITED EDITION
Paul McCartney 1964 Epiphone Texan

A George Harrison "Rocky" replica Stratocaster guitar. Want a Beatles replica guitar? This one would cost you $1,280, though there is no guarantee you will sound like George when you play it.

Image courtesy of Julien's Auctions

John Lennon inspired set of three J-160E guitars sold at auction for $8,960.

Image courtesy of Julien's Auctions

John Lennon Limited-Edition Rickenbacker 325JL: $3,750.
Image courtesy of Julien's Auctions

John Lennon inspired "Revolution" Casino guitar sold at auction for $1,152.
Image courtesy of Julien's Auctions

BRAND ON THE RUN
MARKETING THE BEATLES

There may well be no more coveted—or protected—a brand in the world than the Beatles. This is by design. It's a breath-taking marketing achievement to behold, especially with a long view from the beginning of Beatlemania.

"The Beatles broke up almost 40 years ago, but their brand power is almost as strong today as it was when they first played the 'Ed Sullivan Show' in 1964," wrote Beth Snyder Bulik in Advertising Age Magazine on Sept. 14, 2009, in the article For Beatles Brand, All They Need Is Control. "Moreover, the band built that iconic brand—and continues to promote it, gaining new generations of fans along the way—without the benefit of advertising agencies or formal relationships with PR firms."

When the Beatles took over the world in 1964 after playing The Ed Sullivan Show, the marketing barrage that followed was unheard of. The band so thoroughly captured the attention, and dollars, of its young fan base that a cottage industry sprang up almost overnight. Everyone wanted the Beatles' images on everything.

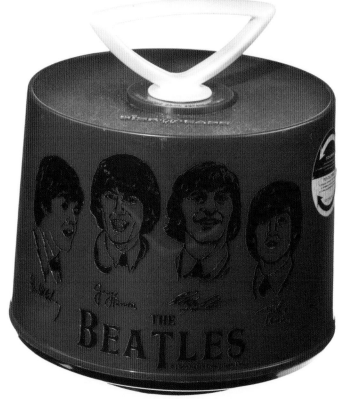

The Beatles Disk-Go-Case record carrier (US, 1966) came in seven fab colors, a twist-off top and spindle for stacking 45s. Importantly, this case still has the instruction sticker, which was typically removed by purchaser. $312.
Image courtesy of Heritage Auctions

BEATLES YELLOW SUBMARINE JUKEBOX: A RARE LIMITED EDITION APPLE RECORDS AUTHORIZED ROCK-OLA JUKEBOX WITH A 100 CD CAPACITY. SERIAL NUMBER YSM1002. THERE WERE ONLY 100 OF THESE ISSUED. THIS ONE BROUGHT $32,000.

Image courtesy of Julien's Auctions

This Beatles 45s record box (Air Flite, US, 1964), shows plenty of wear but remains a popular item at auction, bringing $112.

Image courtesy of Heritage Auctions

AN "OFFICIAL BEATLES FAN" 4"
LITHOPINBACK BUTTON FROM
1964 FEATURING PHOTO IMAGES
OF PAUL MCCARTNEY, RINGO
"RINGS" STARR, GEORGE HARRISON
AND JOHN LENNON. $56
Image courtesy of Heritage Auctions

Originally, the licensing of the Beatles name and image was controlled through NEMS Enterprises (standing for North End Music) a company set up by the band's manager, Brian Epstein, named after the music store his family owned in Liverpool. NEMS didn't directly control every appearance of the Beatles' likeness, but rather brokered its usage through a third-party agent, Nicky Byrne, who then sold the rights.

The result, as Beatlemania caught fire, was an onslaught like none ever seen before. In fact, it's not a far reach to say that the marketing, in large part, drove Beatlemania. The band was the perfect marketing vehicle, having captured the attention of the Baby Boomers, to take advantage of the new affluence of the children of the generation that fought and won World War II. It was magic.

The truth also was, while every single maker of toys and/or novelty items wanted to put the Beatles on their material, it didn't matter whether NEMS or Nicky Byrne approved; they simply went ahead and made them anyway. Before NEMS or any representative of the band could get to them, the product would be sold and the company would be gone.

Group of three unlicensed toy guitars:
Modern issues, two are marked "Made in China," but still great for display. Respectively 11.5", 15.75" and 19" long. Excellent condition. At auction: $575.
Image courtesy of Heritage Auctions

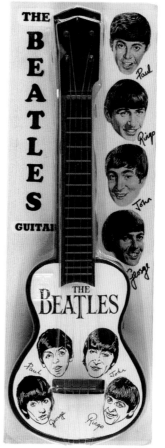

Made by Car Mascot in 1964, the boxed set of Bobb'n Head Beatles is one of the rarest and most coveted Beatles toys. *Single examples, and even the occasional set of four, do appear from time to time, but it's the original packaging that makes it a gem. Even rarer is the cardboard insert that keeps the "bobb'n" heads from "bobb'n." $1,075.*
Image courtesy of Heritage Auctions

Beatles vintage Hofner Guitar String (6th) in original package by Selmer London (Selcol, 1964). *Package contains unused and coiled sixth string "made to the Beatles own specifications." $150.*
Image courtesy of Heritage Auctions

This Beatles Gumball Machine with a set of black plastic record-shaped charms was produced in 1964. Each charm came with a photo of a Beatle with various song titles on the reverse. Sold at auction for $275.
Image courtesy of Heritage Auctions

The Beatles New Sound Guitar (UK, 1963) *at left is a 23-inch long, cream and orange-colored plastic instrument. It's paired with a plastic guitar from Hong Kong, an obvious unlicensed copy. $312.*

Image courtesy of Heritage Auctions

Beatles marketing got much more savvy as the years rolled on and, by the time Apple Corps Ltd. took over control of the band's image in 1968 after Epstein's death, the Beatles emerged as one of the most closely guarded brands in the world, a distinction it still holds today. That's not to say that there are not still a plethora of novelty items to be had—from plush dolls to figurines to band posters and well beyond—it's just that Apple Corps controls all of it. Even more importantly, Apple Corps controls any advertising, TV or film use of the Beatles brand, and they are extremely picky. Examples of this aren't hard to find. Think about the release of The Beatles Rock Band video game in 2009—it revitalized the brand.

This points to a particular brilliance on the part of the Marketing geniuses that control the Beatles brand and music—we'll get to the memorabilia in just a minute—which is their confidence in the music itself, and why not? It's always been all about the music. It's what drew in past generations, what drew us all in

A vintage "Beatle Bugle" Megaphone by Yell-A-Phone (1965). **There are three known color combinations of this 7.5" tall plastic megaphone: bright yellow with green print; white with bright red print; and bright orange with black print. These were sold only at large concert venues on the 1965 North American tour. This is an uncommon item given their tendency to break easily in the crush of concert enthusiasm. At auction: $500.**

Image courtesy of Heritage Auctions

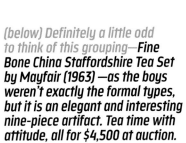

Manufactured in 1964-66 by Mastro Industries in New York, this four-string Beatles Toy Banjo has a nice sound with strings that can be tuned. Offered with a box of the same vintage, but probably not made for this instrument. Finding these in nice condition makes them extremely collectible. See a good one? Get it! This one went for $1,375.

Image courtesy of Heritage Auctions

The Beatles blue Aladdin lunchbox **with its original matching Thermos (1965) is one of the bona fide Holy Grail pieces for lunch box collectors, and equally sought after by Beatles Pop Culture collectors. This was the first Aladdin lunch box dedicated to a rock group and, in the condition you see here – with very little evident wear – expect to pay a pretty penny for it. This one went for $750 at auction.**

Image courtesy of Heritage Auctions

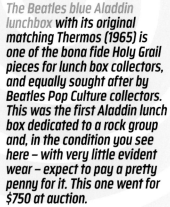

(below) Definitely a little odd to think of this grouping—**Fine Bone China Staffordshire Tea Set by Mayfair (1963)** —as the boys weren't exactly the formal types, but it is an elegant and interesting nine-piece artifact. Tea time with attitude, all for $4,500 at auction.

Image courtesy of Heritage Auctions

BEATLES SNEAKERS BY WING DINGS

John Lennon   Ringo Starr   Paul McCartney   George Harrison

The Beatles marketing team had fans covered from head to toe as evidenced by this pair of white, pointed-toe, low-cut canvas sneakers from 1964. *The sneaks bear a pattern of Beatle faces, logos, and facsimile signatures. The original store display box is included with a handsome graphic on the top of The Beatles, their facsimiles autographs, and the text "Beatles Sneakers by Wing Dings." Made in USA stamped into the rubber sole. $750.*

Image courtesy of Heritage Auctions

and what will continue to draw in future generations, all based on a periodic re-introduction of the band and its music.

After the Beatles split in 1970, their albums and films were periodically re-released through the 1970s, attended by a slew of marketing and materials. This continued through the early 1980s and into the 1990s as specialized compilation albums, featuring remastered tracks and No. 1 singles, were released and were big hits. In the mid-1990s Beatles Anthology was released, a retrospective of the band's career, with extensive interviews with the surviving members of the band as well as "new" Beatles tracks featuring old demos of Lennon singing and playing the piano backed with new instrumentation from the rest of the band. It came with the attendant marketing and marketing materials and, again, a new generation of fans was hooked.

(below) The Fab Four were nothing short of international superstars. Here is a beautiful retail display box with the second series of black and white cards issued in 1964 by O-Pee-Chee for the Canadian market. The box includes 36 unopened packs and sold at auction for more than $4,000.

Image courtesy of
Heritage Auctions

A two-bell, metal wind-up Yellow Submarine alarm clock by Sheffield (UK, 1968) features a bright and colorful psychedelic design. The yellow clock face shows The Beatles and Yellow Submarine in text and images under the glass. Suddenly, waking up in the morning just became a lot more fun. At auction: $875.

Image courtesy of Heritage Auctions

(right) Beatles Colorful Neck Or Table Scarf (UK, 1964): Beautiful, brightly colored Beatles scarf from the UK in 1964 that could be used as a table cloth or a scarf to wear around your neck, or over your hair. 26" x 26", in very good condition. $106.

Image courtesy of Heritage Auctions

This Beatles wristwatch by Bradley Time (1964) certainly stands the test of time. The funny thing is, I would wear this today if I could, and if they were of good quality. Very cool. $600.

Image courtesy of Heritage Auctions

This Beatles set of four Flasher Rings on a display card came from Argentina in 1964. One adjustable lenticular plastic ring for each Beatle with facial images alternating with "I'm John [or Paul, etc.] Beatles". Each ring comes on a perforated tear-off card attached to a header titled "El Anillo Magico" (the magic ring). Part of a varied group of celebrities offered on this display along with Tarzan, Mickey Mouse, Batman, and others (not included). At auction: $87. Image courtesy of Heritage Auctions

NOTHING SAYS YOU LOVE THE FAB FOUR LIKE USING POMADE THAT BEARS THEIR NAME. ORIGINALLY ISSUED IN 1964 BY H.H. CHEMICAL & IND. MFG. OF MANILA, PHILIPPINES, THIS IS LIKELY A 1970S–VINTAGE REISSUE AS IT DOES NOT HAVE THE "10¢" PRICING PRINTED UPON THE BOX, AS DID THE ORIGINAL. $200.

Image courtesy of Heritage Auctions

This was followed in 2009 by the release of the band's entire catalog digitally re-mastered, accompanying the release of the Rock Band video game. The result was another meteoric run through the charts, another gathering of fans. The digital world had a taste of Beatles music in modern format. Still, the Beatles were not present on iTunes. That, however, changed in 2010, as the third in a series of lawsuits between Apple Corps and Apple Computers was finally settled and their albums were available for purchase. In early 2016, when their music debuted on streaming services, the band finally entered fully into the modern model. The result was possibly the most striking yet. Two generations raised on digital music were suddenly able to stream the band's music—the demographics of those streaming it skewed more than half under 44

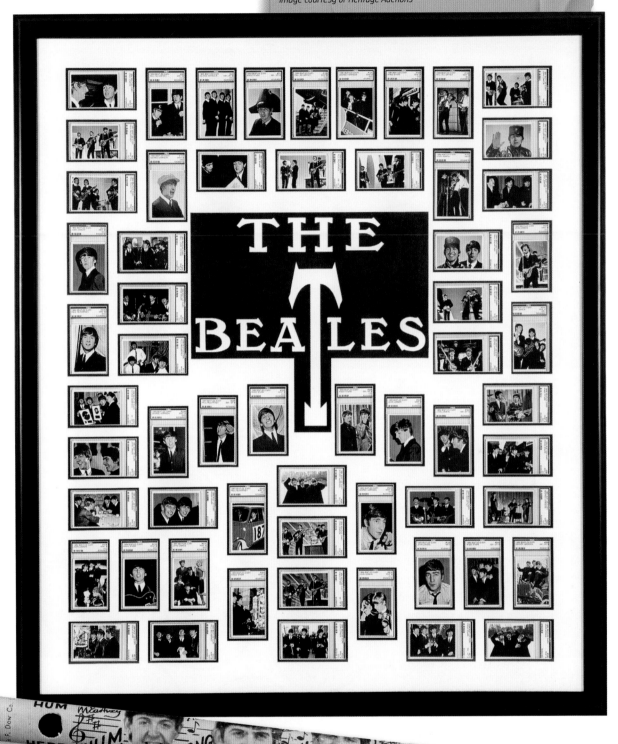

The Beatle Hummer (NEMS, 1964) is a kazoo-like instrument. The 11" long tube features a color lithographed photo of the Beatles and fac-simile autographs. Near Excellent condition. Sold at auction for $350.
Image courtesy of Heritage Auctions

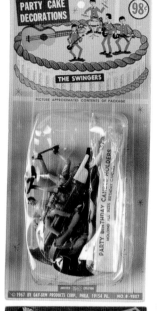

years old. The result? You guessed it: more fans and more merchandising.

That brings us to merchandising as collectibles, which is really the heart and soul of the Beatles memorabilia market. The onslaught of Beatlemania produced millions of items of all kinds, as evidenced by the small fraction of material we're able to show in these pages. It's all evocative of the period, visually compelling and materially scarce. The scarcity is based on the original purpose of the material—it was meant as whimsy, trinkets, and thus was not built to last. In fact, it all broke or fell apart from use. From an original census of millions of pieces, a given example might be reduced to a few hundred, or a few thousand. Condition is important, as is original packaging.

What makes original merchandising great

Seven Vintage Flasher Buttons (US, 1964):
This grouping of seven vintage lenticular lens pinback buttons were all made in 1964 by Vari-Vue of Mt. Vernon, NY. Known as Flasher Buttons, the grouping sold at auction for $312. *Image courtesy of Heritage Auctions*

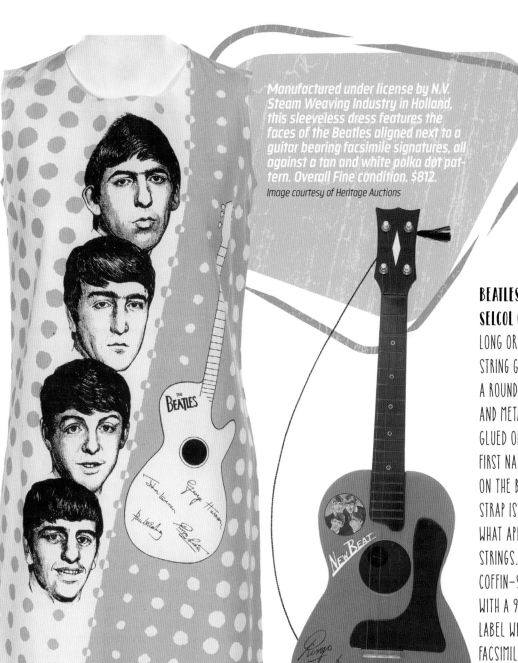

Manufactured under license by N.V. Steam Weaving Industry in Holland, this sleeveless dress features the faces of the Beatles aligned next to a guitar bearing facsimile signatures, all against a tan and white polka dot pattern. Overall Fine condition. $812.
Image courtesy of Heritage Auctions

BEATLES NEW BEAT GUITAR BY SELCOL (UK, 1964). A 32-INCH LONG ORANGE-PLASTIC FOUR-STRING GUITAR WITH A PICKGUARD, A ROUND COLOR BEATLES PHOTO AND METAL "NEW BEAT" ID TAG GLUED ON, AND WITH FACSIMILE FIRST NAME SIGNATURES PRINTED ON THE BODY. THE ORIGINAL NECK STRAP IS STILL ATTACHED AS ARE WHAT APPEARS TO BE THE ORIGINAL STRINGS. THE GUITAR CAME IN A COFFIN-SHAPED CARDBOARD BOX WITH A 9-INCH DIAMETER COLOR LABEL WITH A BEATLE PHOTO, FACSIMILE AUTOGRAPHS AND THE TEXT: "BEATLES NEW BEAT GUITAR." SOLD AT AUCTION FOR $812.
Image courtesy of Heritage Auctions

The Beatles Puritan Shirts promotional poster, circa 1964, with a red background featuring a black and white photograph of The Beatles advertising the arrival of Beatles shirts made by Puritan Fashions Inc. Striking and stylish. At auction: $768.
Image courtesy of Julien's Auctions

EACH AUTHENTIC BEATLE SHIRT CARRIES AUTOGRAPHED PHOTO

JUST ARRIVED!
BEATLE SHIRTS
by Puritan Fashions Corp.

BOYS! GIRLS! MEN!
Sweatshirts! Knit Shirts! Tee Shirts!

collectibles is that, more than any segment of the market besides modern mass-produced material, this stuff is affordable. From as little as $50 up to several hundred and into the low thousands, the merchandise is the most accessible point of the market.

It's also unbelievably entertaining to look at. Some of it is sublime, some very cool, a lot of it completely kitschy but all of it—every last hair band, toothbrush, lunch box or throw rug—brings the band right back to us. If you were there when it happened, it's a nostalgic trip into the past. If you weren't, it's a way to travel back in time and get a taste of it for yourself.

"It's really the merchandizing that has kept the Beatles alive in that there are so many people that can afford at that level," said Julien. "These are things that used to sell for pennies that now bring $600 to $700. It's an attractive and affordable price point and as a result that market's pretty strong right now. The biggest quantity of collectors are at the $50 to $1,000 level. Above that, it's a lot of money to spend."

There's a decided market in modern Beatles collecti-

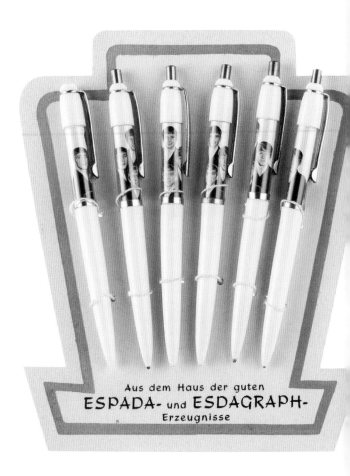

Aus dem Haus der guten
ESPADA- und ESDAGRAPH-
Erzeugnisse

Beatles Style

Ein Hit für den Beatfan. Rassig, jung, faszinierend! Eine Creation aus dem Hause

Filtral
Sonnenbrillen

Two Pairs Of Rare "Beatles Style" Sunglasses By Filtral (Germany, 1966): Two pair of high-quality sunglasses by Filtral (Germany, 1966), one black and one white, each with "Beatles Style" embossed in gold on one of the metal-reinforced earpieces and similar to the ones worn in the movie Help! Sold with reproductions of a color ad for the sunglasses. Near Mint condition. $400. Image courtesy of Heritage Auctions

Twelve Beatles vintage German ballpoint pens on two original display cards (1964). Only offered in Europe. These sold for $500.
Image courtesy of Heritage Auctions

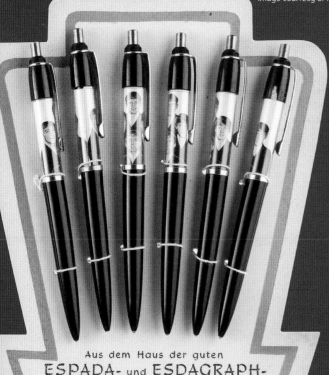

Aus dem Haus der guten
ESPADA- und **ESDAGRAPH-**
Erzeugnisse

(RIGHT) HERE'S A RARELY-OFFERED PIECE OF BEATLE FASHION: AN OFFICIAL LARIAT TIE ON ORIGINAL CARD (U.S. 1964). IN EXCELLENT CONDITION. $350. *Image courtesy of Heritage Auctions*

OFFICIAL
Lariat Tie

THE **BEATLES**

Manufactured under license from Seltaeb, Inc. The ONLY official licensee with exclusive rights for the manufacture and distribution of Beatle Lariat Ties.
Mfg. and printed in USA by PRESS-INitial Corp. Prov. R.I.

THE BEATLES

© Under Licence with " Nems Enterprises Ltd."

Beatles School Bag by Burnel Ltd. of Canada (NEMS, 1964): A 12" x 9" gusseted tan vinyl school bag with a handle and shoulder strap with Beatle images in brown below the flap and on either side of the latch with facsimile signatures between. "The Beatles" is printed in large letters on the flap with sewn black trim all around. Burnel Ltd. of Canada made the bag in 1964. With a $1,750 price tag at auction, I wouldn't carry my homework around in it anymore.
Image courtesy of Heritage Auctions

bles, as evidenced by the fact that so much material is still produced and sold, but this chapter is not terribly concerned with any of that. It is there for the buying if you want it, but often times, for the same price—or saving up what you might spend on three or four modern things—a collector can get something vintage and valuable. That echoes the advice any experienced collector or dealer will give you to do your homework before buying and, in any instance, to buy the very best you can afford.

Beatles Talcum Powder Tin by Margo of Mayfair (UK, 1963). Note the bug antennae on the "B" in Beatles name, as was seen in the very early pieces. This pre-dates the band's appearance on Ed Sullivan. Pure vintage Beatlemania! $937.
Image courtesy of Heritage Auctions

This Beatles Irish linen framed wall hanging was created in 1963. Noted at the bottom: "All Pure Linen Made in Ireland Ulster Copyright Fast Colours." $65.
Image courtesy of Heritage Auctions

If you are a Beatle, even the glasses you drink out of are valuable. These printed Beatles tumblers from Ringo's personal collection brought $1,600 at auction.
Image courtesy of Julien's Auctions

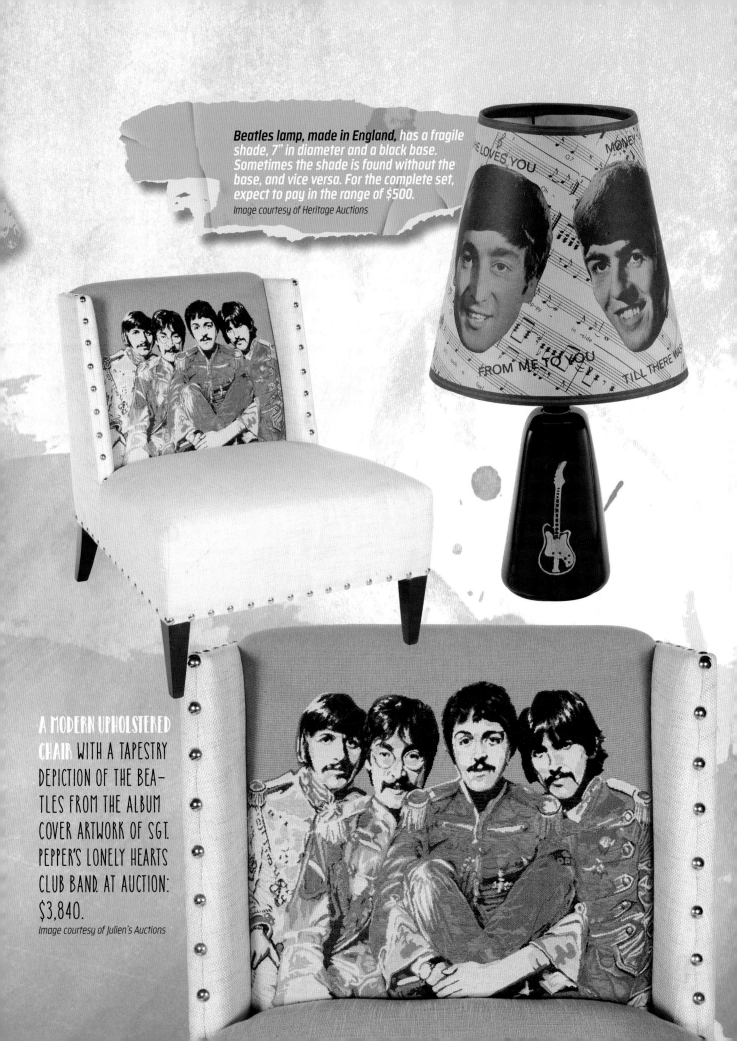

Beatles lamp, made in England, has a fragile shade, 7" in diameter and a black base. Sometimes the shade is found without the base, and vice versa. For the complete set, expect to pay in the range of $500.

Image courtesy of Heritage Auctions

A MODERN UPHOLSTERED CHAIR WITH A TAPESTRY DEPICTION OF THE BEATLES FROM THE ALBUM COVER ARTWORK OF SGT. PEPPER'S LONELY HEARTS CLUB BAND. AT AUCTION: $3,840.

Image courtesy of Julien's Auctions

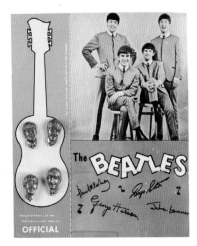

Included in this set from 1964:
"Official Beatles" Guitar Brooch Pin of Ringo, two "Official Beatles" Tie Tacs, one Ringo, one group, "Official Beatle Tac" Guitar Pin with all four Beatles, "Official Beatles" Tie Tack set of all four members and "Beatles Official Tie Tack Pin" set of all four. I would be tempted to wear any of these to the office on any given day were they in my collection. At auction: $312.
Image courtesy of Heritage Auctions

You may not care too much for money but you still need someplace to put it. The Beatles have you covered with this group of vinyl wallets and purses (1960s). Included are two wallets by Standard Plastic Products with various internal compartments and grooming items inside, one red and one yellow; a rare English zippered vinyl coin purse with drawings of the group and the song title "I Should Have Known Better", and a smaller American red plastic coin holder. A chic black vinyl handbag with brass-trimmed handles, and a zippered side compartment, rounds out the grouping. Condition varies, but mostly Good. The group sold at auction for $437. *Image courtesy of Heritage Auctions*

A BRITISH-MADE KANGOL CAP, 1964, IN NAVY. IN VERY GOOD, WEARABLE CONDITION AND JUST AS COOL TODAY AS IT WAS MORE THAN 50 YEARS AGO. $500.

Image courtesy of Heritage Auctions

A Beatles Magnetic Hair Game complete with wand by Merit (UK NEMS, 1964). An 8" x 10.5" heavyweight card with hairless images of the Beatles inside a hard plastic cover full of black magnetic shavings that can be moved into place using the included "magnetic pencil." It's a Beatles take on a classic – it even comes with instructions in case there was one single, solitary human alive who couldn't figure it out. Best is the text saying "It's Dynamic and Magnetic" and that it "Amuses the Whole Family." It obviously moved one collector to the auction tune of $937.

Image courtesy of Heritage Auctions

The Beatles Album Pin Collection presented to Ringo sold at auction for $1,920.
Image courtesy of Julien's Auctions

(above) An extremely rare, 10-foot long full roll of the Crown Company's UK issue of Beatles wallpaper (1964). The roll measures 120 inches long and 22 inches wide (including the sizing strips) and is in Very Good condition. What could show your deep and abiding love of and dedication to Beatlemania more than covering your walls, literally, with the Fab Four? $400.
Image courtesy of Heritage Auctions

Beatles Complete Set of Four Revell Models with Boxes, Completely Assembled and Painted (US, 1964): This complete set of all four Revell models, with original color boxes, makes a tremendously kitschy and cool piece of Beatlemania. The descriptions of the boys are even better. Paul is "The Great McCartney," John is "Kookiest of Them All!," George is "Lead Guitar – Loud and Strong" and Ringo is "Wildest Skins in Town." Notice Ringo's broken arm. At auction, this stellar set brought $687.

Image courtesy of Heritage Auctions

IF YOU WERE A COOL BEATLES FAN IN 1964, THEN YOU DEFINITELY HAD THIS BAD BOY BOARD GAME BY MILTON BRADLEY IN YOUR CLOSET. A RARE PIECE OF BEATLES MARKETING GENIUS. DO YOU THINK THE FELLAS SAT AROUND THE RECORDING STUDIO BETWEEN TAKES AND ROLLED THE DICE? AT AUCTION: $137.

Image courtesy of Heritage Auctions

An unopened black cardboard box containing both the blue photo and orange photo decks of Beatle playing cards as manufactured by the Arrco Playing Card Co. of Chicago in 1964. Samples of each card back are attached to the front and "The Beatles" is stamped in gold on the back. Rare and very cool! At auction: $1,187.

Image courtesy of Heritage Auctions

A rare original Apple watch by Old England, 1967. A very cool, seldom seen and quite fashionable 1.5" square, 21-jewel watch with a black faux suede band. The watch only was sold at the Apple Boutique in Chelsea during its short time in business, December 1967 to July 1968. The clock still runs and keeps very good time when wound. At auction: $1,187.

Image courtesy of Heritage Auctions

One could make that argument that the 1964 Beatles Record Player, with its attractive blue and black cabinet and four-speed turntable, is the most iconic Beatles collectible. This player, graded in overall Very Good condition, sold at auction for $2,750.

Image courtesy of Heritage Auctions

"ALL YOU NEED IS LOVE" PSYCHEDELIC BLACK LIGHT POSTER (CIRCA 1969) BY POSTER PRINTS SOLD AT AUCTION FOR $200.

Image courtesy of Heritage Auctions

A beautiful set of vintage drinking glasses in extraordinary condition, manufactured at the height of Beatlemania by J & L Co., Ltd. in their native England. Each measures 4" high, with a color transfer of each Beatle and full name below. Note some wear, more so to Paul than the others – quite clear who the original owner favored. $450.

Image courtesy of Heritage Auctions

These plates, decorated with Lennon's post-Beatles art, realized $1,920 at auction.

Image courtesy of Julien's Auctions

WHO ELSE WOULD YOU TURN TO WHEN YOU NEEDED TAPE?

ESPECIALLY IF YOU WERE IN THE PHILIPPINES? TWELVE TAPE ROLLS IN PLASTIC BAGS WITH "BEATLES CELLOPHANE TAPE" STICKERS BEARING A GROUP PHOTO, ALL STAPLED TO A COLORFUL 7.75" X 10.25" DISPLAY CARD. THIS APPEARS TO BE A LATER REPRODUCTION AFTER THE ORIGINAL 1960s RELEASE. TALK ABOUT MARKETING PROWESS. AT AUCTION: $175.

Image courtesy of Heritage Auctions

The Beatles "Yellow Submarine" Picture Hangers, set of 4 (1968), is the kind of merchandising that Beatlemania was built on, only this is from the late-Beatles period, not an era known for over-the-top Beatles merchandising. That makes this a rare commodity in any state, let alone in such Excellent condition with the original packing. Two pictured here. At auction: $657.
Image courtesy of Heritage Auctions

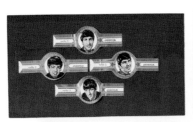

As far as unusual Beatles items, this collection of 28 cigar bands and an oversized cigar (Germany, 1960s) ranks near the top. Likely to avoid licensing issues, some of the labels contain false names for each Beatle (Harie, Benny, Marc and Patrick) for a humorous effect. Sold with a German souvenir Revue cigar featuring a label with Paul's image, with his name changed to "Aristoteles." All Very Good condition, though we question the quality of the cigars these originally were placed on. Cubans? Probably not... Still, these brought $437 at auction.   Image courtesy of Heritage Auctions

BAND-USED GEAR

The spectrum of Beatles collectibles and memorabilia is vast, deep and incredibly varied. If you have $100 or $1 million you can find something to suit your taste and budget. As with any collectible, however, there are levels of both collector and material.

When it comes to The Beatles, if bits of their marketing genius are the most accessible, then surely the pinnacle, the Mount Everest of Beatles collectibles has to be any and all instruments that the band themselves played. These are the tools the master craftsmen used to build their kingdom and they are coveted as the holiest of relics in the church of rock 'n' roll. There are few that could successfully argue that the instruments The Beatles used are not the very foundation of the last 50-plus years of popular modern music.

Even within the rarified circles of Beatles-used gear there are levels. The hobby is replete with examples of instruments that the Beatles have signed—these are at the bottom of the ladder. Though valuable because they are "instruments" with a Beatle signature, they are not usually played by the band. While these can loosely fit in the "Beatles Gear" category, they don't really count as Beatles-used.

The middle tier of the Beatles-used gear sphere is filled with instruments a member of the band played, however briefly. There are plenty of guitars out there that make this claim. This can, however, be a problematic thing to collect, as the provenance on many of these instruments, which has to be rock solid, usually is not. The price tags on these instruments can also often be quite high, from the tens of thousands of dollars up to $1 million or more. As with any investment of this magnitude, buyer beware!

The top level of the world of Beatles-used gear is then, obviously, the instruments that members of the band owned and recorded with. It can be said, unequivocally, that there is no piece of Beatles memorabilia or collectible that is more coveted by collectors.

This is where Andy Babiuk comes in. Babiuk is the owner of Andy Babiuk's Fab Gear, a boutique music shop in Fairport, New York, and author of *Beatles Gear: All the Fab Four's Instruments from Stage to Studio – The Ultimate Edition* (Backbeat Books). Babiuk, a successful musician (a founding member of Chesterfield Kings and current member of the super group The Empty Hearts, featuring Elliot Easton of The Cars, Clem Burke of Blondie and Wally Palmar of The Romantics), author and businessman, is the foremost authority in the world on Beatles-used gear. He is the go-to resource for auctioneers, dealers and researchers needing informa-

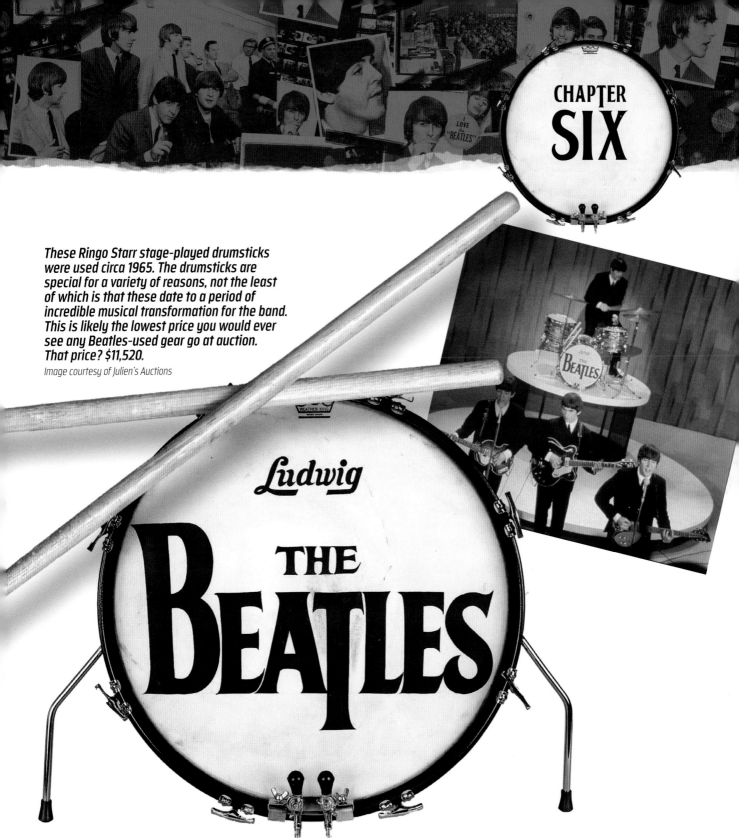

These Ringo Starr stage-played drumsticks were used circa 1965. The drumsticks are special for a variety of reasons, not the least of which is that these date to a period of incredible musical transformation for the band. This is likely the lowest price you would ever see any Beatles-used gear go at auction. That price? $11,520.

Image courtesy of Julien's Auctions

This Ludwig bass drum head, with the iconic "drop-T" logo, was on Ringo Starr's drum kit for The Beatles' debut on The Ed Sullivan Show, Feb. 9, 1964. The show officially launched the British Invasion, changing rock history forever. The Remo Weather King head is painted with The Beatles "drop-T" logo and "Ludwig." It is number two of seven Beatles "drop-T" logo drum heads painted by Edwin Stokes for the band for their first trip to the states. Pre-auction estimates put the value of the drum head at around $1 million. Jim Irsay, owner of the Indianapolis Colts football team, paid $2,050,000 for it. Irsay has a collection of about 175 guitars. Christopher McKinney, who curates the Irsay collection, said in many ways the drum head was more significant to people than a Beatles guitar. "If you showed the guitar to 20 people, one might recognize what it is," McKinney said. "If you show the drum head to 20 people, most will be able to identify with it."

Image courtesy of Julien's Auctions

tion on—or verification of—a Beatles-used instrument.

Babiuk's book is an incredible resource, and his work on it over the last 20 years could rightfully be the subject of a book itself. According to Babiuk's website:

"This book is the first to tell the full story of how the Beatles made their music. It details exactly which guitars, drums, amplifiers and keyboards the Beatles used at the key points of their relatively brief but entirely revolutionary career...from the formation of the Quarry Men skiffle group in the 1950s to the dissolution of the Beatles in 1970.

"It provides a fascinating fresh insight into Beatle history from an entirely new viewpoint, and along the way many myths are exploded and dozens of stories told for the first time, and many more since its first release."

What follows in these pages are images and explanations of a few choice pieces of Beatles-used gear. The fact is, as Babiuk explains, there is really precious little that has been released to the public. The Beatles members and their families have kept, and still have in most cases, every bit of gear they used, especially after they started to get famous. They were keenly aware of the potential worth of the stuff.

That scarcity, however, makes the few examples of personally owned and used Beatles instruments that have surfaced even more exciting and intriguing.

Babiuk took time out of his busy schedule to provide some insight on the band, their instruments, the viability of those instruments as collectibles and on his own journey to

becoming one of the top, most sought-after Beatles experts in the world.

How did you become an expert in Beatles-used instruments?

Andy Babiuk (AB): I've worked in a guitar shop for more than 35 years; it's something I've always done. I have also been a successful musician in a band for more than 30 years. My passion was always the music that we all grew up with—Beatles, Stones, Kinks, the whole British Invasion. I wanted to sound like them when we made records, which meant using the same kind of instruments they used: Gretsch, Hofner and Rickenbacker (guitars).

So we subsequently used that kind of equipment on the first record we recorded and we found out quickly that there was more to it than plugging in and playing on the same type of instruments they used. I started studying how the Beatles did it and became fascinated with it. There was no book on it at that time, so it was really Sherlock Holmes-type of stuff for me to put everything together.

The guitar shop where I worked at the time would have a lot of people come in and they'd have an old Vox amp like the Beatles used in recordings and they would ask about it. The guys I worked with would point to me and say "talk to Andy." In essence what I was doing was teaching them, my co-workers and customers alike. I wasn't bragging, I just knew about it.

So one day, one of my friends—a guy I'm still friends with to this day—he said, "y'know, if you got a case of beer and locked yourself in a house for a weekend and wrote down everything you know about the Beatles you'd have a book," and I thought "Oh wow." Six years later, I had a book.

What was the first Beatles-used instrument you handled?

AB: The first Beatles instrument that I ever held was John's second Gibson J-160E, the one with caricatures of he and Yoko that he drew on it. Gibson had hired me to help with a replica that they were doing, because I had done so much research on it. In order to do it

Andy Babiuk

Photo courtesy of Rob Shanahan

This Ludwig Oyster Black Pearl 3-piece drum kit was the first Ludwig kit ever owned by Ringo Starr and was used on more than 200 live performances and more than 180 studio recordings from May 1963 through Feb. 4, 1964. **The drum kit became a visual trademark as important to The Beatles' stage show as their hair, suits, boots, guitars and amplifiers. In short, it is one of the most iconic instruments on the entire planet.** Eddie Stokes was a local sign painter in London who occasionally worked for Drum City, the store where this kit was bought. Stokes' job was to paint band names on drum heads. He was paid £5 to paint the "drop-T" Beatles logo on the front drum head just under the Ludwig name. Ringo took possession of his new Ludwig kit on May 12, 1963. At $2,110,000 at auction, this writer believes history will bear this price out to be a bargain of the highest order.

Image courtesy of Julien's Auctions

faithfully, I had to measure it and get the perspective right.

It just so happens that, at that time, Yoko was setting up the John Lennon exhibit at the Rock and Roll Hall of Fame. She was very gracious and let me spend a lot of time with it. From there it just took off.

Why is the draw of Beatles gear still so strong?

AB: Because they actually did what they did with these instruments. They were the guys that paved the road for the Stones, Zeppelin and everybody else. If you study their music and see who was doing what at which time—their use of the Rickenbacker 12-string, for instance—then you know that nothing would have been done that way, ever, had they not done that.

Take the idea behind the song "Tomorrow Never Knows," the final track

(left) This is Ringo Starr's 1964 snare drum from his Ludwig #2 Black Oyster Pearl Downbeat kit, also known as the Ed Sullivan kit. This snare came with the kit purchased for The Beatles visit to the United States at Manny's Music store in Manhattan. The kit was also used for filming A Hard Days Night while Starr's Ludwig #1 kit would be used in the studio. For the Beatles first appearance in the United States Starr brought with him a set of his own cymbals, a new Beatles drop-T logo bass drum head and his 1963 Ludwig Jazz Festival snare drum. The 1963 snare drum from his #1 Ludwig kit was Starr's primary snare throughout his career with the Beatles and remains in his collection. This snare does not have a history with the Beatles other than being purchased with the rest of the Sullivan kit but it does have history with Paul McCartney.

In 1969 McCartney was preparing to record his first solo album, McCartney , at his makeshift home recording studio in St John's Wood, London. McCartney, who played all of the instruments on the album, borrowed drum equipment from Starr. The resulting kit was a combination of Starr's Ludwig #1 and #2 kit, which included this snare. Recording of the album took place from December 1969 to February 1970. The kit then traveled with McCartney to his home studio in Scotland. McCartney and drummer Denny Seiwell, used this kit extensively for rehearsing of the newly formed band, Wings, debut album, Wild Life . Ringo is seen playing the kit in McCartney's music video Take It Away, released in 1982. This snare, from Ringo #2 drum set, sold at auction for $75,000.

Image courtesy of Julien's Auctions

on Revolver. Ringo told me that John wanted to record a song with just tape loops. This was, what, 1966? Who would do that? There's just example after example where you see they were way ahead of their time, and then they were gone. They were there for 10 years and then they weren't. What they left behind was amazing.

Is most Beatles-used gear accounted for?

AB: There are about five instruments that are unaccounted for right now, though there are quite a few in total, all of which are in my book. The surviving Beatles themselves, and the Harrison and Lennon estates, have the bulk of their stuff. That's what makes the story of John's J-160, which was stolen so long ago, such a great story. I went on record, before its sale at auction (in November 2015) to say that it would be the highest price Beatles instrument ever sold and it was.

What about Paul's original Hofner? We all know he has it, and would likely never sell it, but what if he did? What could it bring? It's got to be the Holy Grail of Beatles memorabilia.

AB: Paul's Hofner would go much higher—I couldn't say just how high. It's so unique looking. There's no other instrument they call the Beatle Strat or the Beatle Rickenbacker. They call that Hofner the Beatles Bass.

How granular does the pursuit of Beatles instruments go? Meaning, do drumsticks and guitar picks and strings count?

AB: I get that all the time about things like drumsticks or picks, but I usually just can't comment. I get emails and phone calls constantly from people saying, "I've got this or I've got that." Obviously, if I say it's the real thing then they are going to make money on it, so I have to be careful.

I think, with collecting in general, when people like a band or a celebrity or a pro athlete, they like anything that has to do with that person. There then comes a time and a thing where anything that that person has touched is valuable and that can create issues. So, John Lennon played a guitar for a second at a party and it's suddenly more valuable; I always have a problem with some of that stuff because it's so hard to substantiate. When it comes to an instrument they used and recorded with, and it's absolutely backed up by paperwork and photos and anecdotes, it's not only real, it's more valuable.

A Hofner left-handed violin bass with gold-plated hardware and no serial number, custom made for Sir Paul McCartney in 1964, with its original Selmer tweed case. McCartney has used Hofner violin basses since 1961, both with The Beatles and throughout his solo career. The shape, look, and tone of this instrument are so synonymous with his music that the bass is affectionately known as the "Beatle Bass." In exchange for the use of promotional hang tags featuring The Beatles' bass player, Selmer—the distributor for Hofner—paid a small royalty to Brian Epstein's company and supplied a one-off custom-made bass for McCartney himself. The history of this instrument has been well documented in Andy Babiuk's Beatles Gear: All the Fab Four's Instruments from Stage to Studio. A relative bargain at $201,800, as the owner will never lose money on it. Image Courtesy of Julien's Auctions

Image courtesy of
Julien's Auctions

George Harrison's Harptone 12-String Guitar:
George Harrison received this guitar prior to
recording The White Album. While there is
currently no evidence that it was used
on any Beatles recording, it was used
by George and members of Badfinger on the sessions for George's All
Things Must Pass LP set and by Badfinger member Tom Evans at Madison
Square Garden during The Concert
For Bangladesh charity shows. In 1974,
George gave the guitar to Bob Purvis, a
member of the band Splinter, whose debut
LP he had produced. This piece sold more than
a decade ago, just a few years after Harrison's
death, at auction for $35,250 and has not re-
surfaced since. It's safe to say it would bring
significantly more were it to sell tomorrow.
Image courtesy of Heritage Auctions

Life on the road with The
Beatles can be had –
for a price. **This vintage
Ludwig fiberboard drum
case, circa 1960s, was
used by Ringo Starr
while on tour with The
Beatles and sold at auc-
tion for $40,625. You can
clearly see "Ringo Starr
- The Beatles" stenciled
on the lid and side of the
case. The case, which
was used to transport
drum gear and hard-
ware, has its original
leather straps and sits
on caster wheels. Vari-
ous stickers and labels
are adhered to the case.**
Image courtesy of Julien's Auctions

RINGO'S LUDWIG DRUM SET

*This Ludwig Oyster Black Pearl 3-piece drum kit
was the first Ludwig kit owned by Ringo Starr and
was used on more than 200 live performances and
more than 180 studio recordings from May 1963
through Feb. 4, 1964. The drum kit became a
visual trademark of the band. Eddie Stokes was
a local sign painter in London who occasionally worked for Drum City, the store where this
kit was bought. Stokes' job was to paint band
names on drum heads. He was paid £5 to paint
the "drop-T" Beatles logo on the front drum
head just under the Ludwig name. Ringo took
possession of his new Ludwig kit on May 12,
1963. The kit sold at auction for $2,110,000.*

*Fom the catalog for The Ringo Starr and Barbara Bach
Collection, Julien's Auctions, Dec. 2015*

1963 and early 1964 was a very busy and aggres-
sive time for The Beatles and this Ludwig Downbeat
drum kit was used extensively as the band criss-
crossed the UK, playing in England, Scotland, Ireland
and Wales, as well as on the continent in Sweden
and France.

Here are some key moments in its history:

● It was played at the last appearance by The Beatles at The Cavern Club on Aug. 3, 1963

● It was seen on close to 20 television performances including Thank Your Lucky Stars (May 12,
1963), Ready, Steady, Go!(Oct. 4, 1963), Sunday Night
At The London Palladium (Oct. 13, 1963), the Royal Command Performance from the Prince of Wales
Theatre (Nov. 4, 1963), the Morecambe And Wise
Show (Dec. 2, 1963) and Juke Box Jury from the Empire Theatre in Liverpool (Dec. 7, 1963)

● It was heard on more than 160 songs in 28 differ-
ent broadcast episodes of BBC Radio shows like Sat-
urday Club, Pop Go The Beatles and From Us To
You. Many of the recordings can be found on The
Beatles' Live At The BBC, Volumes I & II as well
as on bootleg recordings. Some of the songs include:
Ain't Nothin' Shakin' (But The Leaves On The Trees),
All My Loving, A Shot Of Rhythm And Blues, Boys,
Carol, Clarabella, Devil In Her Heart, Don't Ever
Change, Do You Want To Know A Secret, Everybody's
Trying To Be My Baby, From Me To You, From Us To
You, Glad All Over, Hippy Hippy Shake, I Got To Find
My Baby, I Just Don't Understand, I'll Get You, I'm
Gonna Sit Right Down And Cry, I Saw Her Standing
There, I Wanna Be Your Man, I Want To Hold Your
Hand, Johnny B Goode, Lend Me Your Comb, Long Tall
Sally, Lucille, Memphis Tennessee, Misery, Mon-
ey (That's What I Want), Please Mr. Postman, Please
Please Me, Roll Over Beethoven, Thank You Girl, She
Loves You, Soldier Of Love, Some Other Guy, Sure To
Fall, Sweet Little Sixteen, Thank You Girl, That's All
Right Mama, There's A Place, Three Cool Cats, Till
There Was You, Too Much Monkey Business, Twist
And Shout, Words Of Love, Young Blood, You Really
Got A Hold On Me

(right) An amazing, special and moving piece of Beatles gear, this is a 1964 Rose-Morris Rickenbacker, model 1996, nick-named "The Beatle Backer," owned by John Lennon and later gifted to Ringo Starr. **Rose-Morris, the official UK importer of Rickenbacker, originally gave the guitar to Lennon when his 1964 Rickenbacker 325 was damaged during a Christmas performance. John played this guitar for the remaining 1964 Christmas shows. It is also seen in 1967 photographs taken in Lennon's home music-room. In 1968 Lennon gave the guitar to Starr. According the Julien's catalog from the 2015 auction in which this sold, "in 1968, when tensions were rising among the Beatles, Starr briefly left his bandmates who were recording The Beatles aka the 'White Album.' When he returned, fresh with new material he had written, Lennon gave him this Rickenbacker. Lennon thought the guitar would fit Starr well and wanted to encourage Starr to write more songs." The Beatles Backer brought $910,000 when it sold at auction. A bargain by Beatles standards!**

Image courtesy of Julien's Auctions

Any advice to collectors?

AB: Stay far away from places online where you'll find fake stuff. I worked too hard to get where I am and forge these relationships with these musicians to ever touch any of that stuff, there's so much of it. I'll always look at it, of course—you never know—but it's often nonsense and I don't have the time for it, I just don't want to debate that stuff.

I have a lot of clients that look for the real thing—Beatles-used and otherwise—and buy at auction or privately and I have to say, when it comes to the real thing, the auction route is probably better for them because auction houses take the time usually to research and vet the material, they are people that aggressively look for the equipment. With Beatles gear, good luck. There's just not that much out there and when you see the prices, as much as $1 million or more, you have to be very careful. There's a lot of bogus stuff out there.

Lastly, I have to know, what's it like to hang out with a Beatle?

AB: They happen to be popular musicians, but in the end they're just guys. You're sitting and talking with a person. I'm a musician and I play and I travel all over the world so a lot of the musicians I've worked with are just friends. It's not anything weird. First time I hung out with Ringo, I was a little nervous, but once that initial thing is out—that he was a Beatle—he's really just a nice guy, which is what has made him so successful.

I always relate this story when asked: I've met thousands of musicians in my life and, back in the day in the 1980s, I ran a big music store in Rochester, New York, where I used to set up a lot of in-store performances with the popular bands where they would come in and play, a lot of metal bands and lots of flash-in-the-pan bands. The interesting thing to point out, what has really stuck with me, is how many of them that came in and were real a**holes and prima donnas, how many of them simply aren't in it anymore. Furthermore, nobody cares where they are. All the guys that are really nice guys are still around. That certainly goes for The Beatles.

(below) This is a simply stellar piece of Beatles-used gear, George Harrison's 1962 Rickenbacker 425 guitar. Originally purchased by George at Fenton's Music store, then refinished from a Fireglo finish to the black George requested to match John Lennon's similar Rickenbacker. Among the truly great Beatles instruments and a piece that is supremely evocative of Beatlemania. It sold for $657,000 at auction in 2014. If it came back up for auction today, I would guess that it would easily dwarf even that impressive price.

Image Courtesy of Julien's Auctions

(right) George Harrison played this Maton Mastersound MS500 electric guitar on stage in the summer of 1963. According to Andy Babiuk, Harrison's Gretsch Country Gentleman guitar was experiencing problems and brought to Barratts music store in Manchester to be repaired. The Maton was given to Harrison to use while repairs were made. After his Country Gent was returned Harrison kept the Maton and played it in concert at Margate (July 8-13), in Liverpool (Aug. 2), at The Cavern (Aug. 3) and when the Beatles played Guernsey, Channel Islands (Aug. 6-10). As one would expect with well-documented Beatles gear, this brought a huge price at auction: $485,000.

Darren Julien, President and CEO of Julien's Auctions, **holds a custom-made prototype VOX guitar played by George Harrison and John Lennon during The Beatles 1967 Magical Mystery Tour. Harrison played the semi-hollow-body guitar, distinguished by two symmetrical flared shoulders on the upper body, while practicing "I Am The Walrus," and Lennon used it in a video session for the song "Hello, Goodbye." The VOX guitar was a prototype instrument custom-built for Lennon in 1966, according to Martin Nolan, executive director of Julien's. Lennon gave the VOX guitar as a gift in 1967 to Yanni "Magic Alex" Mardas, who was the electronics engineer for the band's Apple Records label. The guitar sold for $408,000 in 2013.**

AP Photo/Kirsty Wigglesworth

Image courtesy of Julien's Auctions

John Lennon Gibson J-160-E: Gibson J-160E, Serial number 73157, Flattop acoustic/electric sunburst with mahogany back and sides, three-ply laminated spruce top, bound rosewood fingerboard, crown pearl inlays three-on-a-side keystone-tip Kluson tuners, tortoiseshell pickguard, single Gibson P-90 single-coil pickup, single volume control, output jack at side. This lovely little acoustic is the most important early Beatles-used instrument in existence. In 1962 and 1963 when Lennon and Paul McCartney went to write songs, this was the J-160E that Lennon used to compose. The songs "I Want to Hold Your Hand," "Please, Please Me," "From Me to You," "All My Loving," "This Boy" and others, all were written by Lennon and McCartney on this instrument. Just a taste of the recordings this amazing little axe contributed to?

The UK singles:
"Love Me Do" / "P.S. I Love You",
"Please Please Me" / "Ask Me Why",
"From Me To You" / "Thank You Girl"

The albums:
Please, Please Me, With the Beatles, Introducing... The Beatles, The Early Beatles, Meet the Beatles!, The Beatles' Second Album, The Beatles One, Live At the BBC, Anthology 1

The EPs:
The Beatles (No. 1), The Beatles' Hits, Twist and Shout

At some point, Lennon was separated from this guitar, though how it happened is lost to history. Was it stolen? Misplaced? Forgotten? Given away? We may never know. The story of how it was discovered, detailed in the sidebar accompanying this piece, is quite amazing. The record shows it was bought by Tommy Pressley in the summer of 1967 from a music store in San Diego. He had no idea it once belonged to John and later re-sold it to a friend named John McCaw, who owned it for decades before, in 2008, becoming curious about its history. From a simple search for the year his guitar was made unfolded an incredible investigation that, ultimately, led him to Andy Babiuk, author of Beatles Gear: All the Fab Four's Instruments from Stage to Studio – the bible of Beatles gear. Babiuk receives calls almost daily from people who believe they have a real Beatles-used instrument, but the day he got the call from McCaw, something was different. Someone actually did find John Lennon's lost J-160E. Ultimately, in 2015, this beauty realized a record price of $2,410,000 at auction.

Image Courtesy of Julien's Auctions

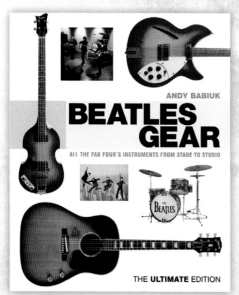

ANDY BABIUK

BEATLES GEAR

ALL THE FAB FOUR'S INSTRUMENTS FROM STAGE TO STUDIO

THE **ULTIMATE** EDITION

A CLASSIC LOST AND FOUND STORY

by Andy Babiuk

Excerpt from Beatles Gear –
The Ultimate Edition

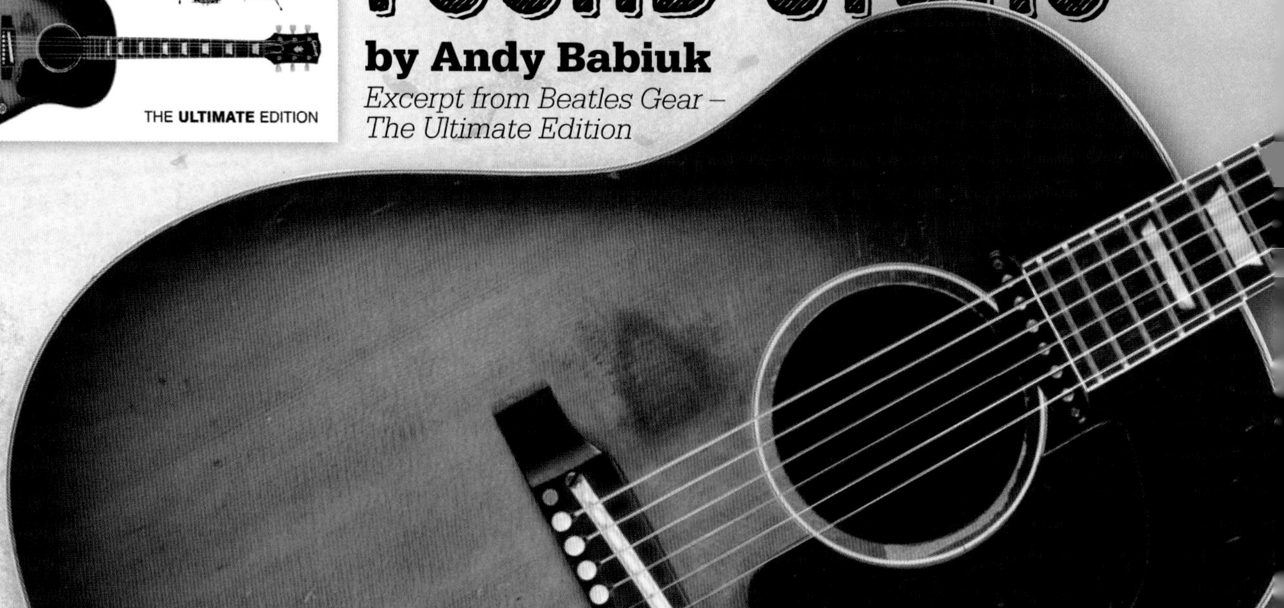

Returning to Liverpool from the September 4 [1962] studio session, [The Beatles] continued with daily live shows. Earlier in the year, just after Abbey Road staff had complained about the poor state of much of the group's gear, Lennon and Harrison had ordered a pair of new Gibson electric-acoustic J-160E guitars, and word now came through that these had arrived.

Gibson launched the J-160E, an unusual hybrid, in 1954. It looked like a regular flattop acoustic, but it was fitted with an electric-guitar type pickup and controls. This meant that it could be used unplugged as a regular acous-

tic guitar, for example for songwriting on the road, or plugged-in to give an amplified approximation of an acoustic guitar, either on stage or in the studio. Lennon and Harrison's Gibson J-160Es were identical sunburst-finish guitars, each with a 16-inch round-shouldered body built with mahogany back and sides, a three-ply laminated spruce top with internal ladder bracing, a mahogany neck with a bound rosewood fingerboard inlaid with crown-shape pearl markers, three-on-a-side keystone-tip Kluson tuners, a tortoiseshell pickguard, and an adjustable ceramic saddle mounted in a rosewood bridge base. Each of the guitars was fitted with a single Gibson P-90 single-coil pickup between the end of the neck and the soundhole, with a single volume and tone control mounted on the body's lower face and an output jack on the side. The guitars arrived in

brown Lifton cases with pink-lined interiors.

The group ordered the J-160Es from Rushworth's – one of the few shops in Liverpool where musicians could buy American-made instruments. The J-160E was not one of the Gibson models generally on sale in the UK through distributor Selmer, so Lennon and Harrison had to order the guitars from a catalogue and wait for them to be sent specially to the store from the United States.

The two guitarists may have been influenced in their choice of this unusual model by Tony Sheridan. "At the time everybody was using a cricket bat," Sheridan says, "a piece of wood with strings on it. Not too many people were into big jazz guitars, but I was. So I guess it rubbed off on the Liverpool crowd. I think that had something to do with The Beatles using those big hollow-body acoustic guitars." Sheridan believes that Lennon and Harrison intended to order the archtop Gibson ES-175 – the model he had used in Hamburg and that the two Beatle guitarists had tried – but that they somehow ended up with the flattop J-160E. He says that they had enjoyed using his Gibson ES-175 and would refer to it as "the jumbo".

Perhaps Lennon and Harrison liked Sheridan's 175 so much that, when it came to shopping for new guitars, they really did mean to get that model for themselves. The two guitarists certainly did refer to their Gibson J-160Es later as "the jumbos". Maybe when Lennon and Harrison ordered the Gibson guitars at Rushworth's they asked for "the Gibson electric jumbo", with the intention of ordering a model like Sheridan's "jumbo". Early-60s Gibson catalogues list the J-160E as the "Electric Jumbo Model" – hence the J and the E. The ES-175 is listed as an "Electric Spanish Model". Maybe this accounts for Lennon and Harrison ending up with their J-160Es. Sheridan also points to a more attractive second theory: that it may have been the influence of another guitar he used in Hamburg, his pickup-equipped Martin D-28E, an instrument much closer in style to the J-160E.

Whatever inspired their purchase, Lennon and Harrison's J-160Es were certainly specially ordered through Rushworth's. The total credit price noted for Lennon's Gibson J-160E (and presumably Harrison's too) was a cool £161/1/- (£161.05, about $450 then and around £3,100 or $4,600 in today's money). Tracing the serial number 73161 listed on Lennon's original hire-purchase receipt to the log still in Gibson's archives shows that this J-160E was shipped by Gibson on June 27. The receipt also reveals that Epstein paid for the guitar in full almost exactly a year later.

We'll learn later how Lennon and Harrison would swap their J-160Es and that Lennon's Gibson would go missing at the end of 1963. In 2014, that long-lost J-160E of Lennon's was found. This author was contacted by John McCaw, who had seen an earlier edition of Beatles Gear and noticed that the serial number published in the book for Harrison's 160 was very close to the one he owned. McCaw bought his used J-160E from a friend in southern California in the late '60s after serving in

THE RECORD THAT STARTED "BEATLEMANIA"

ENGLAND'S SENSATIONS

JUST DID
JACK PAAR SHOW
(JAN. 3)

COMING UP
ED SULLIVAN
(FEB. 9 & FEB. 16)

FEATURED IN TIME, LIFE, NEWSWEEK

THIS IS THE RECORD THAT STARTED IT ALL

PLEASE, PLEASE ME
AND
FROM ME TO YOU
BY
THE BEATLES
[VJ]
VEE-JAY RECORDS

VJ-581

(PROMOTION COPY)

the military in Vietnam, and he has owned it ever since. As he looked at the photo of Harrison's guitar, he thought about how similar it looked to his own. When he read further and found out that Lennon's guitar had gone missing in the early 60s, McCaw wondered if his guitar could possibly be Lennon's. This author compared the wood grain patterns in McCaw's guitar with those in photos of Lennon and his 160, and they provided an absolute match. The guitar was indeed Lennon's original Gibson J-160E. The serial number on the guitar is 73157, and this is listed on the same page of Gibson's shipping records as Harrison's 73161, just a few lines apart. Both guitars were shipped from Gibson on the same day, June 27 1962.

When did the group start to use their new J-160E guitars? They may have been sent by sea from the USA, which would account for them taking more than two months to arrive. Rushworth's boast in Mersey Beat that the guitars were "specially flown to England by jet from America" was probably just part of the promotional hype. That receipt for Lennon's Gibson is dated Sep-

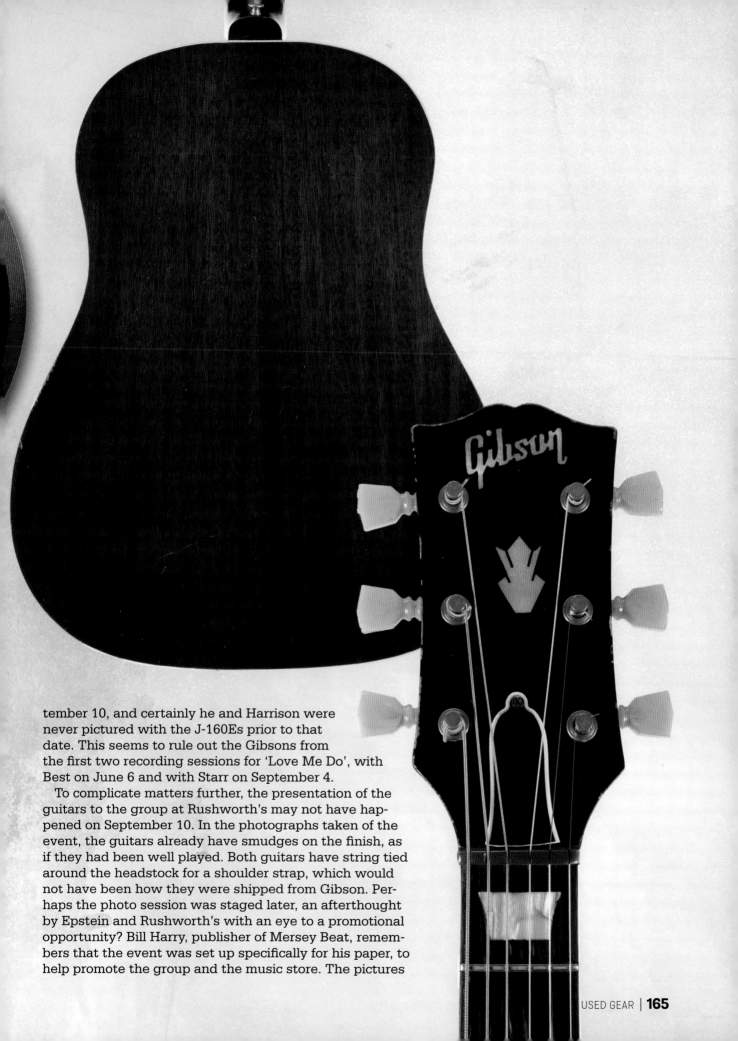

tember 10, and certainly he and Harrison were never pictured with the J-160Es prior to that date. This seems to rule out the Gibsons from the first two recording sessions for 'Love Me Do', with Best on June 6 and with Starr on September 4.

To complicate matters further, the presentation of the guitars to the group at Rushworth's may not have happened on September 10. In the photographs taken of the event, the guitars already have smudges on the finish, as if they had been well played. Both guitars have string tied around the headstock for a shoulder strap, which would not have been how they were shipped from Gibson. Perhaps the photo session was staged later, an afterthought by Epstein and Rushworth's with an eye to a promotional opportunity? Bill Harry, publisher of Mersey Beat, remembers that the event was set up specifically for his paper, to help promote the group and the music store. The pictures did not appear in Mersey Beat until October.

On September 11, the day after Rushworth's sold them their new guitars, The Beatles once again visited EMI's Abbey Road Studio 2 in London to try again to record their first single… The group once again recorded 'Love Me Do' and 'PS I Love You'. All three versions – June 6, September 4, September 11 – have since been released, and all bear a similar guitar sound. So maybe the same guitar was used for all three sessions – meaning either Lennon's Rickenbacker or Harrison's Duo Jet. It is of course possible that the J-160Es were used for the recording on the 11th. When Lennon and Harrison first used their Gibson J-160Es in the studio, they recorded them by plugging the guitars into their amplifiers – the guitars were not recorded acoustically, and the tone came from a miked-up amplifier. If one plays a J-160E, a Rickenbacker 325, or a Gretsch Duo Jet today through an A.C.30, it's relatively easy to get the same sound quality from all three guitars – essentially a very clean and full tone.

The Helen Shapiro package tour started on Saturday February 2. During the tour, Epstein managed to fill The Beatles' days off with sporadic shows at the Cavern and a full schedule of live radio and television appearances to help promote the new single. Amid all this work, producer George Martin and Epstein managed to book another recording session at EMI. On Monday Febru-

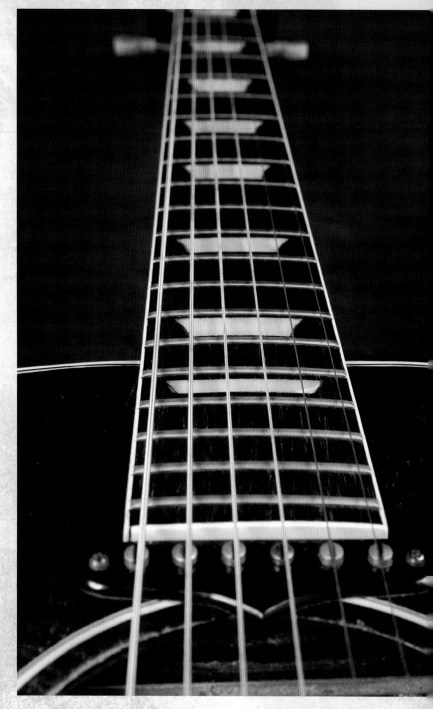

ary 11, The Beatles entered Abbey Road Studio 2 and recorded their first full-length LP, the 14-track Please Please Me. The whole album was recorded in one grueling day. Judged by today's standards, when one day is unlikely to produce a decent drum sound, this seems a remarkable achievement. The session was recorded on to a two-track tape machine, almost entirely live and with few or no overdubs. The instruments and amplification that the group used for making Please Please Me were the same as for their live performances during the Shapiro tour: the '58 Rickenbacker 325, Gretsch Duo Jet, both Gibson J-160Es, both Vox A.C.30 Twin amps (without Top Boost), and the Hofner bass played through the studio's Leak power amp and a Tannoy 15-inch speaker cabinet. Ringo played his Premier drum set.

By February 22, the band's second single 'Please Please Me' neared the top of the British charts. Epstein's program of never-ending promotion had paid off perfectly. On February 17, The Beatles had recorded a performance for the influential British television show Thank Your Lucky Stars, miming a performance of the hit 45. McCartney played his Hofner bass, Harrison and Lennon both used their Gibson J-160E acoustic-electric guitars, and Starr played his Premier drum set with the new bug Beatles logo displayed on the front drum-head.

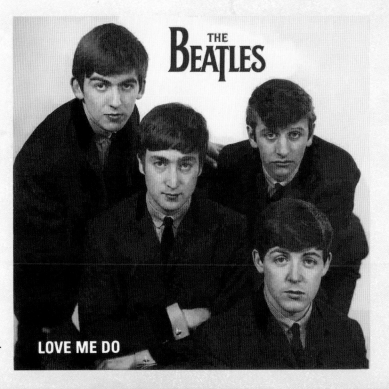

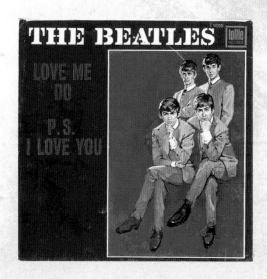

By mid-1963, it must have seemed that the group's success was providing its own momentum. On Monday July 1, they were again summoned to Studio 2 at EMI's recording base in Abbey Road for another recording session, where they recorded their fourth single, 'She Loves You' backed with 'I'll Get You'. Photographs from the session show Starr playing his Ludwig drum set and Lennon with his Gibson J-160E plugged into his Vox A.C.30 amp. McCartney played his Hofner.

By the beginning of November, the group had started their fourth package tour – but this time they were the headliners. Billed as The Beatles Autumn Tour, the month-and-a-half round of English theatres (plus a gig each in Dublin and Belfast) featured an almost daily ritual of live shows. A mix of radio and television interviews and performances were fitted into the schedule wherever possible. The equipment they used on the Autumn Tour saw little change. Starr played his Ludwig drum set, Lennon his Rickenbacker 325 as his main guitar and the Gibson J-160E when required, through his '63 Vox A.C.30 amp. McCartney used his new '63 Hofner bass, with his original '61 as a spare, played through the A.C.30 head and T.60 bass cabinet, while Harrison used his '63 A.C.30, playing his Gretsch Country Gentleman.

> Recalls John: 'George and I often took a jumbo home with us, so nobody noticed until the end of the season that one was missing. A week or two afterwards I asked Mal where he'd put my jumbo. It was only then that we realised the guitar had been pinched, at Finsbury Park. No, I never got it back." Mal Evans, the group's roadie, also recalled the grim moment: "The worst of all was at the Finsbury Empire in London, when I lost John's guitar. It was one he'd had for years, as well. It just disappeared. 'Where's my jumbo?' he said. I didn't know – it's still a mystery."

During the group's Autumn Tour, they made an appearance on the Granada television programme Scene, taping a performance of 'I Want To Hold Your Hand' and 'This Boy' on November 25. The television studio's stage was set up with large headlines from a fictitious Daily Echo newspaper and a drum riser made to look like a camera lens. When they mimed 'This Boy', Harrison and Lennon both used their Gibson J-160E guitars – one of the last occasions that Lennon would be filmed with his, because the instrument was stolen soon afterward. On November 22, the group's second LP, With The Beatles, was released in the UK on Parlophone (PMC 1206 mono, PCS 3045 stereo) with advance orders of 300,000 copies. The album featured (side one:) 'It Won't Be Long', 'All I've Got To Do', 'All My Loving', 'Don't Bother Me', 'Little Child', 'Till There Was You', and 'Please Mister Postman', (side two:) 'Roll Over Beethoven', Hold Me Tight', 'You Really Got A Hold On Me', 'I Wanna Be Your Man', 'Devil In Her Heart', 'Not A Second Time', and 'Money'. A week later, on November 29, the single 'I Want To Hold Your Hand' backed with 'This Boy' came out on Parlophone (R 5084), with over one million advance orders. The Beatles had conquered Britain.

It was at the Christmas shows in London that Lennon noticed his Gibson J-160E had gone missing. An account of the Gibson's abduction published a couple of years later in The Beatles Monthly Book described how Lennon and Harrison took pride in their Gibson "Jumbos" and how they'd saved up their money for the hire-purchase deposits with much determination. "By the time of the Finsbury Park show," ran the report, "the total collection of Beatle guitars had grown, but John and Paul were using their Gibson jumbos in the dressing room and they were there as stand-by replacements if strings snapped during a performance. Recalls John: 'George and I often took a jumbo home with us, so nobody noticed until the end of

the season that one was missing. A week or two afterwards I asked Mal where he'd put my jumbo. It was only then that we realised the guitar had been pinched, at Finsbury Park. No, I never got it back." Mal Evans, the group's roadie, also recalled the grim moment: "The worst of all was at the Finsbury Empire in London, when I lost John's guitar. It was one he'd had for years, as well. It just disappeared. 'Where's my jumbo?' he said. I didn't know – it's still a mystery."

At some point between September 1962, when they acquired their Gibsons, and December 1963, Lennon and Harrison had in fact swapped their guitars. Perhaps it was because of playability or sound preference. Or maybe, because the instruments were identical, the guitars were unknowingly switched, and neither Lennon nor Harrison noticed … or cared. So Lennon's Gibson guitar, serial number 73157, that went missing in 1963 was actually the one that had been registered to Harrison under the hire-purchase deal made at Rushworth's music shop. And the J-160E guitar that Harrison still owned decades later, serial number 73161, was the guitar that was logged to Lennon on the original hire-purchase document.

FOR THE RECORD

When it comes to the Beatles, no matter where your collecting interests lie, it all—always—comes back to the music. The image is key, the personalities important, but in the end it's just about the fact that the band never missed a trick musically. That translates, in terms of collectibles, into the backbone of the category.

"It all started with the records," said Garry Shrum, a Beatles expert and Music Consignment Director at Heritage Auctions. "That's the first connection we all have to the band and certainly the first place that most collectors started."

There is a startling array of Beatles records that were produced, from true first UK editions of all their early albums, to the US releases of those same songs on differently named LPs, to the myriad foreign releases, bootleg releases, early 45s and on and on. It goes deep and it's varied.

For the right Beatles collector, and there are plenty of them, vinyl is the only way to go. The collective vinyl of the Beatles tells the story of the band itself in its purest form: the notes and words they recorded. Not including "Best of" compilations or "Greatest Hits" albums, the band released 13 EPs, 12 LPs in the UK and 17 in the US, and 33 singles in total. With each recording, thousands and thousands of copies were released.

Beatles Yesterday And Today Sealed First State Stereo "Butcher Cover" LP in GEM MINT 10 Condition (Capitol, 1966): **A very high grade, and rare, copy of the band's most controversial record cover, the ninth US release by Capitol Records, June 20, 1966. This was strictly a U.S. release and is a mishmash of tunes – most notably Yesterday – with two cuts from the UK Help! LP, four tracks from the UK version of Rubber Soul, both sides of the single "Day Tripper/We Can Work it Out" and three songs from their not-yet-released Revolver album. The Beatles, who put a lot of thought into the order of their albums, resented the treat-**

ment. The "butcher" photo was taken early in 1966 by Robert Whitaker and actually has a title: A Somnambulant Adventure. Was it a protest against their treatment by Capitol Records, or a protest against the burgeoning war in Vietnam? Who really knows. What we do know, however, is that the reaction by the American public was swift, ferocious and negative. Capitol recalled all the "offensive" albums and glued what's generally called the "Trunk Cover" over it (known as a "second state"). This is how most people have seen it. The original albums that were saved from destruction or the glue-over process, such as this one, are known as being "first state." These unaltered versions of the album are extremely desirable for collectors. As with all collectibles, condition is king. This one, still in shrink wrap, is a rarity among rarities. That's why it's worth $75,000. Other "first state" copies have sold for as much as $32,000 in mint condition. Other examples in lesser condition realize decreased yet still impressive results, but this pristine beauty remains the highest valued version of this classic to date. *Image courtesy of Heritage Auctions*

NEW IMPROVED FULL DIMENSIONAL STEREO

SCHWANN
LIST PRICE $4.79
OUR LOW PRICE
$3.47

File Under: The Beatles   ST 2553

YESTERDAY · DR. ROBERT
I'M ONLY SLEEPING · AND YOUR BIRD CAN SING
WE CAN WORK IT OUT · DAY TRIPPER
NOWHERE MAN · WHAT GOES ON?
DRIVE MY CAR · IF I NEEDED SOMEONE
ACT NATURALLY

The Beatles
Yesterday
And Today

Beatles Yesterday And Today Second State Butcher Cover Stereo LP (Capitol ST 2553, 1966): Pristine copy of a paste-over second-state "Butcher Cover" with the original shrink wrap and price tag. Well worth the price at $1,875.

Image courtesy of Heritage Auctions

It's not hard to see why records are the most abundant, and perhaps the most popular, of all Beatles collectibles. "Records are so popular because we all remember having them and we all wish we had saved the first ones we bought," said Shrum. "There are still many copies of Beatles records floating about, including copies that people still play; that's why collectors look for the best, earliest copies of each record, with the lowest possible serial number. The earlier the pressing, the higher the corresponding value and the greater the bragging rights."

Shrum is in a unique position to comment on the trade in Beatles records; he's been a collector in general since he was a child and a Beatles collector since 1964, when he saw them on The Ed Sullivan Show.

"My mind was blown just like everyone else," he said. "I would go out and get the records right away, but I would also go out and get the magazines and the books. That's where it started for a lot of collectors."

American collectors, in particular in the early days, collected what Capitol Records released, not knowing that the track listings were different from the records released in the UK—this was the '60s, after all, and there was no Internet—and in many cases, completely different records. I would even go so far as to say that Americans weren't really "collecting" at that point, just buying records for listening. What this resulted in, in the end, was that a lot of those early copies were simply played through and worn out. Those that survived, often, are in thoroughly-played condition, rough around the edges of the sleeves, so to speak.

That means that the records that survived in good condition—and better—are the ones that bring a premium. Among those that bring that premium, the earlier the pressing the better and the rarer the record the better. For American Beatles collectors, especially that first generation of Beatles fans that morphed into the early collectors, that meant when they started collecting with passion, there was a whole new world out there for them beyond replacing their worn out American Beatles records.

Beatles Yesterday and Today Stereo 3rd State Peeled Butcher Cover (Capitol ST 2553, 1966): The ninth Capitol album, not counting the narrative album The Beatles' Story, it was the eighth to hit No. 1 on Billboards' Top 200 list, holding down the top position for five weeks in-between Rubber Soul and Revolver. This is an outstanding example of the rarer Stereo version cover with a very good peel job. At auction: $687.

Image courtesy of Heritage Auctions

There were, in fact, more than a dozen separate UK pressings of the same material in a different order on different vinyl.

The great variety and the great availability, distinct in a wide array of conditions, all serves to make records the ultimate gateway collectible into Beatles memorabilia. Within the hierarchy of the records, however, there are a few that stand out as the most desirable, and none more so than the infamous "Butcher" cover.

The "Butcher" Cover

Yesterday and Today was released on June 20, 1966, with the famous cover of the boys, dressed in smocks and covered with dismembered doll parts—fake blood, pieces of meat and all—and was almost immediately, universally criticized in the conservative United States. The negative reaction came from advance copies sent to DJs and distributors all over the nation and was so strong that Capitol, as the first pressings were making their way across America, recalled 750,000 copies to replace the cover with the now familiar more formal and staid image of the band.

The controversy didn't hurt the record, nor did the new pasted-on covers, as it hit No. 1 on the record charts in July of '66 and stayed there for five weeks. It does, after all, feature the songs Yesterday (the most covered song in the history of music), Day Tripper, We Can Work It Out, Nowhere Man, Drive My Car and several other great Beatles tunes.

Capitol Records, however, had unknowingly created an absolute classic collectible. Those records that were bought and stashed away are now what's known as "First State" Butcher covers, untouched, and the most sought after of them all. Those that have the "new" image pasted on them are known as "Second State." Within these "states" there are variations such as sealed or unopened that make a BIG difference in price, as you can see by some of the examples in these pages..

So, given the widespread condemnation of the cover, how exactly did it come about?

The Beatles were slated in late March of '66 for a photo session with photographer Robert Whitaker. Whitaker had a conceptual piece in mind, titled Somnambulant Adventure. He dressed the band up and covered them in chunks of meat and dismembered doll parts. You can imagine that the band, who had suffered through hundreds of mind-numbing photo sessions up to that point, were probably intrigued to do something more experimental.

There is no evidence that the photos from the session were ever meant to be used as an album cover. Something about the images appealed to the Beatles though, and they submitted the photo to Capitol, among others, to consider for the cover. In fact, former Capitol Records President Alan Livingston told Mojo Magazine in 2002 that it was Paul who pressed the hardest to use the cover and that it was the band's "comment on the (Vietnam) war," a sentiment Lennon had also expressed.

Harrison, though, neither liked the photo, nor defended it. When The Beatles Anthology was released he was quoted as saying, the photo "was gross, and I also thought it was stupid. Sometimes we all did stupid things thinking it was cool and hip when it was naïve and dumb; and that was one of them."

It's also commonly thought that the cover was a protest against Capitol Records itself since the band was tired of the Label "butchering" their track ordering on the records, something the Beatles put a lot of thought and time into, when they were released in the states.

The Butcher Cover was released in the states on the front of the album. Another photo, from the same session, showing the band bloodied *(opposite) Beatles Rarest Promo 45 - "Ask Me Why"/ "Anna" (Vee-Jay Special DJ No. 8, 1964): Purportedly as few as five copies of this promotional 45 were ever produced in the US. There was never a commercial release combining these two songs, although they both appeared on the more common version of the Introducing The Beatles LP and on the Vee-Jay EP. The price on such rarity? For this copy it was $35,000.* Image courtesy of Heritage Auctions

Beatles Help! Sealed Stereo LP, (Capitol 2386, 1965). Released Aug. 13, 1965, the US version of Help! is a true soundtrack album, featuring Beatles hits like the title track and "Ticket to Ride" interspersed with selections from the instrumental score by Ken Thorne. Still sealed, with the price written on the plastic in the top left corner. $106.

Image courtesy of Heritage Auctions

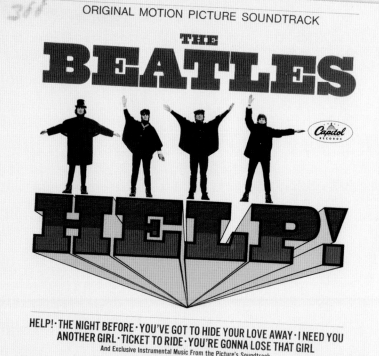

and baby-part bedecked, was used in advertising and promotion, most notably in England with the release of the "Paperback Writer" single, as well as for a June 1966 British music magazine, *Disc*.

From the beginning, good First State Butcher covers have been widely sought after, now routinely bringing as much as $75,000 for the very best examples. Many of the top Butcher covers trading hands today came from Alan Livingston's own collection. He released 24 pristine First State copies that are considered, to this day to be the very finest copies, pedigreed as they are to him and his times as President of Capitol Records at the time of the album's release. When you hear about a really high-grade copy selling—including the top ones you see in these pages—there is a good chance that it originated in the Livingston stash.

No 0000001

No 0000001

The BEATLES

The BEATLES

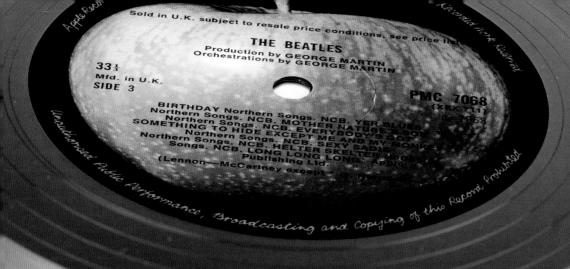

APPLE RECORDS
Sold in U.K. subject to resale price conditions, see price list
Recorded work control

THE BEATLES
Production by GEORGE MARTIN
Orchestrations by GEORGE MARTIN

33⅓
Mfd. in U.K.
SIDE 3

PMC 7068
(XEX 711)

BIRTHDAY Northern Songs. NCB. YER BLUES
Northern Songs. NCB. MOTHER NATURE'S SON
Northern Songs. NCB. EVERYBODY'S GOT
SOMETHING TO HIDE EXCEPT ME AND MY MONEY
Northern Songs. NCB. SEXY SADIE
Northern Songs. NCB. HELTER SKELTER
Songs. NCB. LONG LONG LONG Apple
Publishing Ltd.
(Lennon—McCartney except

Unauthorised Public Performance, Broadcasting and Copying of this Record Prohibited

The Most Expensive Beatles Record in the World

This is the single most valuable record in the world,
the first pressing of the UK mono copy of the double
LP, The Beatles, aka The White Album, owned by Ringo
Starr. It was widely known among collectors that the four
members of the band kept numbers 1 through 4. It was not,
however, commonly known that Starr had No. 1, which he
kept in a bank vault in London for more than 35 years.

Back in the U.S.S.R. : Dear Prudence : Glass Onion :
Ob-La-Di, Ob-La-Da : Wild Honey Pie :
The Continuing Story of Bungalow Bill :
While My Guitar Gently Weeps : Happiness is a Warm Gun :
Martha My Dear : I'm so tired : Blackbird : Piggies :
Rocky Raccoon : Don't Pass Me By :
Why don't we do it in the road? : I Will : Julia :
Birthday : Yer Blues : Mother Nature's Son :
Everybody's Got Something to Hide Except Me and My Monkey :
Sexy Sadie : Helter Skelter : Long, Long, Long :
Revolution 1 : Honey Pie : Savoy Truffle : Cry Baby Cry :
Revolution 9 : Good Night :

An anonymous buyer paid $790,000 for this piece of history at Julien's Auctions in Los Angeles, during the auction of The Ringo Starr and Barbara Bach Collection. The sale price smashed a record set in 2015 when Elvis Presley's first acetate recording sold at auction for $300,000.

The ninth studio album by the Beatles was pressed in 1968. Since the record manufacturing plant certainly had every machine available simultaneously pressing copies of this album it is impossible to say with certainty which records were truly the very first off the press, but these discs were certainly among the very first. The album covers, however, were numbered in sequence, ensuring that Ringo's No.0000001 sleeve is the very first finished cover.

Both discs were pressed from the very first Masters as indicated by the -1 matrix numbers on all four sides. The records are housed in their original black inner sleeves and feature "Factory Sample Not For Sale" labels on the whole-apple side of disc 1 and on the cut apple side of disc 2. All labels feature the "Sold in UK." text but omit the "An EMI Recording" text found on later editions. Also included in the sale were the four original UK portrait photos and UK lyric poster, both in mint condition.

Image courtesy of Julien's Auctions

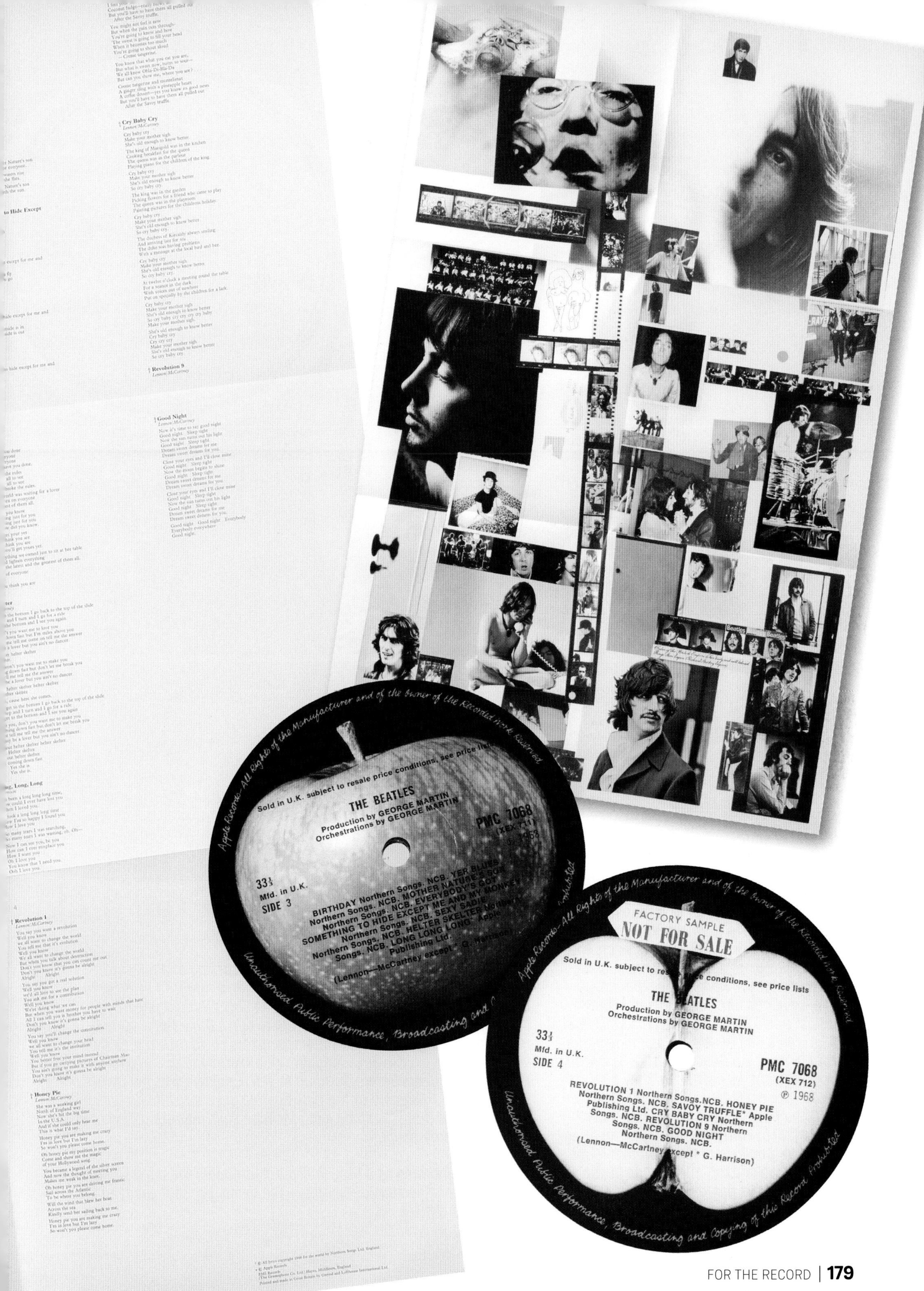

THE BEATLES
Production by GEORGE MARTIN
Orchestrations by GEORGE MARTIN

Sold in U.K. subject to resale price conditions, see price lists

33⅓
Mfd. in U.K.
SIDE 3

PMC 7068
(XEX 711)

BIRTHDAY Northern Songs, NCB. YER BLUES Northern Songs, NCB. MOTHER NATURE'S SON Northern Songs, NCB. EVERYBODY'S GOT SOMETHING TO HIDE EXCEPT ME AND MY MONKEY Northern Songs, NCB. SEXY SADIE Northern Songs, NCB. HELTER SKELTER Northern Songs, NCB. LONG LONG LONG Apple Publishing Ltd.

(Lennon—McCartney except * G. Harrison)

Apple Records—All Rights of the Manufacturer and of the Owner of the Recorded Work Reserved

Unauthorised Public Performance, Broadcasting and Copying of this Record Prohibited

FACTORY SAMPLE
NOT FOR SALE

THE BEATLES
Production by GEORGE MARTIN
Orchestrations by GEORGE MARTIN

Sold in U.K. subject to resale price conditions, see price lists

33⅓
Mfd. in U.K.
SIDE 4

PMC 7068
(XEX 712)
Ⓟ 1968

REVOLUTION 1 Northern Songs, NCB. HONEY PIE Northern Songs, NCB. SAVOY TRUFFLE* Apple Publishing Ltd. CRY BABY CRY Northern Songs, NCB. REVOLUTION 9 Northern Songs, NCB. GOOD NIGHT Northern Songs, NCB.

(Lennon—McCartney except * G. Harrison)

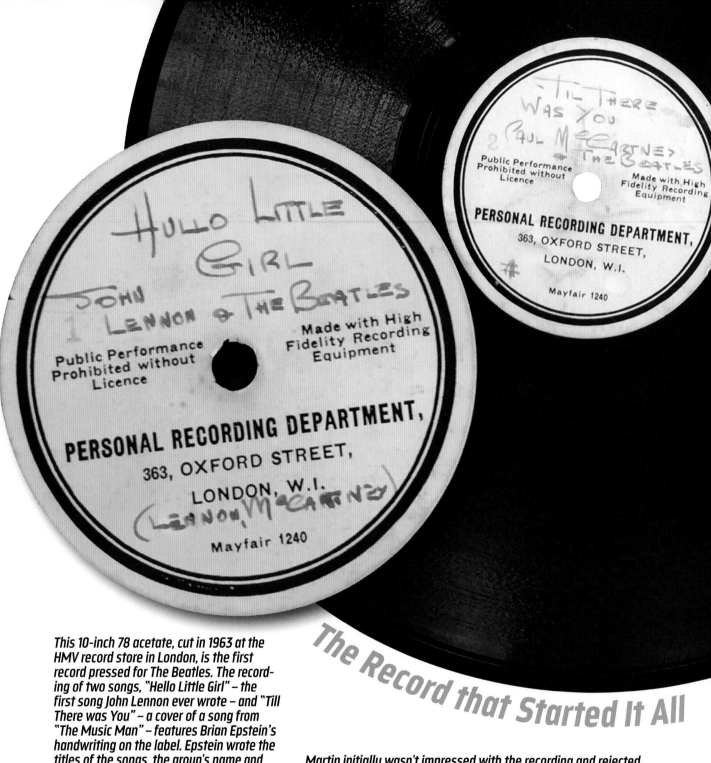

The Record that Started It All

This 10-inch 78 acetate, cut in 1963 at the HMV record store in London, is the first record pressed for The Beatles. The recording of two songs, "Hello Little Girl" – the first song John Lennon ever wrote – and "Till There was You" – a cover of a song from "The Music Man" – features Brian Epstein's handwriting on the label. Epstein wrote the titles of the songs, the group's name and the band member who sang each tune – " 'Hullo (sic) Little Girl,' John Lennon & The Beatles" and " 'Til (sic) There Was You,' Paul McCartney & The Beatles." Epstein took the record to producer George Martin "in a desperate attempt" to get The Beatles a recording contract, according to Omega Auctions, the UK auction house that sold the record for $110,000 in March of 2016. "This meeting was to eventually lead to the breakthrough they were looking for," the auction house said, with Martin going on to produce the Beatles chart-topping first albums for the EMI label.

Martin initially wasn't impressed with the recording and rejected the Fab Four, returning the acetate to Epstein, but Martin eventually changed his mind and signed the group to EMI's Parlophone label. Later in 1963, Epstein gave the acetate to Gerry & the Pacemakers member Les Maguire so that the Pacemakers could record their own version of "Hello Little Girl." Maguire, who stored the disc in a loft for more than 50 years before deciding to sell it, said he was not aware of the history of the record at the time Epstein gave it to him. "It was just another demo that was in my loft," McGuire said, admitting, "I wasn't a big fan of memorabilia."

Today the 78 stands as a Holy Grail piece, arguably the most significant record ever pressed by The Beatles – the demo disc that changed the music world forever.

Photos courtesy Omega Auctions

The Beatles ("The White Album") Lowest-Possible Numbered A0000001 Copy LP, U.S. Pressing (Apple 101, 1968): A Mint 10 album sleeve with, including the original poster and four individual photos along with a set of two EX 7 records (not original to this album), this sleeve is the lowest possible printing that could be found in the U.S. This is an extraordinary discovery, which is reflected in its auction sale: $35,000.

Image courtesy of Heritage Auctions

A0000001

The Beatles (Tony Sheridan and the Beat Brothers) "My Bonnie"/"The Saints" Rare 45 (Decca 31382, 1962): *Among the rarest of the US Beatles singles, even rarer than the pink label promo version of the record. Re-released in 1964 when Beatlemania began in earnest, this single managed to climb to #26 before quickly falling off Billboard's Hot 100 charts. Both The Beatles and Sheridan regularly played Hamburg's Top Ten Club, often together. The Beatles were noted on the 45 as the Beat Brothers because it was thought the name would resonate better with fans than The Beatles. Now that collectors are historians, this release has attained stature as an extremely rare item, possibly one of only 20+ copies in existence. This is one of the nicest you will ever see.* $30,000.

Image courtesy of Heritage Auctions

Beatles Souvenir of Their Visit to America Rare "Ask Me Why" Promo Sleeve (Vee-Jay EPI-903, 1964): *A super-rare promo sleeve that most Beatles collectors – and fans – have never even seen. Part of a Vee-Jay records promo campaign in the mid-1960s. Such rarity – sleeve only, mind you – brought a very respectable $8,437 at auction.*

Image courtesy of Heritage Auctions

ask me why the beatles

[an E.P. that is selling like a single ...at single record prices]

here is your special D.J. promotion copy — EPI-903

VEE-JAY RECORDS

STILL ONLY # 8 IN SALES

THE BEATLES' STORY

A NARRATIVE AND MUSICAL BIOGRAPHY OF BEATLEMANIA ON 2 LONG-PLAY RECORDS

SPARTAN ATLANTIC *Best Centre*
SPECIAL SALE
$1.57
2 for $3.00

includes
SELECTIONS FROM THEIR HIT RECORDS
INTERVIEWS WITH THE BEATLES AND THEIR FANS
MANY NEW PHOTOS
THEIR WHOLE STORY ON RECORD . . . FROM BEGINNING TO FABULOUS FAME!

Capitol RECORDS
HIGH FIDELITY

THE BEATLES' STORY STILL SEALED DOUBLE LP (CAPITOL 2222, 1964). COMPRISED OF SONG SNIPPETS AND INTERVIEWS RELEASED AS THE SIXTH U.S. BEATLES ALBUM IN 1964, THIS DOUBLE ALBUM IS MORE OF A MUSICAL BIOGRAPHY THAN A PROPER BEATLES ALBUM. IN DECENT CONDITION A SMART BUY AT $119.

Image courtesy of Heritage Auctions

Beatles Signed "Love Me Do/ P.S. I Love You" 45 (Parlophone R4949, 1962): "Love Me Do" was the Beatles first single on Parlophone, released on Oct. 5, 1962. This copy includes very early Beatle signatures. George has signed on the pushout center spindle with Ringo, Paul and John around the label (clockwise). They have all added XXXs to their signatures. The original EMI sleeve is included. At $6,250 at auction, that's a really nice price on a very rare get.

Image courtesy of Heritage Auctions

Beatles Sgt. Pepper's Lonely Hearts Club Band Sealed Mono LP (Capitol MAS 2653, 1967): This revolutionary album from 1967 charted on Billboard's Top 200 longer than any of the Beatles other albums: 175 weeks total with 15 weeks at #1. One of the most important albums ever. Capitol stopped making mono albums in 1968, making this sealed copy very rare. At auction: $4,000

Image courtesy of Heritage Auctions

Beatles Magical Mystery Tour Sealed Mono LP (Capitol MAS 2835, 1967): Released only a few months after, and overshadowed by Sgt. Pepper's, Magical Mystery Tour still managed to top Billboard's album charts for eight weeks in late 1967 and early 1968 with such legendary songs as "I Am The Walrus," "All You Need Is Love," "Strawberry Fields Forever," "Penny Lane" and "Hello Goodbye." A pristine copy of the rarer mono version. At auction: $812.

Image courtesy of Heritage Auctions

BEATLES VI

THE WORLD'S MOST POPULAR FOURSOME! JOHN · PAUL · GEORGE · RINGO

YOU LIKE ME TOO MUCH · TELL ME WHAT YOU SEE · BAD BOY · DIZZY MISS LIZZIE · EIGHT DAYS A WEEK · YES IT IS!
WORDS OF LOVE · KANSAS CITY · I DON'T WANT TO SPOIL THE PARTY · EVERY LITTLE THING · WHAT YOU'RE DOING

RECORDED IN ENGLAND

Capitol RECORDS

T 2358

Beatles VI Sealed Mono LP (Capitol 2358, 1965): *One of four albums the Fab released during 1965 to spend multiple weeks at the top of Billboard's Top Pop Albums chart, Beatles VI spent six weeks at #1 in-between Beatles '65 and Help! Good condition on this still-sealed copy of the rarer mono version. $1,625.*

Image courtesy of Heritage Auctions

Beatles Hey Jude Sealed LP (Apple SW-385, 1970): **Released in-between Abbey Road and Let It Be. The title cut was the group's biggest single and headlined this compilation. Notably, the front and back photos of this cover were the last photos ever taken of The Beatles together – they certainly rank as this writer's favorite Beatles pics. At auction: $500.**

Image courtesy of Heritage Auctions

The Beatles (aka The White Album) Sealed #A2457672 LP (Apple 101, 1968): A pristine, still sealed copy of this absolute masterpiece, in Mint condition.
At auction: $687.
Image courtesy of Heritage Auctions

A2457672

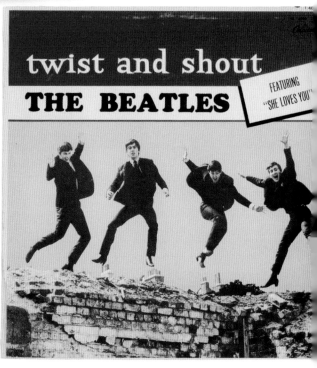

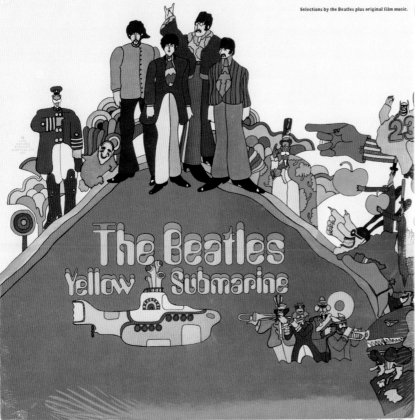

Selections by the Beatles plus original film music.

Beatles Yellow Submarine Sealed Stereo LP (Capitol 153, 1969): **Released in-between The White Album and Abbey Road, this album featured one of the most striking covers of all-time. One side of vocal cuts from The Beatles and one side of George Martin instrumentals, all from the title movie. Rare and in Good condition. $750.**

Image courtesy of Heritage Auctions

BEATLES EARLY CANADIAN LPS MONO GROUP (CAPITOL, 1964): CANADA EXPERIENCED ITS OWN BEATLEMANIA IN 1964, BUT WITH ITS OWN COVERS AND ALBUM SONG SELECTIONS DISTINCT FROM THE US COUNTERPARTS. INCLUDED HERE: BEATLEMANIA (CAPITOL 6051), TWIST AND SHOUT (6054), AND LONG TALL SALLY (6063), ALL RELEASED IN 1964, ALTHOUGH THE COPY OF THE LATTER ALBUM HERE IS A REISSUE FROM THE 1970S OR 1980S. FAIRLY PRICED AT $112.

Image courtesy of Heritage Auctions

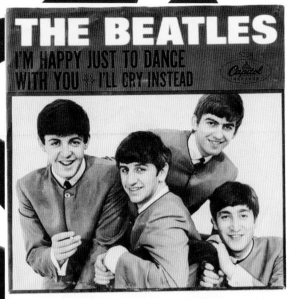

THE BEATLES
I'M HAPPY JUST TO DANCE
WITH YOU ** I'LL CRY INSTEAD

THE BEATLES
"SHE LOVES YOU"

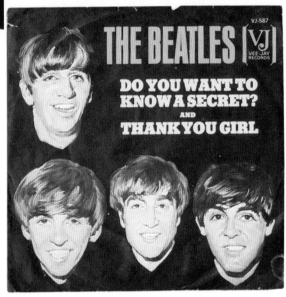

THE BEATLES
DO YOU WANT TO
KNOW A SECRET?
AND
THANK YOU GIRL

the BEATLES
TICKET
TO RIDE
YES IT IS

THE BEATLES
SHE'S A WOMAN
I FEEL FINE

THE BEATLES
AND I LOVE HER
IF I FELL

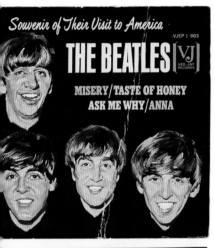

Beatles US Singles and EP Collection (1960s): "My Bonnie," "A Hard Days Night," "Do You want To Know A Secret," "Ticket To Ride," "Help," "Eight days A Week," "Matchbox," "I Feel Fine," "And I love Her," "Eight Days A Week," "I Want To Hold Your Hand," The Beatles EP "4X4," "I'm Happy Just To dance With You," "She loves You" and "Beatles VJ EP." Conditions vary, but generally good. This grouping brought $625 at auction.

Image courtesy of Heritage Auctions

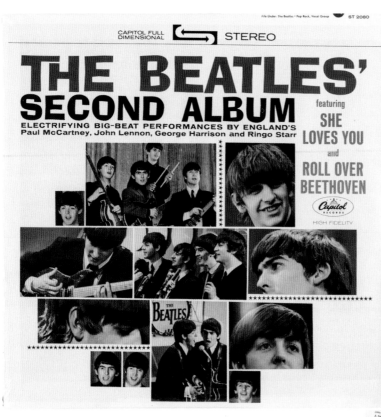

The Beatles Second Album Sealed Stereo LP (Capitol 2080, 1964): *More than any other, this early album shows how great of a cover band the boys were: "Roll Over Beethoven," "Money," "Please Mr. Postman," "Long Tall Sally" and other great recordings. Mint condition and still-sealed state equal a rarity at auction: $625.*

Image courtesy of Heritage Auctions

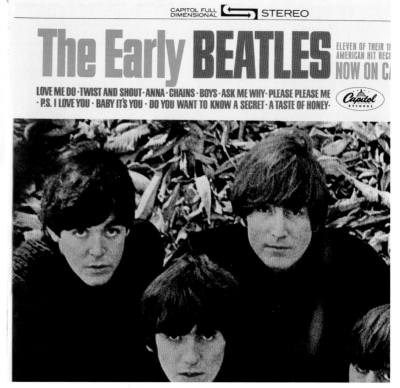

The Early Beatles Sealed Stereo LP (Capitol 2309, 1965): *Capitol's release of the pre-1964 tunes originally offered in the US by Vee-Jay Records on the seminal album Introducing The Beatles. Not often do you see a sealed stereo copy of this album. $625.*

Image courtesy of Heritage Auctions

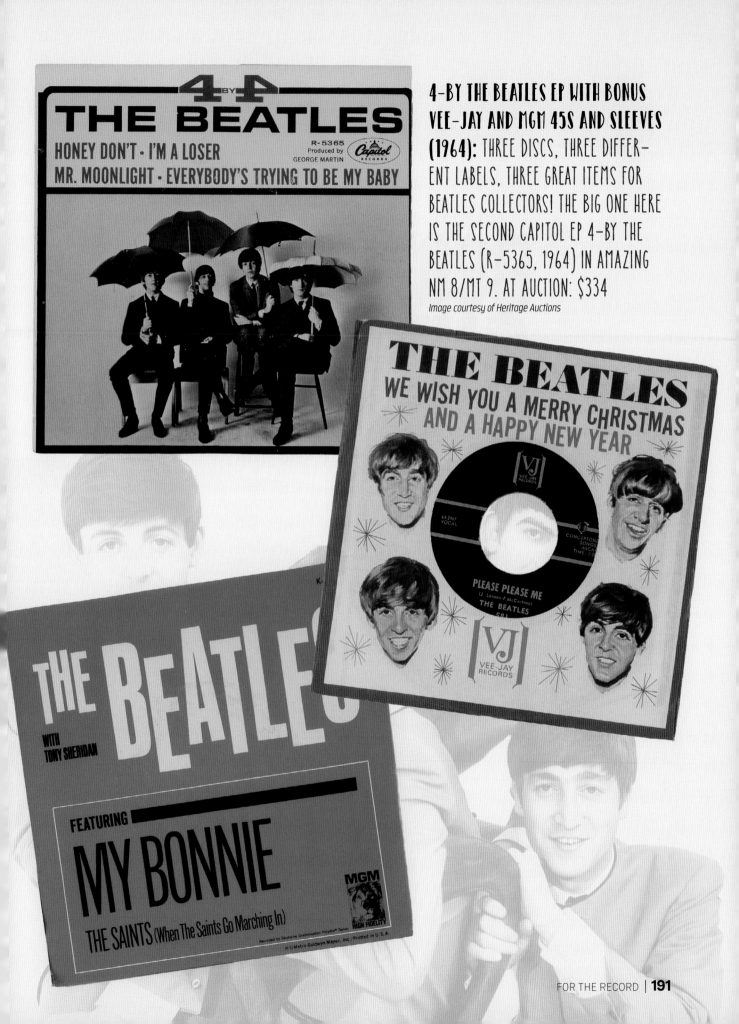

4-BY THE BEATLES EP WITH BONUS VEE-JAY AND MGM 45S AND SLEEVES (1964): THREE DISCS, THREE DIFFERENT LABELS, THREE GREAT ITEMS FOR BEATLES COLLECTORS! THE BIG ONE HERE IS THE SECOND CAPITOL EP 4-BY THE BEATLES (R-5365, 1964) IN AMAZING NM 8/MT 9. AT AUCTION: $334

Image courtesy of Heritage Auctions

Beatles AUTOGRAPHS

The story of The Beatles, the good, the bad and the fake, is all writ large in the pursuit of the Fab Four's autographs. The band's signatures provide an overview of the world's greatest rock 'n' roll band in a way that few other niches can. The troughs and the crests of the their careers together, and separate, are laid out clearly before collectors, who have to exercise their due diligence, do their homework and deal with reputable sources in the pursuit of those famous names.

"There are a ton of Beatles signatures out there but not all of them were signed by the band," said Garry Shrum of Heritage Auctions. "In the early days, the band would sign all the autographs that were put before them, but as they got more popular it became more and more difficult for them to sign them all."

In the early days, in Hamburg and Liverpool, the boys were popular, but not so popular that they were unable to meet the kids that came to see them. Whether it was for members of the early fan club, or just fans that

THE BEATLES

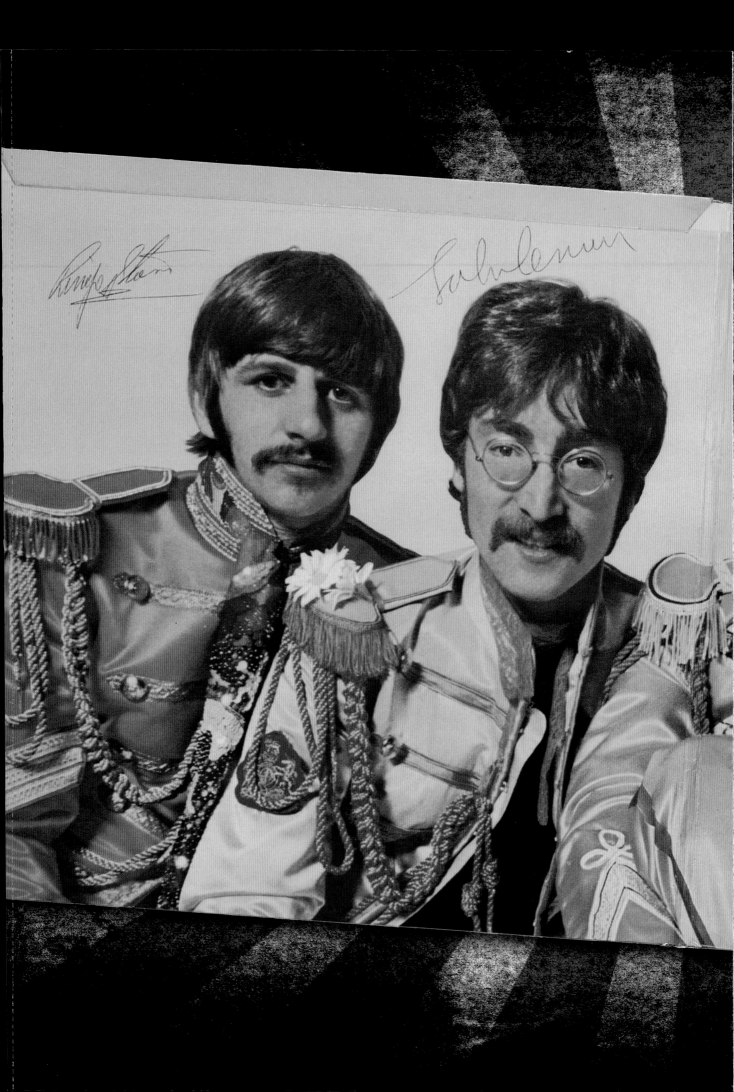

A great set of blue ink autographs from The Beatles on a Star-Club promo photo, Shrewsbury, Dec. 14, 1962. Astrid Kirchherr took the photo during a session commissioned by Brian Epstein to highlight the band's new "cleaned-up" image. At auction: $9,375. Image courtesy of Heritage Auctions

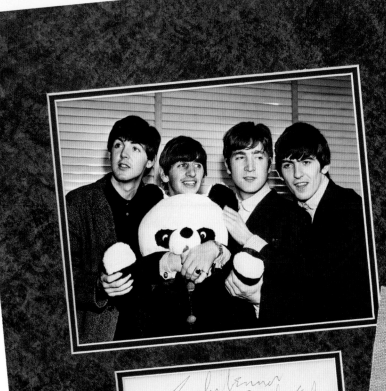

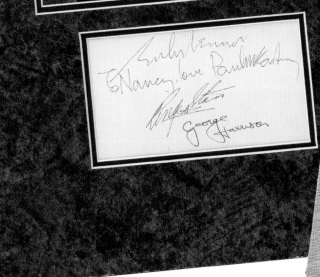

they got to know night after night. Things got a little more complicated as 1962 and '63 wore on and dizzying fame approached. As the number of fans increased, along with the demands on the band's time, the autographs changed. Often, one member of the band would end up signing for all the members, so-called "clone" autographs. Still valuable and

desirable as collectibles, but not as much as the original signatures of all the members.

When the band really took off in England, after being signed by Brian Epstein, recording with George Martin and appearing all over English television, the band had no time for the hundreds of requests sent to them on a weekly basis. It was still possible to get all four member to sign a photo, a poster, a magazine or an autograph book if a fan managed to get backstage at a performance or a press event, but direct access

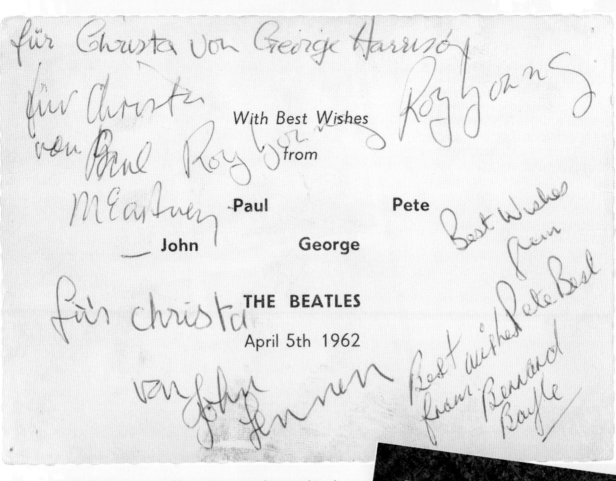

Beatles Rare Early Signatures with Roy Young and Bernard Boyle (Hamburg, 1962): **Also signed by the founder of the first-ever Beatles Fan Club (and a sometime Beatles roadie) Bernard Boyle. A deckle-edged black-and-white glossy photo of the boys in their black leather outfits not long before they would, literally, storm the world – without Pete Best, of course. These photos were given out at a Cavern Club concert honoring the Official Fan Club. Also signed by Roy Young, a British Rock singer and pianist who had some success in the late 1950s on various Pop music TV shows. A great early artifact: $12,500.**

Image courtesy of Heritage Auctions

became a difficult thing—let's just say that the boys were not always thrilled to face their screaming, awestruck, rabid fans.

"They just couldn't keep up," said Shrum. "Something had to give."

Into this gap stepped Epstein and the band's merchandising and road manager, Neil Aspinall, among others. It became routine for those that worked in the Beatles organization to sign the headshots and other autograph requests sent to the boys. It is these very autographs that now create complications for collectors, especially the inexperienced.

"You have to always go through reputable sources that provide authentication in some form," said Darren Julien. "If you're buying from an online source that provides no oversite of who is selling what, then you are likely going to get stuck with a fake."

Original 1963 English prototype poster, 17.25" x 22", featuring a terrific set of four concert images capturing each Beatle in the midst of a performance and beautifully signed by all four on their corresponding images. The poster was signed during the Beatles' Autumn Tour starting Nov. 1, 1963, which included their now famous Royal Command Performance in front of the Queen Mother on Nov. 4. The Beatles almost never signed images of themselves with instruments and this item holds the incredible distinction of being the only known signed poster showing the entire band with their instruments. Professionally restored, excellent condition. Sold at auction for $20,315.

Image courtesy of Heritage Auctions

It's buyer beware, certainly, but these non-Beatle Beatle autographs are not always bought by would-be collectors. They are often in the hands of fans that have cherished them for decades, believing the signatures they have of their beloved Mop Tops to be the authentic article. "I get calls every single week," said Shrum, "and every single week I have to break someone's heart."

Maybe their mother got the "autographs" in the 1960s and they've been holding on to them for decades. Maybe they themselves wrote to the band and received a signed 8 x 10 in return for the effort. Depending on the year, in so many cases, they're fakes. Well-intentioned fakes, perhaps, but fakes.

Within the hobby there are places that will be able to offer both opinions and authentication. A good auction house will have an expert on staff that can help, and dealers that are worth their salt can help you too. Bring your autographs to any Beatlefest, if you are not sure, and find someone. Consult a major name in the authentication business, like Frank Caiazzo or John Reznikoff. Better yet, check their websites or the websites of Julien's Auctions, Heritage Auctions or any

number of dealers. There will be examples of authentic autographs on these sites that the uninitiated collector can, at least, compare against.

So that's the bad news about Beatles autographs. The good news is that there are a lot of great, authentic autographs out there and plenty of people who can help you get what you're after. Examples of all four members signing something from the late 1960s are rare, meaning their value is going to be considerably more. These autographs provide a bookend of rarity and value for the band when paired with the bookend of the best and most early Beatles autographs.

Collectors would also do well to seek out the autographs of the band members in individual form, more rarely from their days together and more commonly from their solo careers. Many a fine display of Fab Four autographs has been made by assembling individual examples and framing them nicely together with a Beatles image or an album.

The availability of autographs is interesting in terms of how it mirrors the journey of the band itself. As the Beatles were starting out they were eager to please their fans and to grow together as a musicians. As they grew more famous, their desire to please their fans was still there, but they began to grow apart interpersonally. The years of their peak

This 5.75" x 4" deckle-edged, black-and-white glossy promotional photo of the Beatles (Hamburg, 1962) shows them in their black leather outfits with their instruments. On the back is printed "With Best Wishes from Paul Pete John George. The Beatles. April 5th 1962". Surrounding are neat and dark blue ballpoint signatures as follows: "für Monika viele grüße von George Harrison" ("many regards for Monika"), "To Monika, best wishes John Lennon", "To Monika from Paul McCartney", and "Best Wishes to Monica from Pete Best." These promo cards were given out at a Cavern Club concert honoring their newly-formed Official Fan Club on the above date and it's quite likely that any extras were taken with them to Hamburg for the Star-Club grand opening performances that started just a few days later. The German sentiment from George would indicate that this one was signed in Hamburg. $8,750.

A color centerfold image of The Beatles from the June 15, 1963, issue of Boyfriend magazine from Ringo's personal collection. The "Boyfriend Star Portrait" is signed in blue ink by George Harrison, Paul McCartney and John Lennon and signed in black ink by Ringo Starr. The magazine poster was discovered in a trunk full of press clippings and ephemera gathered by Starr's mother. Pre-Beatlemania treasures like this bring a premium, as evidenced by the $44,800 price tag. It doesn't hurt that it came from Ringo's collection directly.

Image courtesy of Julien's Auctions

fame, sick of the grind and the demands on their time, they were not together near as much—making it difficult to procure all four signatures at one time—and they were solely a studio band, effectively withdrawing from public performance and from each other. The late period of the band's tenure, therefore, produces very little in the way of traditional autographs, save some letters here and there and signed checks (a very popular option).

Once the Beatles split up, however, and were fully ensconced in their solo careers—and free from the pressure of being Beatles—the floodgates on autographs opened. The post-Beatles period is actually the best source of autographs for the band with the former Beatles signing plenty of autographs as solo artists.

"They were free then in a certain way, weren't they?" said Shrum. "They were also all promoting their own projects at that time, which made them want to sign more. The result is that, today, those signatures are easier to get."

It's also nice to think that, after the later years of turmoil and heartbreak in the ranks, they reached a place within themselves that allowed them to reconnect with their fans and, ultimately, with one another as evidenced by the guest appearances each band member made on the other's solo projects.

"I think they were all at peace with themselves and with the end of the band," said Julien. "They were all already working on solo music and taking on other projects."

There is a rich world of Beatles autographs awaiting the right collector out there, and the reward is as satisfying as almost any niche in the hobby. It takes patience, temperance, due diligence and a firm hold on one's budget, but good examples are out there to be had.

Designer Peter Blake worked with the Beatles to stage the cover of Sgt. Pepper's Lonely Hearts Club Band, which was filled with life-size cardboard likenesses of famous figures (Mae West, Bob Dylan, Marlon Brando, etc.) behind the Beatles. Among the smaller items in the foreground was this garden gnome, which appears on the cover to the right of George's leg. At the end of the cover session on March 30, 1967, the gnome was chosen as a memento by an assistant to cover photographer Michael Cooper, and it was signed by the Beatles immediately following the shoot. The gnome is in two parts—both front and back were created by Blake for the shoot, and presumably joined together, which may explain the small holes at the top and bottom of each. The Beatles have all signed the back in the lower, lighter portion in green marker. There appears to have been a liquid spill on the back after the signing, which has affected the Ringo and John signatures. Very Good overall condition. This superb Beatles artifact brought $42,500 when it crossed the block.

Image courtesy of Heritage Auctions

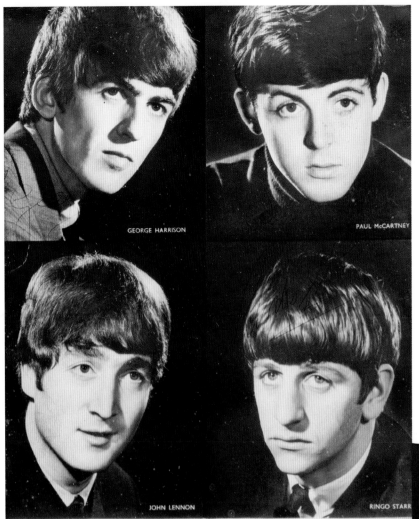

GEORGE HARRISON

PAUL McCARTNEY

JOHN LENNON

RINGO STARR

THE BEATLES

The $3,520 price paid at auction for this signed publicity image *seems to be on the low end. If a similar opportunity presents itself to you, you have my full permission to go for it.*

Image courtesy of Julien's Auctions

These Beatles signatures on an Austrian menu were obtained during the filming of Help! (Obertauern, March 17, 1965). This 4.25" x 6.25" daily menu card in Obertauern, Austria, listing the courses for Lunch and Dinner – likely from the Edelweiss Hotel where the Beatles stayed during the filming of HELP! – is one of the coolest signed Beatles pieces I can think of. Signed on the back in dark blue ink by all four, it is paired with a black-and-white glossy photo of them sitting in an Austrian restaurant holding beer steins. A quick thinking waiter or waitress got the boys to sign the menu they ordered lunch from, which in turn provides us with a simply spectacular collectible. A good price at $12,500.

Image courtesy of Heritage Auctions

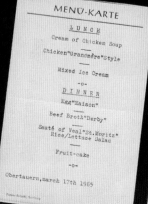

INVOICE

HUNTER FILMS LIMITED

LICENCE/INVOICE No. 3568

16mm. FILM DISTRIBUTORS

174 WARDOUR STREET
LONDON, W.1

Telephone:
01-734 8527
Two lines

Directors:
COLIN HUNT
PETER DARVILL

J. Lennon Esq.,
Beatles Ltd.,
5/6, Argyll Street,
W.1.

19th January 1967

To licensing

TAXI TO TORBRUK							
GERVAISE							
SATURDAY NIGHT OUT							
STOPOVER TOKYO insurance							

one day

	7	10	0
	7	15	0
	8	0	0
	9	10	6
	£33	1	0d

PAID - 8 FEB 1967

> **John Lennon signed invoice:** One partially printed page, 8" x 7", London, Jan. 19, 1967. This invoice from Hunter Films Limited was sent to Lennon for the rental of four movies: Taxi to Torbruk, Gervaise, Saturday Night Out and Stopover Tokyo, totaling £33.1.0. John Lennon signed at lower left acknowledging pament on Feb. 9, 1967. Payment for this cost the collector $1,375.
>
> *Image courtesy of Heritage Auctions*

> A signed first pressing of the Beatles' groundbreaking first UK album, Please Please Me (Parlophone PMC 1202, 1963) is enough to make most any collector swoon, let alone one in as fantastic condition as this one with such wonderful, strong signatures. This album was the first of what would be many chart-topping LPs released by the Beatles over a short but productive seven-year period. The album is ranked No. 39 on Rolling Stone's 500 Greatest Albums of All Time list. At auction: $62,500.
>
> *Image courtesy of Heritage Auctions*

Please Please Me
THE BEATLES

■ GEORGE HARRISON (lead guitar)
■ PAUL McCARTNEY (bass guitar)
■ JOHN LENNON (rhythm guitar)
■ RINGO STARR (drums)

SIDE ONE

1. I SAW HER STANDING THERE
   (McCartney-Lennon)
2. MISERY
   (McCartney-Lennon)
3. ANNA (GO TO HIM)
   (Alexander)
4. CHAINS
   (Goffin-King)
5. BOYS
   (Dixon-Farrell)
6. ASK ME WHY
   (McCartney-Lennon)
7. PLEASE PLEASE ME
   (McCartney-Lennon)

SIDE TWO

1. LOVE ME DO
   (McCartney-Lennon)
2. P.S. I LOVE YOU
   (McCartney-Lennon)
3. BABY IT'S YOU
   (David-Williams-Bacharach)
4. DO YOU WANT TO KNOW A SECRET
   (McCartney-Lennon)
5. A TASTE OF HONEY
   (Scott-Marlow)
6. THERE'S A PLACE
   (McCartney-Lennon)
7. TWIST AND SHOUT
   (Medley-Russell)

Recording first published 1963

LONG PLAY 33⅓ R.P.M.   E.M.I.

TONY BARROW

Pop picking is a fast 'n' furious business these days whether you are on the recording studio side listening out, or on the disc-counter side listening in. As a record reviewer I find myself installed halfway in-between with an ear cocked in either direction. So far as Britain's record collecting public is concerned, The Beatles broke into earshot in October, 1962. My natural hometown interest in the group prevented me taking a totally unbiased view of their early success. Eighteen months before their first visit to the EMI studios in London, The Beatles had been voted Merseyside's favourite outfit and it was inevitable that their first Parlophone record, LOVE ME DO, would go straight into the top of Liverpool's local hit parade. No other team had joined the best-sellers via a debut disc. But The Beatles were history-makers from the start and LOVE ME DO sold enough copies during its first 48 hours in the shops to send it soaring into the national charts. In all the busy years since pop singles first shrank from ten to seven inches I have never seen a British group leap to the forefront of the scene with such speed and energy. Within the six months which followed the Top Twenty appearance of LOVE ME DO, almost every leading deejay and musical journalist in the country began to shout the praises of The Beatles. Readers of the *New Musical Express* voted the boys into a surprisingly high place via the 1962/63 popularity poll ... on the strength of just one record release. Pictures of the group spread themselves across the front pages of three national music papers. People inside and outside the record industry expressed tremendous interest in the new vocal and instrumental sounds which The Beatles had introduced. Brian Matthew (who has since brought The Beatles to many millions of viewers and listeners in his "Thank Your Lucky Stars", "Saturday Club" and "Easy Beat" programmes) describes the quartet as *visually and musically the most exciting and accomplished group to emerge since The Shadows*. Disc reviewing, like disc producing, teaches one to be wary about making long-term predictions. The hit parade isn't always dominated by the most worthy performances of the day so it is no good assuming that versatility counts for everything. It was during the recording of a Radio Luxembourg programme in the *EMI Friday Spectacular* series that I was finally convinced that The Beatles were about to enjoy the type of top-flight national fame which I had always believed that they deserved. The teen-audience didn't know the evening's line-up of artists and groups in advance, and before Muriel Young brought on The Beatles she began to read out their Christian names. She got as far as John ... Paul ... and the rest of her introduction was buried in a mighty barrage of very genuine applause. I cannot think of more than one other group — British or American — which would be so readily identified and welcomed by the announcement of two Christian names. To me, this was the ultimate proof that The Beatles (and not just one or two of their hit records) had arrived at the uncommon peak-popularity point reserved for disc-dom's privileged few. Shortly afterwards The Beatles proved their pop power when they by-passed the lower segments of the hit parade to scuttle straight into the nation's Top Ten with their second single, PLEASE PLEASE ME.

This brisk-selling disc went on to overtake all rivals when it bounced into the coveted Number One slot towards the end of February. Just over four months after the release of their very first record The Beatles had become triumphant chart-toppers!

Producer George Martin has never had any headaches over choice of songs for The Beatles. Their own built-in tunesmith team of John Lennon and Paul McCartney has already tucked away enough self-penned numbers to maintain a steady output of all-original singles from now until 1975! Between them The Beatles adopt a do-it-yourself approach from the very beginning. They write their own lyrics, design and eventually build their own instrumental backdrops and work out their own vocal arrangements. Their music is wild, pungent, hard-hitting, uninhibited ... and personal. The do-it-yourself angle ensures complete originality at all stages of the process. Although so many people suggest (without closer definition) that The Beatles have a trans-Atlantic style, their only real influence has been from the unique brand of Rhythm and Blues folk music which abounds on Merseyside and which The Beatles themselves have helped to pioneer since their formation in 1960. This record comprises eight Lennon-McCartney compositions in addition to six other numbers which have become firm live-performance favourites in The Beatles' varied repertoire. The group's admiration for the work of The Shirelles is demonstrated by the inclusion of BABY IT'S YOU (John taking the lead vocal with George and Paul supplying the harmony), and BOYS (a fast rocker which allows drummer Ringo to make his first recorded appearance as a vocalist). ANNA, ASK ME WHY, and TWIST AND SHOUT also feature stand-out solo performances from John, whilst DO YOU WANT TO KNOW A SECRET hands the audio spotlight to George. MISERY may sound as though it is a self-duet created by the multi-recording of a single voice ... but the effect is produced by only one 'trick duet' and that is on A TASTE OF HONEY featuring a dual-voiced Paul. John and Paul get together on THERE'S A PLACE and I SAW HER STANDING THERE: George joins them for CHAINS, LOVE ME DO and PLEASE PLEASE ME.

(above) This 8.5" x 6.5" black-and-white photo of the Fab Four on stage at Liverpool's Empire Theatre, Dec. 7, 1963, was taken during a free concert for the Northern Area Fan Club convention. An original photograph taken by legendary Beatle chronicler Dezo Hoffman, bearing his imprint at lower left. This performance was taped by the BBC and shown as It's The Beatles. $35,000.

Image courtesy of Heritage Auctions

A detached center-page spread from the Meet the Beatles magazine of 1963, signed by John, Paul, George and Ringo in black ink next to their respective images. Signed photos of The Beatles in their collarless suits are very rare. Signed in December 1963, mere weeks before the band embarked on their historic tour of the United States. Items autographed by the band after 1963 are difficult to find, and, after 1969, extremely scarce. After the band stopped doing live concerts in 1966, they came together as a group mostly just for recording sessions, and that only until production concluded on Abbey Road in August 1969. In Very Fine condition. This is a great relic with an appropriate price of $17,925 at auction.

Image courtesy of Heritage Auctions

Beatles Meet the Beatles! Stereo LP Signed at the Deauville Hotel in Miami, the Day Before Their Second Ed Sullivan Show Appearance (Capitol ST 2047, 1964): **While this is a beautiful example of the first Beatles album to be released on Capitol Records, it's the quartet of signatures – and the date they were placed there – that make this a truly spectacular artifact. You'd be hard-pressed to get a stronger set of autographs from the band and you could hardly hope for better timing as a typed label states the date and place of the signing: "The Beatles/ Deauville Hotel- Miami/ Feb. -15th-1964," the night before the Beatles made their second appearance on The Ed Sullivan Show in a live simulcast from the hotel, a week after setting the world on fire with their first appearance on Feb. 9, 1964. It brought $56,250 when it crossed the block.**

Image courtesy of Heritage Auctions

(below) This Beatles signed Pan Am Airways route map was obtained on the band's flight to America, Feb. 7, 1964. The Beatles signed this 15.75" x 9" (overall) printed Pan American Airways System world map on their flight across the Atlantic on their way to The Ed Sullivan Show. This was among the last few possible moments the boys would ever have of not being the most famous musicians on the planet. Beautiful autographs obtained by a First Class passenger on Pan Am Flight 101. Two nights later, nervous and unsure of how they would be received, The Beatles played before 73 million people on TV and, overnight, the world changed. Hard to find a piece of Beatle memorabilia more evocative of that first American visit. At auction: $23,750.

Image courtesy of Heritage Auctions

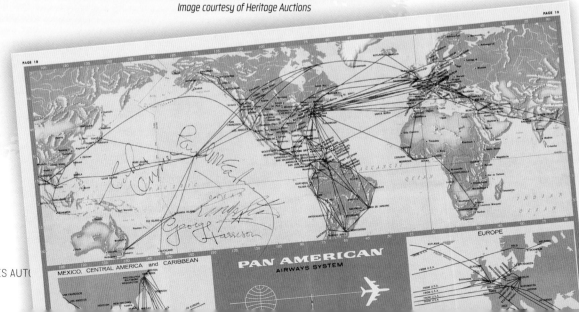

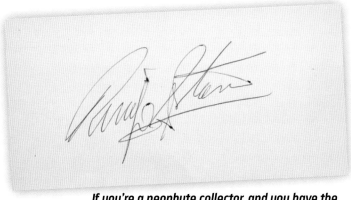

If you're a neophyte collector, and you have the funds, this Ringo Starr signed cut sheet is a great place to start. Well priced at $640.
Image courtesy of Julien's Auctions

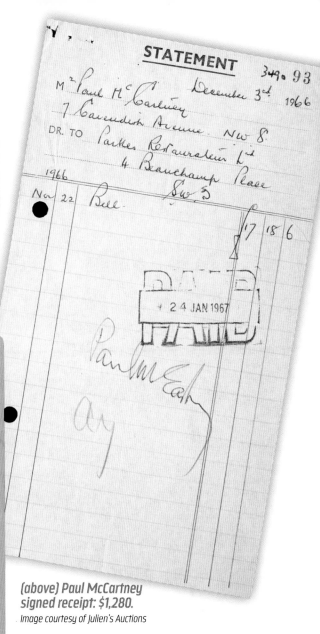

(above) Paul McCartney signed receipt: $1,280.
Image courtesy of Julien's Auctions

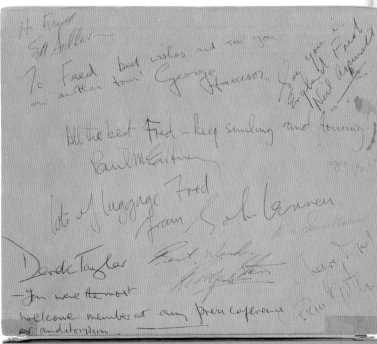

The Beatles, Ed Sullivan, and Brian Epstein-Signatures from their Historic First American Appearance on the Ed Sullivan Show, February 9, 1964: An early 8" x 10" glossy of the Fab Four, signed at inarguably the most important single performance of their careers. Signatures in black, with three bearing personal sentiments, almost certainly, to Fred Kaps, a fellow performer on the show: "To Fred best wishes and see you on another tour! George Harrison,", "All the best, Fred - keep smiling and touring! Paul McCartney," "lots of luggage Fred from John Lennon," and "Best Wishes Ringo Starr." Also signed by the legendary host, "Hi Fred Ed Sullivan," and the band's manager, "Cheers Fred Brian Epstein." A true piece of Pop Culture history from, arguably, one of the greatest nights in Pop Culture history. What more can be said? It brought $125,000.
Image courtesy of Heritage Auctions

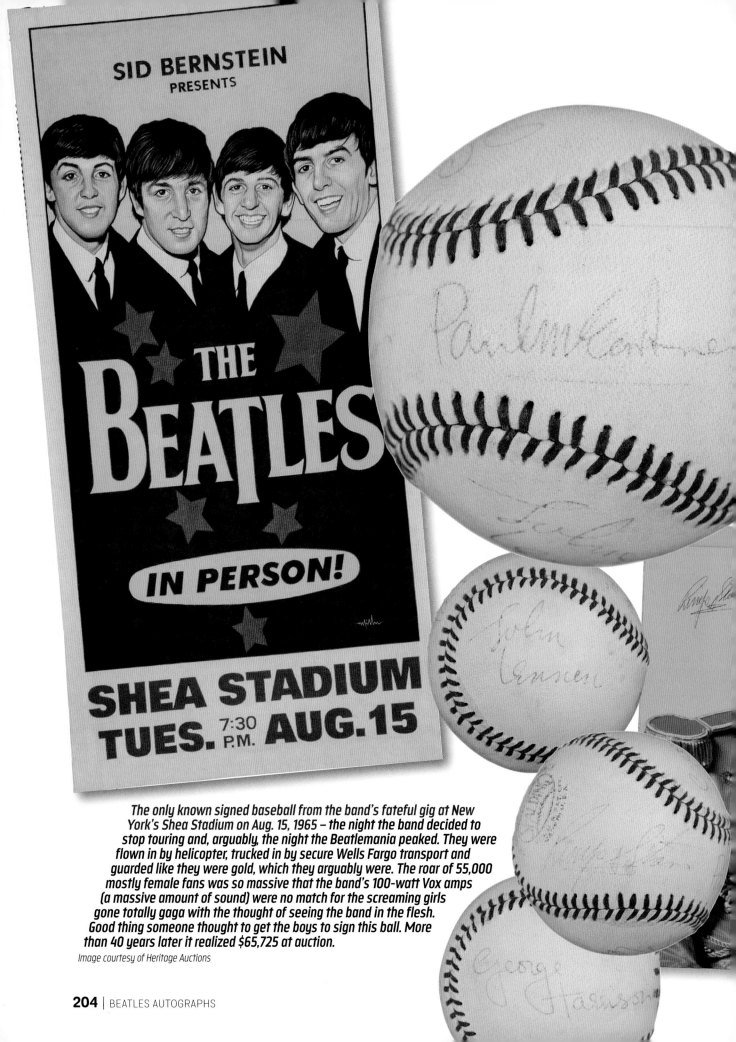

The only known signed baseball from the band's fateful gig at New York's Shea Stadium on Aug. 15, 1965 – the night the band decided to stop touring and, arguably, the night the Beatlemania peaked. They were flown in by helicopter, trucked in by secure Wells Fargo transport and guarded like they were gold, which they arguably were. The roar of 55,000 mostly female fans was so massive that the band's 100-watt Vox amps (a massive amount of sound) were no match for the screaming girls gone totally gaga with the thought of seeing the band in the flesh. Good thing someone thought to get the boys to sign this ball. More than 40 years later it realized $65,725 at auction.

Image courtesy of Heritage Auctions

The BEATLES

Not sure, but I'm almost willing to bet a copy of this Paul McCartney signed White Album masterpiece signed by one of the geniuses that created it would definitely sound better than an un-signed copy. Well worth the $1,280 paid at auction.

Image courtesy of Julien's Auctions

Beatles Signed Sgt. Pepper's Lonely Hearts Club Band mono UK Gatefold Cover (Parlophone PMC 7027, 1967): **A true jewel among Beatles collectibles and among the most spectacular Beatles autographs of all time. All four of the lads have signed this, the gatefold of their most iconic record. This beauty, when it was auctioned in 2013, led renowned Beatles expert Perry Cox to aver, "... being thoroughly immersed in Beatles collectibles for over 30 years, it takes something extraordinarily special to excite me, but I consider this to be one of the top two items of Beatles memorabilia I've ever seen – the other being a signed copy of Meet The Beatles." It realized $290,500 at auction, though I would imagine it would top that price easily were it to show up again today.**

Image courtesy of Heritage Auctions

THIS JOHN LENNON AND RINGO STARR SIGNED MENU SOLD FOR A TASTY $1,280 AT AUCTION.

Image courtesy of Julien's Auctions

Oh, to have been a fly on the wall at 565 Perugia Way in Bel Air, Calif., on the night of Aug. 27, 1965, when The Beatles drove to meet Elvis Presley.
The Beatles were on the eve of playing Balboa Stadium in San Diego; Elvis was in the midst of shooting Paradise, Hawaiian Style in Hollywood. That night, between 10 pm and 11 p.m., John, Paul, George and Ringo arrived in limousines and were personally greeted by The King. The nights was to become known as the "summit meeting" of Pop and Rock. "If you guys are going to stare at me all night," joked Elvis, "I'm going to bed!" In fact, Elvis was also awed, but the ice broke and the evening found the men playing music, admiring Elvis's new sauna, laughing at a fan who had infiltrated the house and discussing the terrors of fame. Jerry Schilling, a member of Elvis's "Memphis Mafia," got the autographs of all four Beatles on a piece of Elvis Presley's personal stationery, dating the event "8/27/65." A truly magical relic of rock 'n' roll royalty. $59,750.

Image courtesy of Heritage Auctions

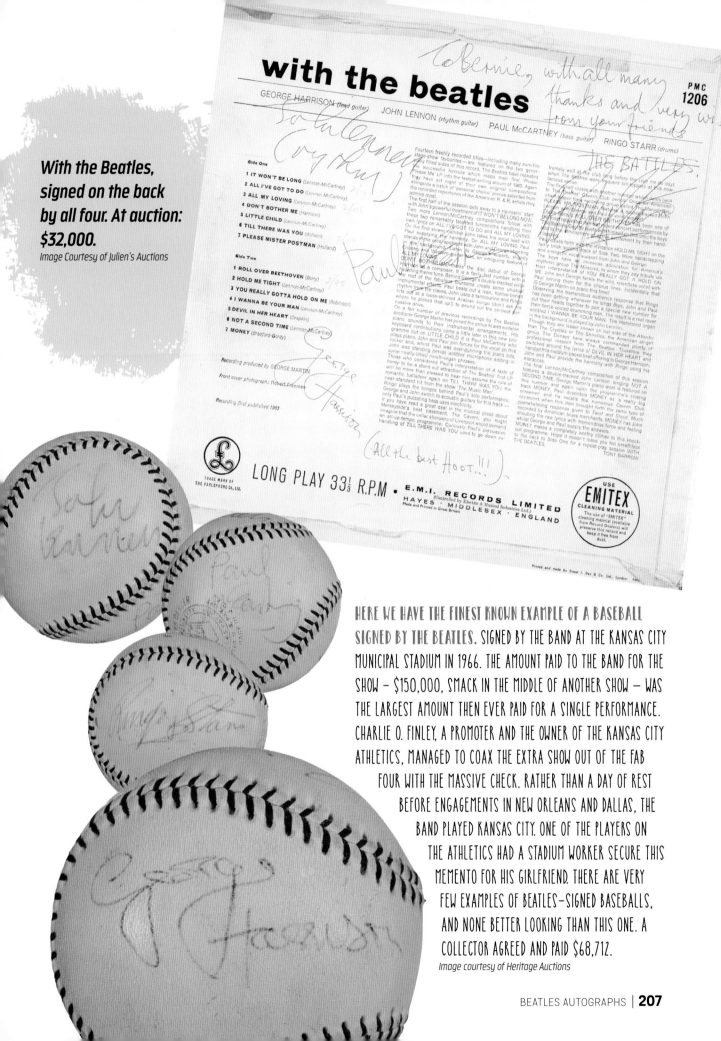

With the Beatles, signed on the back by all four. At auction: $32,000.

Image Courtesy of Julien's Auctions

HERE WE HAVE THE FINEST KNOWN EXAMPLE OF A BASEBALL SIGNED BY THE BEATLES. SIGNED BY THE BAND AT THE KANSAS CITY MUNICIPAL STADIUM IN 1966. THE AMOUNT PAID TO THE BAND FOR THE SHOW – $150,000, SMACK IN THE MIDDLE OF ANOTHER SHOW – WAS THE LARGEST AMOUNT THEN EVER PAID FOR A SINGLE PERFORMANCE. CHARLIE O. FINLEY, A PROMOTER AND THE OWNER OF THE KANSAS CITY ATHLETICS, MANAGED TO COAX THE EXTRA SHOW OUT OF THE FAB FOUR WITH THE MASSIVE CHECK. RATHER THAN A DAY OF REST BEFORE ENGAGEMENTS IN NEW ORLEANS AND DALLAS, THE BAND PLAYED KANSAS CITY. ONE OF THE PLAYERS ON THE ATHLETICS HAD A STADIUM WORKER SECURE THIS MEMENTO FOR HIS GIRLFRIEND. THERE ARE VERY FEW EXAMPLES OF BEATLES-SIGNED BASEBALLS, AND NONE BETTER LOOKING THAN THIS ONE. A COLLECTOR AGREED AND PAID $68,712.

Image courtesy of Heritage Auctions

Cool early Beatles publicity still – the boys take a break at a street market to have a bite – signed by Ringo. It brought $1,250.
Image courtesy of Julien's Auctions

(right) Ringo Starr signed invoice: $750.
Image courtesy of Julien's Auctions

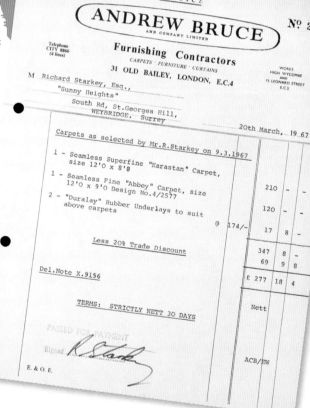

ENGRAVED COLOR CHECK ISSUED BY DISTRICT BANK LIMITED, SERIAL NUMBER R079611, DATED DEC. 28, 1967, FOR 10 BRITISH POUNDS SIGNED BY JOHN LENNON AT THE BOTTOM. ABOUT FINE CONDITION. LIKELY BOUGHT BY JOHN FOR A QUICK GETAWAY TO MOROCCO FOLLOWING THE CRITICAL FAILURE OF MAGICAL MYSTERY TOUR. SOLD FOR $4,000 AT AUCTION.
Image courtesy of Heritage Auctions

The Beatles signed Please Please Me album cover: High grade, strong signatures, what more do you need from your early signed Beatles albums? This one has it all and a $26,875 price tag to prove it.

Image courtesy of Julien's Auctions

COLLECTING BEATLES IN ACTION

On the morning that I meet Jeff Augsburger in early December of 2015 at the LBJ Library in Austin, Texas, I walk in expecting an aging hippie, definitely with long hair, likely flashing peace signs and saying everything was "groovy."

Perhaps I'm exaggerating the last part, but the aging hippie part was on my mind as I checked into the library. I had driven down from Dallas to meet with Augsburger to get a personal tour through the exhibition "Ladies and Gentlemen... The Beatles!" of which Augsburger provided a significant number of the collectibles on display. He along with three other major collectors (Mark Naboshek, Russ Lease and Chuck Gunderson) have generously given of their time and massive collections to provide the meat of the exhibition, which focuses on the first half of the band's career, ending right when the band stopped touring.

Augsburger's name is well known to me, as it is to so many Beatles collectors, since he's the author of the definitive Beatles price guide The Beatles Memorabilia Price Guide Paperback (Antique Trader Books, 1997), every bit the collecting bible of the hobby. His is a name that looms large among collectors, and rightly so. Just perusing the book it's obvi-

ous that the author possesses an encyclopedic knowledge of the band and its related collectibles. The price guide, and its legacy, leads me to assume that, besides meeting a genial, long-haired, peace sign-flashing hippy, that he is likely about 10-feet tall, a giant of the hobby.

Thus I'm taken somewhat aback when I am approached by Augsburger, a man of average size and cropped, graying hair. He presents a gentle and all together ordinary—in the best possible sense of the word—countenance. Quickly, however, as we walk through the exhibition together, with Augsburger pointing out the various pieces in the cases from his own collections and those from his collecting compatriots, I learn that he is a man of great curiosity, keen intellect and possessing an incredible knowledge of all things Beatles and Beatles collecting. It's a massive subject, daunting as it is intriguing and very difficult to master.

Augsburger, however, is just that: a master of the form. He's been a fan of the band's music since the beginning, starting his collection the way so many others did, by collecting records when they came out and buying the various Beatles marketing and ephemera that he came across along the way. As he grew into adulthood, establishing himself in his home state of Indiana as the proprietor of a successful plumbing business, he found himself, in the mid-1980s, beginning to collect more and more. It was, he soon found out, in his blood.

"I was already a big music fan as a kid," said Augsburger, who saw The Beatles in concert in Chicago in 1966. "I'm pretty sure I became completely crazy about the Beatles as soon as I heard the single 'Please Please Me' and the B-side, 'P.S. I Love you.' I started scouring record stores for the singles I didn't have. The Beatles, as I saw it, really broke the funk that American music was in at the time. This was until I was about 16, when I became interested in a few other things and stopped collecting."

THE BEATLES
MOBILE MUSEUM
BUY SELL TRADE

Beatles
Memorabilia
exhibit

The scope of Augsburg-er's collection is vast, as shown here at a Beatlefest. Well-organ-ized and easy to follow, it's a virtual template for collectors to follow as they assemble their own groupings.

T-shirts, pillows, post-ers and toys, all carefully curated by Augsburger and presented by his careful and discerning eye.

Yards of Beatles on display, laid out impeccably by Augsburger. The posters present a portrait of rarity and variety, while the various ephemera on the tables is given ample room to be seen and enjoyed – not to mention bought and traded – by the various collectors who frequent the mobile display.

His teen dalliance with those "other things" would prove a mere a divergence. Within a decade of stopping, he was back in it. His journey toward elite collecting status is one that is familiar to any hardcore collector, whatever their niche. It was 1973, Augsburger was 23. The Beatles had broken up, but he was still obsessed with the band. He began to look for other ways to fulfill his Beatles need.

"I found myself wanting to get a Beatles lunchbox for my shelf at home," Augsburger said. "Once I got that, I thought to myself, 'there must be a lot of other things out there with their faces on it. It was a straight journey from there."

Augsburger tapped directly into the burgeoning Beatles collecting zeitgeist. These were the early days of the Capitol Records Beatles swap meets in Los Angeles, the same time that all the other Beatles-obsessed Baby Boomers were coming into their own money and careers. Even if Augsburger didn't

know it, he was not operating in a vacuum; the collecting bug was biting thousands of others. "I started joining clubs and going to flea markets and swap meets," he said. "A lot of people had records I didn't, bootlegs, memorabilia, you name it."

It was not long before the pursuit of the next, and best, Beatles collectible was happily filling his spare time. It was also not long before his collection outgrew the meager space on his shelves he had set aside. His obsession with amassing a substantial collection became undeniable.

"I started running ads in local papers and shoppers," he said. "It was a goldmine. I can't tell you how many times I would get calls from women telling me that they had daughters at college and rooms full of stuff they wanted to get rid of. I don't imagine those girls were too happy when they came home from school, but their loss was my gain."

Like so many, Augsburger's collection was in full gear. The difference, however—and this is key in collecting anything—is that Augsburger is possessed of that rarest and most special collecting commodity: The Eye.

"The Eye" is the thing that separates the wheat from the chaff in collecting and it is the one thing that cannot be taught. A neophyte collector can learn the ins-and-outs of collecting, how to identify the rare date or design—all of these things are easily transmitted from a willing teacher. That is not equal to the intangible that is "The Eye." There are collectors that have a knack for finding that rare piece, for getting a great deal on it and for trading up at the most opportune time. It's a rare gift, the thing that makes the top collector and dealers in any hobby and the thing that puts certain people at the very top of the form, making them sought after for their advice and their inventory.

This is just what Augsburger became as the 1970s and 1980s progressed. It was a revelation to him. "In '76 I went to Beatlefest in Boston; it was one of the first gatherings of its kind," he said. "There were vendors there of all kinds and thousands of collections. I soon realized, happily, that I wasn't alone."

Indeed he wasn't. He soon found himself part of an exuberant and growing club. Moreover, he was rapidly climbing the ranks as one of the top. "I'd say that I got lucky a lot," he said. "There was lots of luck and lots of missed opportunities along the way."

Luckily for Augsburger, he was able to make up for any mistakes. With collecting in his heart, his energy, when not working, was fully invested in the pursuit. As he says, if there was something out there he didn't have and wanted, he would pursue it doggedly until he was in a position to "go out there and grab it."

His attendance at various swap meets and Beatlefests soon changed the nature of his participation in the hobby; he became more than just a seeker of material. "I had so much material that I was soon setting up," he said. "It became a chance not only to acquire good things I didn't have, it allowed me the opportunity to display my full collection as well as to sell pieces I no longer needed." Today, Augsburger's collection, which he does not display at home—minus a few select special pieces, as there's just too much—sits in the range of 1,500 pieces, give or take.

The sheer range of Augsburger's collection/display is mind-boggling. It's deep in all areas, from the early days and the first singles, paper ephemera and marketing products that were produced by NEMS up through the harder to corral late-Beatles period and into their solo years. The key is that Augsburger has remained both flexible and patient in his pursuit. He spends at least an hour a day organizing what he has and looking through online listings from other collectors. He obsessively pours through the digital listings, looking for key words and dates that set off the alarm in his brain that he may be on to something special. It's all about the chase.

"I'm not in it for the money," he said, "and I don't trust anyone that's in it for that reason. I'm in it because I love it. That's it. The fun for me is in finding and buying some obscure little thing that no one has any idea of, something like a local poster or promotional piece from some small city the band played in before they stopped touring. That's where the thrill is."

This passion may be what marks Augsburger's pursuit, but it has to be noted that he also has a tireless dedication to finding pieces that complement each other. It's one thing to spend a good bit on original Beatles hand-written lyrics, or a page from Stuart Sutcliffe's artist's notebook, but it's another thing to seek out that perfect photo, autograph or piece of ephemera that perfectly balances that piece. The right image can relay context and increase value and this is exactly where Augsburger is a master, as evidenced by his array of Beatlemania accessories and toys.

"I always like to find things that originally went together," he said. "If I can find, say, a dozen Beatles wristwatches, or a pair of canvas shoes, then I immediately start looking for an original cardboard display for those watches, or the original show box in great shape. Put these things together and you have the original context in which they were presented. It's a thrilling thing when it works."

These days, when Augsburger isn't actively

So much room and so much to choose from in Augsburger's Beatles Mobile Museum. This image gives you a good sense of the size and scope of his collection, fully laid out. Extensive collections such as Augsburger's are almost impossible to display at home because of space limitations.

Notice the variety display as well as the coordination of the material. One of Augsburger's great talents as a collector is a knack for understanding what goes well together.

buying, scouring listings or loaning gems from his collection to travelling Beatles exhibitions organized by the Grammys, he and his impressive collection can be found at most every Beatlefest. There he shares his knowledge with beginners, trades with old friends and does his best to find that next, best, most elusive piece.

Is there advice, then, that Augsburger is willing to give to anyone that has just entered the hobby, or is seriously thinking about entering?

"Yes," he said. "You have to immerse yourself in it. Go to shows, read up online, talk to knowledgeable dealers and collectors. Most of all, buy because you love it. Buy it because you want to live with it—never because you are looking to make money."

Augsburger also stresses that, for younger collectors, this is a good time to get into it.

"The future of the hobby is pretty wide open right now, as a lot of older collectors are aging out of actively collecting. This means that there are a lot more things available than there would have been before at the same time as many of these older collectors are starting to parse out their collections."

That mean it's a Buyer's Market and, for the intrepid, dedicated collector, it puts a collection of quality and rarity—granted, maybe not as spectacular as Augsburger's collection—well within reach.

Ladies & Gentlemen... THE BEATLES!

Ladies & Gentlemen... THE BEATLES!

"Ladies and Gentlemen... The Beatles!" – an exhibition overview

Ladies and Gentlemen...The Beatles! is an exhibition assembled by four of the greatest Beatles memorabilia collectors of all time: Jeff Augsburger, Mark Naboshek, Russ Lease and Chuck Gunderson. This traveling exhibit details the early part of the Beatles career, told through the incredible collectibles, worth millions of dollars, assembled by its creators and presented in a comprehensive, attractive display by the Grammy Museum.

The exhibition takes collectors on a ride through the early 1960s and the re-birth of rock 'n' roll as focused through the lens that was the four lads from Liverpool. Covering Beatlemania, primarily 1964-1966, the collectibles tell the story of how the Beatles affected nearly every aspect of American pop culture, from music and television to fashion, art and advertising.

A journey through the exhibition is a journey through every aspect of the lives of the band members. There are dozens of Beatles-related pop culture artifacts on display, all of them complemented by correspondence, instruments, posters, photographs, interviews and interactive displays, with an oral history booth in the middle where visitors can leave their own statements about the Beatles and talk about how this incredible group affected their lives.

For more information, and future exhibition locations and dates, check the exhibition website at:
FabFourExhibits.com.

Exhibition attendees are presented with a fully interactive display detailing the meteoric rise of the Fab Four.

(opposite) The entrance to the exhibition, the beginning of a trip through the spectacular first part of the Beatles' amazing career.

Replicas of the band's instruments are on display, presented as they were used during the Beatles' world-changing appearance in February 1964 on The Ed Sullivan Show.

A Hamburg-era set list, one of Augsburger's prized Beatles possessions and a wonderful look inside the early performances from the band.

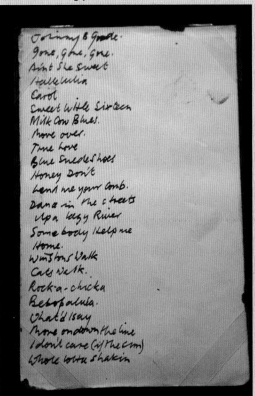

Beatlemania in full effect in this evocative display. Notice the amazing and rare white Beatles sweatshirt on the right side – a great piece! The drum is a replica of the bass drum from Ringo's Ludwig #1 set.

This display in the exhibition, curated by Augsburger, with material from his collection, depicts what the room of a young female Beatles fan may have looked like in the mid-1960s.

A fan studies up on early Beatles material, including a grouping of early 45s from artists that influenced the band.

A collection of early Beatles singles and ephemera in the form of articles on the boys in Mersey Beat, a seminal British 1960s music magazine.

1966-1969

A display focusing on the last part of the Beatles career. While the exhibition focuses largely on the early years of the band, Augsburger and his collaborators are knowledgeable in all areas of the band's career and collectibles.

(left) A superb grouping of Beatles accessories and toys. Much of this comes from Augsburger's collection and displays his signature style – notice how the collectibles are paired with good condition displays.

I'M WITH THE BAND

A great number of people – and places – played influential roles in the lives and careers of The Beatles. Here's a look at some who had a profound effect.

PETE BEST

Pete Best (born Nov. 24, 1941) is, of course, most widely known as the first drummer for The Beatles. One has to wonder what it would be like to be Best, watching his former band fire him, replace him and go on to become the greatest rock band in history, with the attendant wealth and glory that comes with it. It's easy to think that he would sink into bitterness, perhaps even madness, but by all accounts, Pete Best is a decent man who has made a good life for himself and who has enjoyed the modicum of fame bestowed upon him by his brief association with The Beatles—even if it took him many years to come around to it. Let's face it, if you're going to be a footnote in Pop Culture history then it might as well be as one attached to the most famous musicians of the 20th century.

It was in 1959 that Pete Best's mother, Mona, opened The Casbah Coffee Club, a rock music venue, in the basement of their Liverpool home. It was a hotspot, to be sure

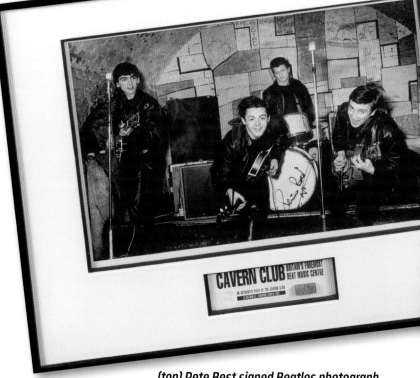

(top) Pete Best signed Beatles photograph outside of The Cavern Club. $640 at auction.
Image courtesy of Julien's Auctions

(above) Pete Best signed this photo of The Beatles playing at The Cavern Club, something the band did 292 times. Even the ex-Beatle can command good prices for autographs, as evidenced by the price this one garnered at auction: $1,280. *Image courtesy of Julien's Auctions*

**CHAPTER
TEN**

and all the local bands played there, including Best's own band The Black Jacks and the Quarrymen (John, Paul and George). By 1960, McCartney had asked Best to join the band for a series of gigs in Hamburg. It was a legendary time in the development of the group, and rock 'n' roll in general, and Best stayed with the band through their trips to Hamburg, recording with them as the Beat Brothers backing up the popular singer Tony Sheridan on "My Bonnie."

Best was still with The Beatles at their first EMI recording session in June 1962 when George Martin suggested using a better session drummer instead of Pete—a common thing to do at the time. The rest of the band saw it as an opportunity to oust Best permanently from the group, as he was perceived to be the weak link musically and anti-social off-stage. On Aug. 16, 1962, Epstein fired Best from the band. Ringo was soon in and history was on its way to being written.

Best tried his hand at other musical ventures post-Beatles, but eventually, lacking any success, left the business altogether and became a civil servant. In 1988, after refusing to embrace his past, Best played drums in public for the first time in decades. He has since toured the world several times over with his own band and regularly makes appearances at Beatles-related events.

STUART SUTCLIFFE

Stuart Fergusson Victor Sutcliffe, born on June 23, 1940, in Edinburgh, Scotland, was not the bass player in The Beatles long, but his impact was significant in many ways. He may not have been near as good a musician as the other band members, but he was easily the most handsome and stylish of the first Beatles line-up and, by all accounts, the most charismatic.

Sutcliffe's real passion was art. It was, in fact, at the Liverpool College of Art that a friend introduced Sutcliffe to John Lennon. Lennon was intrigued and drawn to Sutcliffe, who was a superior artist to Lennon, and the two became very good friends. The two even shared an apartment for a time in 1960. Lennon, at that time, was playing music with McCartney and the two, after talking one night at the Casbah Coffee Club—owned by Pete Best's mother—convinced Sutcliffe to buy a Hofner bass guitar. Sutcliffe, who had studied music as a child, and played piano and acoustic guitar, joined Lennon, McCartney and Harrison in May of 1960, when the band was known as The Silver Beetles.

Sutcliffe was never regarded as, and never claimed to be, a great musi-

cian. He was competent, certainly, but somewhat artless and unspectacular. His personal charisma made up for whatever shortcomings there were as a musician. It was Sutcliffe, in fact, that drove the early image, and thus the popularity, of the band. McCartney himself admitted decades later that he was jealous of Sutcliffe's relationship with Lennon and bothered by how popular Sutcliffe was with the fans at those early Beatles performances.

While that early Beatles image, so cool and rough (as clearly evidenced in the magnificent photos of the band at the Hamburg Fun Fair taken by his girlfriend and soon-to-be fiancée, Astrid Kirchherr) was directly reflective of Sutcliffe's sense of style, he was never fully invested in becoming a musician.

Photograph of Stuart Sutcliffe taken by Astrid Kirchherr during a photo session in 1960. *Image courtesy of Heritage Auctions*

The handwritten journal page reads:

Notes: John's descriptions of painting.
"I'm not against anything, but I'm more for myself. I don't know who I am, but I'm not them anymore."
"When you've got to ask what it is you'll never really know" (L. Armstrong.).
"Revolted against awesome dominance of Paris and the far flung shadow of Pablo Picasso."

Strange anatomical images and fragments of observed nature.

The cult of any meaninglessness, proof of the emptiness of our existence in industrial society.
"A brave new world - unfettered".

"The Human mind is an instrument it gives coherence to perception, and dominates the impulses which we call instinct and emotion. (felt the impulse to flee mundane world of appearances. Its like a young woman who is quite capable of having children but not producing them until the seed inside her is fertalised by another mature source."— (try and enlarge this).
- "Everything in life has its hmm."
"No human work could possibly be devoid of content, and how can a painted work conform to the same requirements as a written text."
"Nowadays we are more attracted by the ways things are presented, we are less interested in things in themselves. We are more interested in the manner in which a man walks rather than where he is walking to." (enlarge on the comparison of Rembrandt and De Staël.).
"I always have a point of departure, but I transpose it.
"Painting is the truth, it draws the nearer to beauty, in the same light it transposes things as rock etc, and replaces them by ..."

When they turn up, pages from Stuart Sutcliffe's journal are always desirable. This page brought $1,152 at auction.
Image courtesy of Julien's Auctions

During those legendary days in Hamburg, falling in love with Kirchherr and playing epic sets in seedy clubs, it became clear to Sutcliffe that his heart was in becoming a visual artist, an area where he clearly had talent.

So it was, in early July 1961, that Sutcliffe decided to leave the band and pursue his art by enrolling at the Hamburg College of Art. He remained friendly with the band, was engaged to a talented, successful and gorgeous photographer in Kirchherr and, as it all looked, was on his way to achieving exactly the life he wanted. Fate, however, had other plans.

It was around this time that Sutcliffe began suffering from severe headaches and light sensitivity, some of which even temporarily blinded him. In early 1962 the symptoms grew worse. In April he collapsed in the middle of an art class. German doctors were unable to determine the exact problem, so he went to England for treatment. There he was told there was nothing wrong with him. He returned to Hamburg and Kirchherr in the spring, where his symptoms continued to worsen.

On April 10, 1962 he collapsed once more. Kirchherr called an ambulance and rode with him to the hospital. It was too late, however, as he died in Kirchherr's arms on the way due to what was later determined to be a brain aneurysm. What caused it is unknown, but it's now believed the problem may have stemmed from a fractured skull he received in a fight after a show at Lathom Hall in Liverpool in 1961. Sutcliffe never received medical attention for it.

Understandably Kirchherr was devastated, as was Lennon. For Kirchherr, she had lost the love of her life and would never fully get over it. For Lennon, he had lost his best friend and artistic compatriot. Lennon did not speak often in public of Sutcliffe, but he carried his memory close the rest of his life. For the rest of the world, though time has illuminated his talent and influence, Sutcliffe's death would go largely unnoticed.

This untitled, original watercolor painting by Stuart Sutcliffe was purchased directly from Sutcliffe's sister Pauline in the 1990s. It sold at auction for $10,240.
Image courtesy of Julien's Auctions

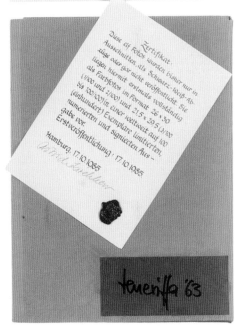

A rare portfolio titled "Teneriffa '63," dating to 1985 – the first and only time that the color Tenerife photos were produced in a professional edition from the original negatives by Astrid Kirchherr. Originally envisioned as an edition of 100, only 15 portfolios were produced, and only a few – including this one – were sold as complete, unbroken sets. Each print is 11.5" x 8" and signed by Kirchherr and numbered 11/100. Kirchherr, along with friend and artist Klaus Voorman joined The Beatles (John Lennon was in Spain with Brian Epstein) during a 12-day break in Tenerife, in the Canary Islands. The group stayed at the Voorman family home located on the island. These rarely seen photos show the boys and Kirchherr relaxing by a swimming pool near the ocean, free from the pressures of Beatlemania that had recently been unleashed in England. Kirchherr took these with her portable camera, in color no less, and captured an amazing moment in time: when the band returned home they were never again free to be out in public and not be recognized. The first taste of fame had been experienced and there was no going back for the boys. This set brought $6,250 at auction. *Image courtesy of Heritage Auctions*

ASTRID KIRCHHERR

Astrid Kirchherr (born May 20, 1938), a German photographer and artist, is probably the photographer most widely associated with The Beatles—especially in the early years. Kirchherr's amazing photos did as much to define the early image of the band as anything did and, to this day, her evocative images from Hamburg, Germany in 1960, '61 and '62 are the definitive look at the hungry young lads from Liverpool as they careened toward fame.

Kirchherr captured Sutcliffe in this full-length studio portrait in Hamburg in 1961. Kirchherr signed the large-format photograph (18.5" x 23.25"), which brought $312 at auction.
Image courtesy of Heritage Auctions

Although Kirchherr has taken very few photographs since 1967, her early work has been and still is widely celebrated and has been exhibited extensively around the world, including in Hamburg, Bremen, London, Liverpool, New York City, Washington, D.C., Tokyo, Vienna and at the Rock and Roll Hall of Fame in Cleveland. She has also published three limited-edition books of photographs.

Kirchherr was an art student in Hamburg in 1960 when, with her then-boyfriend (and important friend to The Beatles) Klaus Voormann, she saw The Beatles at the Kaiserkeller club. She very quickly realized that her mission was simply to be as close to The Beatles as she could get. It was not long before she asked the band if she could take pictures of them. The next day, with her famous Rolleicord camera, at the Hamburg Fun Fair, she took a series of the most famous rock photos of all time, featuring the young Beatles (minus Best, who had skipped the shoot). It was the beginning of a beautiful friendship between she and the boys.

In terms of Stuart Sutcliffe, however, it was much more than friendship. Sutcliffe was obsessed with Kirchherr and the two soon fell deeply in love, though it was not to last. Less than a year after leaving the band

to pursue his studies in art—his true artistic passion—Sutcliffe would die of a brain hemorrhage, wrapped in Kirchherr's arms, in the back of an ambulance, on the way to the hospital. The impact on Kirchherr, as you might expect, was profound.

Kirchherr continued photographing The Beatles, including her very famous "behind the scenes" photographs of The Beatles during the filming of "A Hard Day's Night," through 1967.

Kirchherr is often credited with inventing The Beatles' signature "mop-top" haircuts, though she has denied it in the past, even telling the BBC in 1995 that "all my friends in art school used to run around with this sort of what you call Beatles haircut. And my boyfriend then, Klaus Voormann, had this hairstyle, and Stuart liked it very very much. He was the first one who really got the nerve to get the Brylcreem out of his hair and asking me to cut his hair for him."

Whether or not she created the hairstyle can certainly be debated. One thing is for certain, though: through her lens and her pictures of the band, Kirchherr certainly played a crucial role in creating The Beatles' image as they and their music stormed the planet.

Klaus Voormann

Klaus Voormann (born April 29, 1938) is a German artist, musician and record producer best known for creating the original artwork for The Beatles' 1966 masterpiece Revolver. For most of us, just being known to history for that one album cover would be enough, but for Voormann it is just one of many feathers that he has in his cap across an extremely interesting and storied career. Not only did Voormann get to be a good friend to The Beatles, designing artwork for them and playing music with them throughout the 1970s, he also has put together a successful career as a studio musician and artist outside of his association with The Beatles, most notably as the bassist for Manfred Mann from 1966 to 1969.

Voormann, along with Astrid Kirchherr and Jurgen Vollmer, were among the very earliest friends The Beatles had in their legendary stint in Hamburg. In fact, it was because of Voormann that the trio of Germans became so close to the quartet of Brits. As an art student in Hamburg, while dating Kirchherr, Voormann wandered down the Reeperbahn, in the St. Pauli district of Hamburg, after an argument with her and Vollmer. It was not a neighborhood he would usually frequent, but after hearing The Beatles in the Kaiserkeller club, he convinced Kirchherr and Vollmer to come see the band the next night. All three were soon spending every spare moment they had with The Beatles.

In 1966, Voormann was asked by Lennon to design the artwork for Revolver. The now famous collage-style image is part of Rock history. While he was only paid £40 for the work, he won the Grammy Award for Best Album Cover in 1966, assuring his name a place in the annals of Rock history. He would later design the cover art George Harrison's 1988 single, "When We Was Fab."

Around the same time Voormann was hired to design the cover for the Bee Gees first album, followed the next year by artwork on the American edition of The Bee Gees' album Idea. In 1973, he created the album sleeve and booklet artwork for Ringo's album Ringo, on which he also played bass.

In 1966 Voormann became a member of the 1960s band Manfred Mann, having turned down offers by The Hollies and The Moody Blues. In the 1970s he became a session musician, playing on solo projects by Lou Reed, Carly Simon, James Taylor and Harry Nilsson. He was a member of Yoko Ono and Lennon's Plastic Ono Band. He also played in Harrison's assembled band at the 1971 The Concert for Bangladesh. After The Beatles disbanded, there were rumors the band would re-form as "The Ladders," with Voormann on bass. While this never happened, the line-up did perform in various combinations on Lennon's albums, John Lennon/Plastic Ono Band (1970) and Imagine (1971).

In 1980, besides a cameo in the Robert Altman film "Popeye," he produced three studio albums and a live album by the German band Trio, including the hit "Da Da Da." In 1995 he designed the covers for The Beatles albums. Voormann designed the cover of Scandinavian Leather for the Norwegian band Turbonegro in 2003 and, in 2007, designed the artwork for the album Timeless by Wet Wet Wet.

Voormann released his first solo album in 2009, called A Sideman's Journey. It featured performances by McCartney, Starr, Yusuf Islam (formerly known as Cat Stevens), Don Preston, Dr. John and Joe Walsh among many others.

BRIAN EPSTEIN

Brian Samuel Epstein (Sept. 19, 1934-Aug. 27, 1967) was the most important—and enigmatic—figure in the history of The Beatles, minus the lads themselves, of course.

When looking at Epstein's early life, it's not immediately apparent that he was on a crash course with history, but all of his moves seemed to position him perfectly. After a stint in the military, he studied acting at the Royal Academy of Dramatic Arts (RADA) in London in the late 1950s, but dropped out after three semesters, driven more by his business sense than his sense of drama. Epstein quickly proved himself a keen businessman in the family business, the famous NEMS, short for North End Music Stores. Epstein was put in charge of the newly opened store on Great Charlotte Street in Liverpool, quickly turning it into one of the biggest musical retail outlets in the North of England. The business achieved so much success that Epstein was asked to write a column for Mersey Beat magazine, which featured The Beatles on its second cover—an issue, it should be noted, that Epstein would have sold many copies of at his store. By the time he first saw the band, Epstein's own regional fame may well be said to have rivaled, if not surpassed, their own.

So it was in November of 1961 that Epstein famously saw and met The Beatles for the first time at The Cavern Club, a short while after hearing the band as "The Beat Brothers" backing Tony Sheridan on the "My Bonnie" single recorded in Germany.

After the performance, Epstein briefly met the boys, who all knew him from NEMS. While he didn't propose it at the time, Epstein was already thinking about becoming The Beatles' manager. It wasn't until almost a month went by—with The Beatles playing at The Cavern and Epstein at every performance—before he met with them to propose a management arrangement on Dec. 3, 1961. After further meet-

Brian Epstein was at the center of The Beatles world during their remarkable rise to fame. When he died in 1967 many regarded the moment as the beginning of the end for the group. This mounted photo and autographs sold for $4,000 at auction. Image courtesy of Heritage Auctions

Brian Epstein Typed Letter Signed to Peter Eckhorn of the Top Ten Club in Hamburg (Liverpool, January 24, 1962): A one page letter on Epstein's personal stationary, to Peter Eckhorn, signed in full in black ink. He mentions their conversation about a possible March appearance for The Beatles at his club, stating they are booked at the suggested time, but may be available later. The other engagement he mentions is the grand opening of the Star-Club. The Beatles would never play again at the Top Ten. A great piece of early Beatles history sold for $6,562. at auction.

Image courtesy of Heritage Auctions

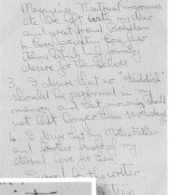
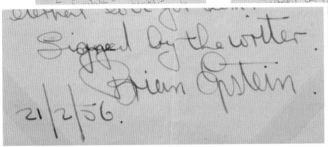

Brian Epstein Last Will and Testament: A rather macabre but nonetheless interesting and important piece of Beatles history relating to death of Brian Epstein on Aug. 27, 1967. Epstein was a brilliant, caring man, but his life was complicated, especially when word got out after his death about his sexual orientation, his penchant for gambling and his drug use – the last of which was not going to go unnoticed, as he died of a drug overdose. His death marked the beginning of the end for the Beatles, so, in many ways, this document marked the slow start of the band's dissolution. $4,480 at auction.

Image courtesy of Julien's Auctions

ings on Dec. 6 and 10, 1961, The Beatles signed a five-year contract with Epstein on Jan. 24, 1962. They signed a new contract later that same year, in October, which would give Epstein 25% of the band's revenues after expenses. It was an exorbitant amount, though The Beatles accepted it.

At the same time Epstein began to shape the image that would make The Beatles so famous. He changed their on-stage outfits, slowly, from blue jeans and leather jackets to the collarless suits that would define their Beatlemania image. He also helped refine their performances, insisting that they didn't swear, smoke, drink or eat on stage. He also instituted their famous synchronized bow at the end of performances.

Once he remade the image of the band, which was rewarded with better gigs at bigger venues, Epstein—after being rejected by every major record label in London—got the band a recording contract with EMI's Parlaphone label, working with George Martin.

The Beatles story after that point is well known, as they literally stormed the world. Via non-stop touring, television and film work between 1963 and 1965, the band and Epstein became incredibly famous, incredibly rich and incredibly burnt out. By summer of 1966, The Beatles had had enough of touring and, after their Aug. 29, 1966, performance at Candlestick Park in San Francisco, they called it quits. Epstein wanted them to continue touring—so much of his involvement with and management of the band, not to mention the 25% of revenues he made, was tied up with touring—but the band had simply had enough of life on the road.

While Epstein still managed a few other bands (Gerry & the Pacemakers, Billy J. Kramer and the Dakotas, among them), the end was written in The Beatles decision to stop playing live. Without the constant touring and television, Epstein knew that his contract with The Beatles was going to change and that his percentage was going to drop. His sweetheart deal with the band, which had trusted him so implicitly, was going to end. The Beatles had become much more interested in their finances, in the rights to their songs and their percentage of marketing revenues, and they had begun to figure out that Epstein, who they still loved, was neither giving them a great deal nor being forthright with them about their

cut or his dealings on their behalf.

It's ironic that the period of The Beatles greatest success as musicians was a dark time for Epstein, but it seemed to be just that. As he contemplated his future, and swung ever more deeply into drug abuse and addiction, which he had battled since the early '60s, Epstein would reach the end point—via a deadly accidental overdose combination of the sleeping pill Carbitral and alcohol—on Aug. 27, 1967. The Beatles were riding high on the success of Sgt. Pepper's Lonely Hearts Club Band, they had just released the most important album of their careers, and Brian Epstein was dead.

After his death, when news of his drug abuse and homosexuality surfaced—a widely known fact amongst his friends, family and inner circle—Epstein's demise became the subject of much more public scrutiny. He was the manager of the most famous band in the world and he had lived a lifestyle that most of the public had no idea even existed. More importantly, too, his death would soon come to be regarded as the beginning of the end The Beatles. While it certainly cannot be found fully responsible for it, it's hard to not to see in Epstein's death the dissolution of the last link that was tying the band together. Less than three years after his death, The Beatles would no longer exist.

In a 1997 documentary interview with the BBC, McCartney had the following to say about Epstein's importance to the band's history: "If anyone was the fifth Beatle," he said, "it was Brian."

GEORGE MARTIN

While no one can claim the credit for the magical music of The Beatles—besides the members of the band themselves—their one-and-only producer, George Martin (Jan. 3, 1926-March 8, 2016), certainly figures more prominently than any other in that amazing sound. The amazing thing to consider is that Martin, who had produced mainly comedy records for EMI's Parlaphone label in the 1950s and early 1960s, had almost no experience at all with Pop Music before signing the band.

The story of how Martin became The Beatles producer is the classic rock story. Epstein was in London, trying everywhere he could think of, to get a recording contract for the band. He was turned down by everyone—including, famously, Decca Records—before, finally, getting a meeting with Martin at Parlaphone. While Martin thought that Paul was a promising vocalist, he was unimpressed overall with the band. Still, because he liked Epstein, he decided to give the band a shot.

The first time the boys entered the studios at Abbey Road with Martin was early June of 1962 to record "Love Me Do." This recording session, ultimately led to the dismissal of Best on the drums. On Sept. 4, 1962, with Ringo on drums, they recorded it again. Martin still didn't think the sound was right. They recorded the song again on Sept. 11, 1962, with session player Andy White on drums and Ringo, unhappily, on tambourine and maracas. The song hit #17 in England, prompting another session on Nov. 26, 1962, where Lennon and McCartney begged Martin to let them do another original, this time "Please Please Me." During the session Martin suggested the band speed the song up, as it was written as a ballad. We all know the result.

"Congratulations gentlemen," Martin told the boys when the recording session was finished, "you have just made your first number one record."

There was clearly a synergy between the band and Martin. The boys had the raw talent and the charisma; Martin had the musical knowledge and expertise, the know-how to create a lasting product. He helped The Beatles bridge the gap between wild exuberance and studio polish, perfecting the formula and musical phrasing that would make them all

The Beatles with George Martin in Abbey Road Studios, London, January 1967. *Photo courtesy Apple Corps Ltd.*

household names.

Martin also wrote most of The Beatles' instrumentation and orchestral arrangements, as well as collaborating with the band on the keyboard parts of their early music. He conceived of the idea to put strings on "Yesterday," he insisted on the piccolo trumpet solo in "Penny Lane," he conducted the strings arrangement on "Eleanor Rigby," he did the revolutionary re-mixing of "Strawberry Fields," arranged the ensemble music for "I Am the Walrus" and played the baroque piano on "In My Life," which he then sped up for the final recording. He also did the film scores for "A Hard Day's Night" and "Yellow Submarine." The list of his contributions goes on and on. He also continued producing for the members of the band in their post-Beatles solo careers.

Through the last decades of the 20th century Martin worked with many different and important rock musicians, including: Gerry & The Pacemakers, Billy J. Kramer & the Dakotas, the band America, Jeff Beck, Neil Sedaka, Ultravox, Kenny Rogers, Cheap Trick, Elton John, Celine Dion, Dire Straits and many more. In 1992 he worked with Pete Townshend on the Broadway production of Tommy, for which he won a Grammy Award as producer. He oversaw the production of The Beatles Anthology in 1994-95 and, in 2006, remixed more than 80 minutes of Beatles music for the Cirque de Soleil's Las Vegas show Love.

He was, in his own way and with his own abilities, as much of a genius as The Beatles themselves, even if that genius was made manifest by recognizing, improving and expanding on the existing raw genius of the band. He has, by any measure, earned his place in rock 'n' roll history.

APPLE CORPS

While most of the world today thinks of computers when they think of Apple, the fact is that The Beatles got to the name first, creating Apple Corps in 1967 following the death of their manager, Brian Epstein. What followed in the succeeding five decades has been a history of success and failure, ups and downs and everything in-between. Today, with all catalog rights and image control firmly back with the company, Apple is a force in the world of music and entertainment to be reckoned with.

Epstein's death in August of '67 was a huge shock to the band. It also left most of their business dealings in limbo, as Epstein had handled much of it. The result was the formation of Apple Corps, a parent company to the various music, media and business dealings of the band. The first project to come out of the new Beatles-owned company, under the Apple Films subdivision, was the film Magical Mystery Tour, a critical flop.

Next came the Apple Records subdivision, officially founded when The Beatles returned from their 1968 trip to study transcendental meditation with the Maharishi in India. Apple Records was founded, ostensibly, to sign and record new artists (including James Taylor, Mary Hopkin, Billy Preston, the Modern Jazz Quartet and Badfinger among them), but which, as the 1970s wore on, more and more was basically a label to release solo projects of the former Beatles.

In 1969 Allen Klein took over management of Apple (he was manager of The Rolling Stones at the time) and subsequently shut down several subdivisions, including Apple Electronics, while several artists were also dropped from the label. Klein's tenure would last until 1973 and the end of his contract. During his time at the helm, in 1971, Apple re-issued The Beatles entire pre-Apple catalog—though the covers still carried the Capitol Records logo—which proved to be his most lasting legacy with the company. Neil Aspinall, a longtime Beatles insider, took over the company.

What followed, starting in 1976, with the end of Apple's distribution contract with EMI—when the control of the entire Beatles catalog reverted back to EMI—was a 10+ year-long court battle and a flirtation with oblivion in an effort to get those rights back. The lawsuit was settled in 1989 and new projects finally began to come together, including the much-lauded Live at the BBC album and The Beatles Anthology project.

Apple Records was back in the news again in 2006, as Apple Corps and Apple Inc. (Apple Computers) went to court over the name and trademark disputes, a battle that dated intermittently back to 1978. In 2007 the company was reported in conjunction with another lawsuit, this one again with EMI, this time over royalties. The dispute was settled and it was announced that Aspinall would retire and be replaced by American music industry exec Jeff Jones, who was coming over from Sony. By November 2010 The Beatles music was available for purchase on Apple's iTunes store and, by January 2016, The Beatles music was available for streaming on both pay and free digital music services such as Apple Music and Spotify.

Apple Corps now not only controls the rights to all of The Beatles catalog, it also controls the rights to The Beatles image, a commodity that is almost as valuable as the music itself.

DEZO HOFFMAN

Dezider Hoffmann (May 24, 1912-March 29, 1986), more commonly referred to as Dezo, is a Czech photographer who—outside of Astrid Kirchherr—is most commonly associated with The Beatles. Born in Czechoslovakia, Hoffmann had the good fortune to encounter The Beatles early in the 1960s and, more fortuitous, have the band like him. While he may be best known for his great snaps of the band, Hoffman was no one-trick pony. Among the many Rock and film stars he shot regularly are some of the biggest names in history: The Rolling Stones, Dusty Springfield, Sophia Loren, Marlon Brando, Marilyn Monroe, Laurence Olivier, The Kinks, Tom Jones, Jimi Hendrix, Frank Sinatra, Bob Marley, Duke Ellington, Louis Armstrong, Elton John, Omar Sharif and Pink Floyd.

Showbiz may have made Hoffmann's reputation, but he earned his stripes in Europe before World War II. He received his journalism degree in Prague and was working in Paris for 20th Century Fox when he was sent to Abyssinia to document Mussolini's invasion in October of 1935. After that Hoffmann was sent to Spain to cover "The People's Olympiad," in 1936, which was being staged as a protest against Hitler's 1936 Berlin Olympiad. As fate would have it, the Spanish Civil War broke out while he was on assignment—during this period, legend had it, Hofmann became good friends with Ernest Hemingway. He was injured several times during his war coverage and, after recovering from a final injury that left him with amnesia for several months, Hoffmann moved to London and joined the Royal Air Force (RAF), flying with a squadron of Czech pilots working with the RAF.

Photographer Dezo Hoffman captures The Beatles in the studio in the early to mid-1960s. $896. *Image courtesy of Julien's Auctions*

So it was, after the war, living in London, that Hoffmann began his work as a professional photographer. Landing a gig with Record Mirror in London in 1955, Hoffmann embarked on the career that would define him: photographing celebrities.

It was 1962 when Hoffman was sent to Liverpool to cover the lads for the first time. They were not yet world-beaters, but the promise was there and the band and the photographer struck up a friendship and good working rapport. It was during this first assignment with the band that Hoffmann took 8mm film footage of the band, the first time they were ever captured in color.

Hoffmann would photograph The Beatles for several more years, capturing an amazing variety of images of the band, both personal and private. His were the eyes that captured what the entire world wanted to see and he became both in-demand and famous for these images. Hoffmann would never ever suffer from a lack of work, even after his time with The Beatles was over.

An out-of-print 1982 book, With The Beatles - The historic photographs of Dezo Hoffmann, offers a wonderful look at many of his best shots of the band, taken at the height of Beatlemania. The rights to those photos now belong to Apple Corps, Ltd., minus 100 of them, which Hoffman sold to the Silver K Art Infinitum in Australia, which continued to market and sell editions of archival prints from the selection. The rest of Hoffmann's work, some 1 million images of music and entertainment figures, is owned and managed by Rex Features, which also represented Hoffmann from the 1960s until his death in the mid-1980s.

Dezo Hoffman's "collarless suit" photograph of The Beatles is a great early image for a beginning or intermediate collector, or could compliment a period collectible in a display. Well-priced at $625. Image courtesy of Julien's Auctions

(below) The Beatles jump pose photograph by Dezo Hoffman helped to define the boys' image. $896 at auction. Image courtesy of Julien's Auctions

NEILL ASPINALL

Neil Aspinall (Oct. 13, 1941—March 24, 2008) was the ultimate Beatles insider. He knew the boys in the band since they were pre-teens and he was with them for the entire insane, glorious ride from dingy Liverpool to the top of the world. He was friend, confidant, roadie, driver, fixer, assistant and accountant to the band. He was, in short, closer to the boys than anyone in the world.

Ah, what stories he could tell, yes? What tales of sex, drugs and rock 'n' roll he must have related before all was said and done!

Not so much.

"Neil Aspinall, who died yesterday aged 66, was one of only two people of any importance in The Beatles saga who never told their story," wrote Beatles biographer Hunter Davies in Aspinall's March 25, 2008 obituary in The Guardian. "Which is strange, when you think we've had a thousand Beatles books these last 40 years, from people who never met them, to lawyers who did in passing, chauffeurs who once drove them and scruffs who stood outside their offices hoping for autographs."

Aspinall was fiercely loyal to the band and their families until the very end, just as he had been since the beginning, at 12 years old, when he met Paul McCartney at the Liverpool Institute. It wasn't long before he

A pair of 1969 Beatles signed documents, the first document is headed "Apple Films Ltd." and is signed by Neil Aspinall, Lennon, McCartney and Harrison. The second document is headed "Python Music Limited" and is signed by Aspinall and Ringo, who signed "R. Starkey." Both documents refer to a change of secretary from Mr. B.F. Burns to Moor House Secretaries Limited. Internal Beatles documents always bring good prices, this is no exception at $13,750.
Image courtesy of Julien's Auctions

had become friendly with George Harrison and John Lennon, too. He was there at the very beginning, when The Beatles played at the opening of the Casbah Coffee Club on Aug. 29, 1959, in the cellar of the house owned by Mona Best, Pete Best's mother.

Shortly afterward, Aspinall would rent a room in the house, where he would become good friends with original drummer Pete Best. His stay in the Best house would also prove important as Aspinall fell in love with Best's mother, Mona, 17 years his senior. The relationship, in fact, produced a child, born barely a month before Pete was sacked as the band's drummer in 1962. One can only imagine the turmoil that Aspinall must have felt as his good friend was cut from what would become the greatest band in the world, as his lover railed against the treatment of her son and as he himself weighed what his future with The Beatles would be. In the end, he chose The Beatles, ending his relationship with Mona Best.

Prior to this, Aspinall had become the band's driver, a position he took full time in July 1961 when the band returned from its second residency in Hamburg. The fact is that Aspinall was making more as the band's driver than he was at his day job as an accountant. In 1963 the burly Mal Evans, who doubled as roadie and security guard for the band, joined Aspinall. This freed Aspinall up to act more as a personal assistant to the band, setting up meetings, scheduling appointments and buying the boys whatever they needed, be it clothes, booze, pills or shoes.

In time, in the "Personal Assistant" role, Aspinall was ever-present with the band, his main duties consisting of simply being around when one of the boys needed something. He was with the band on the first trip to America for The Ed Sullivan Show, standing in at the rehearsal for an ailing George Harrison. He was famously tasked by photographer Peter Blake to find photographs of all the people that were shown on the cover of Sgt. Pepper's and, legend has it, that Aspinall suggested the reprise of the song "Sgt. Pepper's Lonely Hearts Club Band" near the end of the record.

When Epstein died in 1967, the band asked Aspinall to take over the management of the newly formed Apple Corps in 1968. Aspinall, uncomfortable with the roll, reluctantly agreed to do it until a suitable replacement could be found. It would be 40 years, give or take a few, that he would be at Apple's helm.

In his time at Apple, Aspinall proved as dedicated a steward of the brand as there could be. He was integral to three different lawsuits that Apple Corps. filed against Apple Computer over the years, starting in 1978, two of which Apple prevailed in, and was the Executive Producer in 1994 on The Beatles Anthology. He, along with George Martin and press officer Derek Taylor are the only non-Beatles to appear in the documentary that accompanied the project.

Aspinall's tenure with the band ended on April 10, 2007, when Apple announced that Aspinall was going to "move on." The truth was he was sick and dying. Before he passed away in March of 2008, he was overseeing the re-mastering of the back catalog of The Beatles for a 2008 re-release.

Derek Taylor

Derek Taylor (May 7, 1932—Sept. 8, 1997), most famous for being The Beatles first publicist and a lifelong friend of both John Lennon and George Harrison, was a journalist and writer well before he met The Beatles and their publicist soon after.

He started his writing career in the late 1940s at the age of 17, working for a local Liverpool newspaper, the Hoylake and West Kirby Advertiser, followed by stints at the Liverpool Daily Post and Echo before nabbing a gig as the North England writer for a chain of national British publications, including the News Chronicle, the Sunday Dispatch and the Sunday Express.

It was the Daily Express that assigned Taylor to review a Beatles concert on May 30, 1963, just as the band was starting to get big in England. The piece was expected to be critical of the band and its music—seen as a teen fad and little else—but Taylor could see what was happening and he could see that The Beatles had real musical talent. It was not long before he befriended the band and was trusted by them.

By 1964 Epstein had hired Taylor as the band's Public Relations Manager. He wrote the press releases for the band and interfaced with the media for them. He also acted as an assistant to Epstein and helped him write his 1964 autobiography A Cellarful of Noise.

On The Beatles' first American concert tour in 1964 Taylor joined the band as its press officer. He witnessed the madness first hand all through the summer of that year, quitting when the tour ended in September.

After a brief stint at the Daily Mirror, Taylor moved to Los Angeles, opening his own PR firm and working—to considerable success— with bands such as the Byrds, the Beach Boys and Paul Revere and the Raiders. He was also a key component of the production team that put on the Monterey Pop Festival in 1967.

The next year, in April 1968, Taylor went back to England to work as the Press Officer for Apple Corps., at Harrison's request, where he was front and center for much of what happened at Apple during the first few years, including John and Yoko's widely publicized 1969 world peace campaign and its attendant anthem, "Give Peace a Chance." His name is even mentioned in the last verse of the song, as he was in the room, with all the other famous names in the verse, when it was recorded.

Taylor left The Beatles again in 1970, during Allen Klein's brief tenure at the company, and would go on to author a prolific career in the music business, working in a variety of functions for Warner Bros., making his mark via work with a variety of prominent stars, including the Rolling Stones, Yes, America, Neil Young, Carly Simon, and Alice Cooper.

Taylor also never stopped writing. In addition to working as editor on Harrison's 1980 autobiography, I, Me, Mine, Taylor authored books such as As Time Goes By, The Making of Raiders of The Lost Ark, Fifty Years Adrift (In An Open Necked Shirt) and It Was Twenty Years Ago Today.

Taylor was asked back to Apple Corps. in the early 1980s to head the company's marketing arm, working on a variety of projects that included the release of the original Apple catalog on Compact Disc, the release of the landmark Live at the BBC recordings and the compilation of the then-upcoming Beatles Anthology.

When Taylor died, on Sept. 8, 1997, he was still working for Apple on The Beatles Anthology book.

THE CAVERN CLUB

There is no other venue more closely associated with The Beatles than Liverpool's The Cavern Club. It's the venue that comes to mind when one thinks of the early Beatles slogging away as young musicians on their journey toward greatness. It conjures images of the lads bedecked in black leather, tough as nails, cigarettes hanging from their mouths as they churn out the rock and roll to the raucous young Merseyside Brits.

Original owner Alan Sytner, who opened The Cavern Club in mid-January, 1957, did not design the club as a Rock venue. Sytner had been inspired by his time in Paris to open a jazz club situated in a cellar like many of those he found in the city. He eventually found a former air-raid shelter in the cellar of a fruit warehouse.

The first time a Beatle, or a soon-to-be-Beatle, stepped foot in the Cavern was on Aug. 7, 1957, when John Lennon's skiffle band, The Quarrymen, played a set between jazz bands. Paul McCartney's first appearance at The Cavern was with The Quarrymen on Jan. 24, 1958. George Harrison first played at The Cavern during a lunchtime session on Feb. 9, 1961 with The Beatles—it was the band's first of what would be 292 performances on the legendary stage.

The ownership of The Cavern Club changed hands in late 1959 and the new owner, Ray McFall, opened it up to more Rock and Blues bands. He had, unknowingly, created the lab that would conduct the experiment that would turn into one of the greatest cultural forces in history. He began to book periodic "Beat Nights" with local bands and it was on one of the first "Beat Nights" at the club, May 25, 1960, that Ringo Starr would

The Beatles performing at The Cavern Club.

make his first appearance at the club as the drummer for Rory Storm and the Hurricanes.

Brian Epstein, The Beatles longtime manager, first saw the band perform at the club on Nov. 9, 1961. The band's last performance at the club would happen on Aug. 3, 1963, just one month after the band recorded "She Loves You" and six months before The Beatles' first trip to America. It was obvious, by the time of this last show, that The Beatles were starting to get quite famous and that the small club could no longer hold the massive crowds streaming in to see them.

The club would close in March of 1973, more than a decade after the last Beatles show and following multiple performances by a variety of legendary acts, including The Rolling Stones, The Yardbirds, The Hollies, The Kinks, Elton John, Queen, The Who and John Lee Hooker. When the doors were locked on the club for the final time in its first incarnation it was torn down and the site filled with concrete by the municipal authority to make room for the Merseyrail underground rail loop.

The Cavern Club would not stay gone, however. It re-opened again, on the same site, in April of 1984 under the ownership of soccer player Tommy Smith, who acquired many of the original bricks from the club to rebuild the venue. It was a noble idea, but the club struggled and, after just five years, closed down once again.

In 1991 The Cavern Club would get another shot as two friends, Bill Heckle, a teacher, and Dave Jones, a taxi driver, re-opened the club. The two have proved, so far, to have the right touch with the legendary space, still running it to this day. While the club sees tremendous traffic as a tourist spot, it still continues to book about 40 musical acts of all kinds each week.

McCartney is the only Beatle to ever return to The Cavern to play a show, doing so on Dec. 14, 1999, playing his last gig of the millennium—in support of his album Run Devil Run—on the famous stage.

What can really be said about Yoko Ono (Feb. 18, 1933) that hasn't already been said? She should be, and is, the subject many books; her legacy has been debated endlessly across the last 50 years. She's fascinating, brilliant, influential, controversial, and everything in-between. I say, with love in my heart for her, that there's not enough room in this volume to fully detail her contributions to the world, or even to begin to illuminate her influence on John Lennon's life and music. Let me apologize in advance for everything that gets left out.

YOKO ONO

Yoko is best known as the widow of John Lennon and, to the uninformed, is often referred to as the woman who broke up The Beatles. In fact, her name has become an adjective unto itself for describing the rock 'n' roll wife or girlfriend that shows up, after a band has achieved success, and acts as wedge between male musicians.

To reduce Yoko to such a trivial role, however, is an insult to her as an accomplished artist, peace activist, singer, songwriter and performer. She is a force of nature, an unbending, unyielding artist who has never had problems expressing herself and who was well-established as an accomplished artist and musician in her own right well before she met Lennon. It was all of these things that attracted him to her when they first met.

The story of that first meeting is the stuff of legend. The most widely accepted version is that the two originally met at artist Gustav Metzger's "Destruction in Art" Symposium at the Indica Gallery in London in September of 1966. Yoko was the only female artist invited to participate in the exhibition. Lennon visited the show in early November of that year and was supposedly unimpressed with the work, except for one piece: a ladder with a magnifying glass on top of it. Intrigued, Lennon climbed the ladder, grabbed the magnifier and looked up to the ceiling. The word he saw there, "YES," hooked him, as it was a rare positive message during a time when conceptual art was largely negative and critical.

It was the beginning of an intense attraction between the two, though the relationship would not be consummated until six months later, in May of 1968. Lennon's wife, Cynthia, was on vacation in Greece. Lennon invited Yoko to his estate in England. The two spent the night recording what would become the Two Virgins album and making love as the sun rose. Thus one of the 20th century's most epic, and complicated, relationships was born. They became inseparable.

It was soon after this that Ono began showing up at Abbey Road Studios with Lennon during recording sessions. There is no doubt that this created tension in the band, but the simple fact is that Lennon trusted her and wanted her artistic input on his music. The band was recording The White Album at the time, their most disparate album, so there was already a good bit of distance between the musicians. She may not have helped the situation, but to blame her for the

John Lennon and Yoko Ono standing in front of the Eiffel Tower circa 1969 while on their honeymoon. The couple signed the photo in black felt tip pen. At auction, the photo sold for $2,750. Image courtesy of Heritage Auctions

Yoko would continue to be an enduring musical partner with Lennon through the last decade of his life. After Two Virgins Yoko collaborated with John for the experimental "Revolution 9" on The White Album, as well as contributing background vocals to Paul's song "Birthday" and one lead line of vocals on John's "The Continuing Story of Bungalow Bill," giving her the distinction of the only instance on a Beatles tune in which a woman sang lead vocals—a rather special distinction.

After The Beatles, Ono and Lennon would form the Plastic Ono Band, recording seven albums, including two indisputably great albums, Mind Games in 1973 and Walls and Bridges in 1974. Those two albums, however, were recorded during a time of separation in their marriage—actually during Lennon's famous "Lost Weekend," a two year affair with May Pang.

Ono and Lennon reunited in 1974 and, in 1975, she gave birth to the couple's son, Sean. Lennon retreated from music and from public life to raise him. This period would, arguably, be the most content and happy of his life. By all accounts Lennon found peace being a stay-at-home dad and developed a very close relationship to Sean.

eventual break-up of the band, as the English press—and most Rock fans at the time—did is grossly unfair. In subsequent years both Yoko and Lennon refuted this, as did the other members of The Beatles themselves. The band was heading for dissolution with or without her.

As the last two years of The Beatles played out, Lennon and Yoko increasingly, as the other Beatles were, forged their own identities outside the band. They became fierce public critics of the Vietnam War, which would have harsh consequences in his life. After the two were married in March of 1969, in Gibraltar, they honeymooned in Amsterdam, spending a week in their hotel room holding their famous "Bed-In for Peace." They planned another in the U.S., but, upon trying to re-enter, were denied as U.S. authorities were in no hurry to welcome him back to the states. Re-adjusting their plan, John and Yoko relocated the second Bed-In to the Queen Elizabeth Hotel in Montreal, Canada. It was during this Bed-In that they recorded "Give Peace a Chance."

It was in early December of 1980, while Ono and Lennon were putting the finishing touches on their landmark Double Fantasy album, the unthinkable happened. Stalked by a deranged fan, Mark David Chapman, Lennon was gunned down outside The Dakota, the Manhattan apartment building where he and Ono lived. Lennon died of his wounds within an hour. The world lost one of its greatest, most influential and beloved musicians. Sean Lennon lost his beloved father. Yoko Ono lost her husband and the love of her life.

While Ono has had several very public spats with Paul McCartney over the decades since Lennon's death over a variety of things—the order of songwriting credit on Beatles tracks most notably—the two now largely get along and the public appreciation of Ono has risen significantly over time. She has come to be highly regarded as an artist and has had several important retrospectives of her work at museums and galleries all over the world.

Still, her greatest contribution has been as the steward of Lennon's music and legacy. She funded the Strawberry Fields memorial section of Central Park in New York, the Imagine Peace Tower in Iceland and the now-closed John Lennon Museum in Saitama, Japan. Ono continues to be a dynamic, influential and popular force of political activism and Beatles music. She continues creating art, creating music and collaborating with Sean on various projects, all-in-all emerging as one of the most fascinating people that the 20th century produced. It's not hard to understand why Lennon loved her so deeply and was so devoted to her.

Beatles Discography

STUDIO ALBUMS

Please Please Me - Released March 22, 1963

With the Beatles - Released: Nov. 22, 1963

Beatlemania! With the Beatles - Released Nov. 25, 1963

Les Beatles (France) - Released November 1963

Introducing... The Beatles - Released Jan. 10, 1964

Meet the Beatles! - Released Jan. 20, 1964

Twist and Shout - Released Feb. 3, 1964

The Beatles' Second Album - Released April 10, 1964

The Beatles' Long Tall Sally - Released May 11, 1964

A Hard Day's Night - Released June 26, 1964

Something New - Released July 20, 1964

Beatles for Sale - Released Dec. 4, 1964

Beatles '65 - Released Dec. 15, 1964

Beatles VI - Released June 14, 1965

Help! - Released Aug. 6, 1965

Rubber Soul - Released Dec. 3, 1965

Yesterday and Today - Released June 20, 1966

Revolver - Released Aug. 5, 1966

Sgt. Pepper's Lonely Hearts Club Band - Released June 1, 1967

Magical Mystery Tour - Released Nov. 27, 1967

The Beatles (The White Album) - Released Nov. 22, 1968

Yellow Submarine - Released Jan. 17, 1969

Abbey Road - Released Sept. 26, 1969

Let It Be - Released May 8, 1970

LIVE ALBUMS

Live! at the Star-Club in Hamburg, Germany; 1962 - Released April 8, 1977

The Beatles at the Hollywood Bowl - Released May 4, 1977

First Live Recordings - Released in 1979

Live at the BBC - Released Nov. 30, 1994

On Air - Live at the BBC Volume 2 - Released Nov. 11, 2013

COMPILATION ALBUMS

My Bonnie (with Tony Sheridan) - Released Jan. 5, 1962

The Beatles with Tony Sheridan & Guests (with Tony Sheridan) - Released Feb. 3, 1964

The Beatles Beat - Released Feb. 6, 1964

Something New - Released Feb. 10, 1964

Jolly What! (with Frank Ifield) - Released Feb. 26, 1964

Ain't She Sweet - Released Oct. 5, 1964

The Beatles' Story - Released Nov. 23, 1964

The Early Beatles - Released March 22, 1965

The Beatles - Released April 1965

The Beatles' Greatest - Released June 18, 1965

The Beatles in Italy - Released July 13, 1965

Dans Leurs 14 Plus Grands Succès - Released Sept. 1, 1965

Los Beatles - Released Nov. 19, 1965

Greatest Hits Volume 1 - Released June 7, 1966

A Collection of Beatles Oldies - Released Dec. 9, 1966

Greatest Hits Volume 2 - Released February 1967

The Beatles' First - Released Aug. 4, 1967

Very Together - Released Nov. 4, 1969

Hey Jude - Released Feb. 26, 1970

In the Beginning (Circa 1960) - Released May 4, 1970

From Then To You/The Beatles' Christmas Album - Released Dec. 18, 1970

Por Siempre Beatles - Released Oct. 8, 1971

The Essential Beatles - Released February 1972

1962-1966 - Released April 19, 1973

1967-1970 - Released April 19, 1973

Rock 'n' Roll Music - Released June 7, 1976

Love Songs - Released Oct. 21, 1977

Rarities - Released Dec. 2, 1978

20 Golden Hits - Released 1979

Rarities - Released March 24, 1980

The Beatles' Ballads - Released March 24, 1980

Rock 'n' Roll Music, Volume One - Released Oct. 27, 1980

Rock 'n' Roll Music, Volume Two - Released Oct. 27, 1980

The Beatles 1967-1970 - Released 1980

The Beatles - Released January 1982

Reel Music - Released March 22, 1982

20 Greatest Hits - Released Oct. 11, 1982

The Number Ones - Released 1983

The Early Tapes of the Beatles - Released Dec. 10, 1984

Past Masters, Volume One - Released March 7, 1988

Past Masters, Volume Two - Released March 7, 1988

Past Masters, Volumes One & Two - Released Oct. 24, 1988

Anthology 1 - Released Nov. 21, 1995

Anthology 2 - Released March 18, 1996

Anthology 3 - Released Oct. 28, 1996

Yellow Submarine Songtrack - Released Sept. 13, 1999

1 - Released Nov. 13, 2000

Beatles Bop - Hamburg Days (with Tony Sheridan) - Released Nov. 6, 2001

Let It Be... Naked - Released Nov. 17, 2003

Love - Released Nov. 20, 2006

Past Masters - Released Sept. 9, 2009

1962-1966/1967-1970 - Released Oct. 15, 2010

Anthology Highlights - Released Nov. 16, 2010

Tomorrow Never Knows - Released July 24, 2012

I Saw Her Standing There - Released April 15, 2013

The Beatles Bootleg Recordings 1963 - Released Dec. 17, 2013

EPs

My Bonnie (with Tony Sheridan) - Released July 12, 1963

Twist and Shout - Released July 12, 1963

The Beatles' Hits - Released Sept. 6, 1963

The Beatles (No. 1) - Released Nov. 1, 1963

All My Loving - Released Feb. 7, 1964

Souvenir of Their Visit to America - Released March 23, 1964

Four by the Beatles - Released May 11, 1964

Long Tall Sally - Released June 19, 1964

Requests - Released July 1964

Beatles Again! - Released July 1964

Hard Day's Night No. 1 - Released July 1964

Beatles No. 2 - Released July 1964

Extracts from the Film A Hard Day's Night - Released Nov. 4, 1964

Extracts from the Album A Hard Day's Night - Released Nov. 6, 1964

4-by the Beatles - Released Feb. 1, 1965

Beatles for Sale - Released April 6, 1965

Beatles for Sale (No. 2) - Released June 4, 1965

The Beatles' Million Sellers - Released Dec. 6, 1965

Yesterday - Released March 4, 1966

Nowhere Man - Released July 8, 1966

Magical Mystery Tour - Released Dec. 8, 1967

4: John Paul George Ringo - Released Sept. 23, 2014